# Rebirthing the Phoenix

## Embodying the Goddess through Rebirthing Breathwork and Immortal Master Babaji

## Sara Dawn

**Gaia Dreaming LLC**

gaia dreaming

# Disclaimer

You are responsible for your health and well being. The contents of this book are for educational purposes only and are not a substitute for medical advice. The contents of this book are not intended to diagnose, treat, cure, or prevent any condition or disease. Consult with a health care provider for medical advice, diagnosis, treatment, or before making any changes to your health regimen. Sara Dawn and Gaia Dreaming LLC are not liable for risks or issues associated with using or acting upon the information within this book.

I am not, nor am I holding myself out to be a doctor/physician, nurse, physician's assistant, advanced practice nurse, or any other medical professional ("Medical Provider"), psychiatrist, psychologist, therapist, counselor, or social worker ("Mental Health Provider"), registered dietician or licensed nutritionist, or member of the clergy.

As a Breathworker, I am not providing health care, medical or nutritional therapy services, or attempting to diagnose, treat, prevent or cure any physical, mental or emotional issue, disease or condition. You agree and acknowledge that I am not providing medical advice, mental health advice, or religious advice in any way.

Do not disregard medical advice or delay seeking medical advice because of information you have read in this book. Do not start or stop taking any medications without speaking to your own or your Medical Provider or Mental Health Provider. The strategies and advice presented in this book are not a substitute for professional counseling or therapy. Seek guidance from qualified professionals for personalized support.

This work depicts actual events in the life of the author as truthfully as recollection permits. While all persons within are actual individuals, names and identifying characteristics have been changed to respect their privacy when requested. In Truth, Simplicity, and Love.

# Foreword

Welcome to my journey, a radical transformation through love and pain, blood and breath, and Spirit embodied. It is a story filled with tears, laughter, ecstasy, and the pure bliss of being merged with the Divine.

My path is marked with many victories and seeming failures with endometriosis, years of being symptom-free, and years of falling back into the abyss of excruciating physical pain. Endometriosis is a chronic, painful disease where tissue similar to the endometrial tissue in the lining of the uterus grows outside the uterus. I share my story with you, hoping it will inspire you along the way, present some exciting ideas, and work as a catalyst for your own process of healing and spiritual awakening.

I am not a doctor, psychologist, guru, or scientist. I am just me. I am as ordinary as any other person. I don't expect you to believe everything I have to say. But please, do take some of it to heart. While the focus of my healing has been on menstruation, the concepts herein can be applied to any disease and this book is intended for all genders. Non-menstruating individuals can still benefit from the ideas presented in this book.

Having said that, I have a special note for my sisters; your femininity is sacred. Your menstrual blood is life-giving. Your power and creativity are more significant than you have ever dared imagine. It is a gift to be a woman. It is time for us to return as embodiments of the Goddess. It is time for us to love and embrace our creative wombs, discover our gifts to the world, and discover our interdependence and connectedness with each other and Mother Earth. It is time to be our true feminine selves in all this means and encompasses.

It is important to note that the spiritual experiences I share with you in this book came about through kundalini (life force energy) activation via Rebirthing Breathwork and meditation. They were wholly unassisted by drugs or plant medicine. Rebirthing Breathwork is a simple, gentle, connected breathing rhythm practiced in individual sessions, as developed by Leonard D. Orr, the founder of the modern day Breathwork movement.

While science is just beginning to define the mechanics of the mystical experiences available through breathwork, it has been a part of humanity's path since time memorial. These mystical experiences are our birthright and destiny. We are each capable of spiritual awakening and kundalini activations through the gentle and simple Rebirthing Breathwork technique. Mystical experiences are a natural part of humanity. Please know that this mysticism is available to you personally as well.

It's my intention that this book be utilized as an action, an experience, and not just a mental–intellectual meandering. I am not interested in what you will know after you read this book. I am interested in how you might put it into practice in your life, how and if it calls to your heart, and what you do with your precious golden life.

Throughout this book you will find Invitations, which are lit-tle calls to action or inner reflection. In this way, it can also be used as a workbook for your own healing journey.

My first invitation to you is to keep a journal, even if you feel a lot of resistance or if all you write is one or two sentences a day. Just start one now. Writing fixes your thoughts onto paper. It enables you to take a good, objective look at your thoughts later when you are no longer in that state of consciousness. If you do not like to write or cannot, you can keep an audio journal by recording your voice.

A valuable journaling exercise that may help you get started would be to create a journal of your thoughts and reactions to the contents of this book. The value of this may become more apparent over time.

In these pages you will also find some of my own journal entries. I decided to include them to keep this book real. I did not want it to be a watered-down version, polished, smooth, and shiny, to make my healing process seem like something it was not.

Male or female, challenged with physical symptoms or perfectly healthy, our bodies and Earth demand that we no longer struggle and strain to fit into a mechanized world that shuns our rhythmic, cyclical, intuitive nature. It is time, our time, to return to the flow of the Universe. We can walk again in the sacred union of the feminine and masculine present within all living things. It is time for us all to reveal the Gods and Goddesses within.

I want to thank and honor my teachers and dedicate this book to their higher purpose and service: Ascended Master Jesus the Illumined Christ, Sri Haidakhan Babaji, and my earthly teachers; Matt Garrigan and Leonard D. Orr. The sea of Divine Grace is immensely vast and unfathomable. I am eternally grateful.

All my love,
Sara

# *She*

*She who ran with the horses*
*and bathed in moonlit skies*
*who roamed the wild forests*
*that soothed her tired, grieving eyes.*
*She who found comfort*
*with ancient native Spirits*
*who witnessed many sunsets*
*setting all life ablaze,*
*with their fiery red rays.*
*She who clung*
*to her precious, vulnerable heart*
*and painted with passion her sacred art.*
*She who found her tribe*
*amongst woodland foxes, deer, owls,*
*herons, and eagles soaring in flight.*
*She who loved.*
*She who survived.*
*She, who to this day is healing*
*and learning to Thrive.*

# The Bliss of Being

**A** soft bed of pine needles supported me from below as I lay comfortably on the forest floor. I watched the winds riding like waves over giant mountain tree tops, massaging me with the sweetest ecstasy beneath a radiant blue sky.

A soft tingle of swirling energy flowed through every cell of my body. My breathing was free and light. The scent and solitude of the forest permeated my entire being. My mind soared as high as the eagles, yet it was calm, quiet, and serene. I felt as though the whole mountain range was holding me, merging with me, loving me.

Just moments ago, I had received darshan, a loving transfer of energy, through visions of whales, dolphins, horses, eagles, mythical-looking extraterrestrials, rocks, and elementals, all of whom gazed in each one's turn deeply into my eyes, loving me, blessing me, thanking me for being. All of life, everywhere, everything, every particle loved me, and I loved it back. Who knew existence could be this blissfully peaceful? This serenity was my new normal. It had not always been this way for me, though. Feeling as light as air and as light as light itself, I lay there filled with a deliciously buzzing aliveness, seemingly lifetimes away from where my journey began years ago...

# The Beginning

Sitting against the closed door of my parent's bedroom, my heart sank to the pit of my stomach.

"Go back to sleep, Sara, it's only a dream," I heard them both call to me from behind their locked door. My heart pounded relentlessly in my head.

Night after night, I was waking with nightmares and climbing into their bed. Laying between the two warm, protecting bodies of both my parents felt like the safest place in the world. I was tired and wanted to sleep and I knew everyone else was tired and wanted to sleep. But I was too afraid of my dreams.

Each time I fell asleep, they came; life-sized demons made of lava and fire chased me through the cul-de-sac outside my home. Their massive bodies struck me with a terror that made my heart pound in my ears and choked out my screams. Barely able to breathe, I ran as hard as I could as more and more of them appeared around me. Encircling me, I moved in slow motion, paralyzed against my will as they reached out to grab me.

Finally able to scream, I awoke as tears streamed from my eyes. I sat up sweating and straining in a panicked torture. The dream repeated night after night, and felt as real as life to me. And now my parents had locked their door. I was alone in my agony.

After weeks of this, one afternoon as my mom watched a television talk show, I heard the idea that people could fall asleep each night telling themselves, *I'm dreaming,* and think of what they wanted to dream about. Night after night, I practiced with my head on the pillow, repeating, *I'm dreaming, I'm dreaming, I'm dreaming,* as I felt myself float off to sleep.

After a few days, I became lucid that I was asleep and dreaming. I began to construct a place to go in my dreams. I was in a fairytale forest with my own home inside a vast, grand oak tree. The door was at its roots. It was a magical sanctuary that only I could see.

Inside was a beautiful, earthy home complete with a fireplace, kitchen, bath, and stairs leading to a main bedroom at the highest point of the tree. Large doors overlooked the forest with a balcony outside. Before long, a graceful, soothing, majestic white pegasus came each night, her hooves clopping on the wooden balcony as she neighed to me with a joyful greeting. She was sensitive to me, and I was to her. She would respond to me without words, and we were interconnected. She carried me across the treetops and mountains, over streams, and into other mythical dream worlds.

Night after night I kept practicing, and found that I could go to her immediately upon sleeping. And for many years, this was my dream life. Finally, in my teenage years, it occurred to me to stop controlling my dreams and see what might happen. Opening the doors to my dream world without any intervention or direction, led me to a vastly rich experience filled with magical guides, spiritual tests, initiations, and deep symbolic meaning. Occasionally, I met people in my dreams before meeting them in real life. My dream life was more meaningful and fulfilling to me than waking life and I held a deep knowing that more is happening in life than most people believe. I would be in my twenties before I learned that not everyone could dream lucidly. It was a real shock to me.

My fairytale home and pegasus were an integral part of my childhood, and I came to understand that the nightmares served a great purpose for me: I had become masterful at lucid dreaming by the age of five, and as a result of this, I had an avenue of wildly creative self-expression through dreaming.

Horses were a lifelong passion of mine. The family joke was that my first word was 'horse.' No one knew where I got my equine fever as no one else in the family seemed to have it. Yet, by age thirteen, I had a whole shrine to horses on my bedroom walls. Years later, when my Grandfather was on his deathbed, he reminded me that I had a poster of a horse looking out over a stall, hanging on my bedroom door. If I could have lived in a stall or the loft of a barn, I would have happily done so. So when my parents announced that they would be giving me a horse on my thirteenth birthday and that they were getting a divorce, I felt a horrendous mix of both joy and agony.

During the first summer of my family's separation, my mother dropped me off at the stable in the mornings and picked me up in the evenings, sometimes well past dark. I packed a small lunch bag and some water, snacked on the apples in the orchard across the lane, or grazed on the abundant blackberries lining the riding trails along the Kalapuya River.

I brushed my horse so smoothly and thoroughly that he shined like a royal king's mount. He was an Egyptian Arabian with a delicately carved face and ears, a beautiful bay color with a white star, and a small spot of white on his nose. His name was Snip. Although Arabians are known for being high-strung, he was as gentle as a rose, without the sharp thorns to remind me of the harsh realities of life. How my parents were able to find him and afford him at such a time was nothing short of a miracle that saved my life. It was the best thing they could have done for me, and I am forever grateful.

My entire summer was spent wrapping myself around Snip. Emblazoned by the hot sun, his coat took on a glorious golden sheen. I often took him for a swim in the river, riding on miles of trails, avoiding the patches of stinging nettles and boggy areas that smelled of a particular dampness found only in an Oregon temperate rainforest. Resting in the cool shade of giant evergreen trees, Snip and I alternated from exploring the forest to leaping over jumps and training for hours in the arena between weekly riding lessons. He was my refuge and my whole life, where I could be free, at ease, and completely myself while the rest of my life seemed to disintegrate.

The drama of a four-year-long divorce proceeding unfolded. I saw less and less of my sister and my dad. I completely lost connection with my cousins and uncles and managed to visit my grandparents and great-grandparents only a handful of times. I suddenly found myself estranged from my family. Even though my mother went with me to see therapists and offered support, no one seemed to acknowledge the intense grief, loneliness, isolation, and loss I experienced. I put on a smile and pretended to be ok, believing I had to be strong and this was the way to survive.

There were times when the emotional pain was so intense that I just wanted to die. I remember the peak of this one day, sitting on my bathroom floor sobbing. I contemplated how I might kill myself, which way might be the less painful. Pills? A knife? By drowning? I mulled it over in my mind. But being raised Catholic, I had an intense fear that if I committed suicide, I would go straight to eternal hell, and there would not be much relief from pain there. My emptiness grew greater, and I abandoned the idea of escaping through suicide. What was the point in life? In suffering? Why was I here? What did it matter?

I found other ways to escape the pain: my art, horses, long walks in nature, and the few close friends I had in school. The days passed, and I quietly blended myself into the crowd, hoping not to attract unwanted attention.

# Menarche - The First Bleed

T hree years passed, and at sixteen years old, I was the last of all of my friends to 'get her period.' Why was I so late? Was something wrong with me? If I didn't start within the next few months, I would have to see the doctor. A few friends reassured me, "It's because you're so tall. All of your body's energy has been going into your height."

It was true; I had grown five inches in one year and sadly had outgrown my beloved horse by the time I was just fourteen. And I continued to grow inches more each year since. I towered above all my friends and some of the boys. But I doubted that my height had anything to do with my delayed menstruation.

Watching with apprehension, I listened as girls walked to the bathrooms together in small groups, complaining about 'being on the rag,' the 'curse,' that seemingly shameful time of the month when girls wished they could ask to be excused from Physical Ed class, but were expected to continue as if nothing were happening. When would that dreaded day come for me as well? Many more months passed until that day finally arrived.

At 4:00 am, my alarm clock went off, striking the dark, silent air with its sharp, piercing sound. I turned it off and leaped out of bed. It was the morning of a horse show, and I would be competing with my young, newly trained Polish Arabian horse for his third show. I had sadly chosen to sell my previous horse, Snip, to a close friend from the stable. With that money, I was able to purchase a beautiful dapple gray, just four years young and trained almost exclusively by my horse trainer.

Excitement pulsed through me as I turned on the lights and began to find my riding clothes. I entered the bathroom and sat down to pee when I noticed a sticky brown substance on my underwear. My period had begun. Of all days for it to finally arrive, this was it? My excitement turned to a fearful dread. What would this day bring me? How much blood will I shed? Will it hurt? Can I still ride my horse? I had been training for months in preparation for this event, and everything was set to go. Now, none of it seemed to matter.

I woke my mother, and she searched her bathroom for the panty liners she had bought for my first flow. But she naturally grew less vigilant at keeping the pads for me in the years of waiting, expecting, and it never arriving. All she had was a box of large tampons. At 4 am, all of our local stores were closed. My mom handed me the tampons and explained how it all worked.

I managed to insert one, but it was uncomfortable, and I could feel it all morning. It was irritating and somewhat painful. Later that morning, at the horse show, I was too embarrassed to tell my trainer what was happening. I took numerous breaks to go to the bathroom and try to readjust the oversized tampon. Thankfully, my mother got to the store as soon as they opened and bought me some pads. I canceled the rest of my competitions that day and went home.

My mother taught me to carefully wrap the used pads and place them in a paper bag beside the garbage. I had to keep the bag closed and make sure there were no signs of blood anywhere. It was clear to me that I shouldn't let people know I was menstruating. Periods were a top-secret nuisance that no one else should know about. And that was it; my initiation into womanhood. The days went on as though nothing noticeable had changed.

## *Invitation - Menarche*

Write out your thoughts about menarche:
What was your first menstruation like?
What were you taught about menstruation?
Did you feel well-informed and prepared?
What were the attitudes and expectations of those around you?

### *For men:*

When and how did you first learn about menstruation?
What were the attitudes, ideas, and mindsets of those around you regarding menstruation?
How did you feel about knowing that women bleed every month?

# *And So it Began*

At age sixteen I left home and briefly lived with my father and stepmother before moving in with my high school boyfriend's family.

My first few periods were irregular and unpredictable, but the following year, they became like clockwork, a fountain of blood that flowed like mad for six to seven days. I changed a heavy flow pad every hour. Sometimes, I doubled up and used an 'ultra' heavy flow tampon combined with a pad and still bled through both in an hour and a half.

Numerous doctors told me that some women have it easy, and others don't. That's just the way it is. They patted me on the head and sent me out the door, telling me to take more ibuprofen. Although I had always had painful and heavy periods, I will never forget the first day I felt the pain of endometriosis.

At just eighteen years old, I crouched over on the edge of the bed, feeling an unbearable, nauseating pain radiating up from the base of my pelvic bowl. It was so intense that I could not move. The only position I could be in without fear of passing out was sitting, leaning slightly forward over my knees. My boyfriend thought I was faking it and got mad at me when I refused to move, drink, or eat for half the day. I did not know it, but this was not the typical pain level of mere menstrual cramps; endometrial lesions were bleeding into my abdominal cavity.

Still maxing out on the dosage of pain medicines, my doctor apologized to me, saying again that "some women just have it bad and others don't." There was nothing he could do unless I wanted to go on birth control, and he offered me no other explanation or advice for the uncontrollable level of pain.

I felt that no one listened to me. I thought there must be something inherently wrong with me because no one else seemed concerned that I was taking the maximum dose of pain medicine and still having excruciating cramps, nausea, and heavy flow. I didn't know that the medical industry was also ignoring countless other women who faced similar problems daily.

Every month, at the onset of my period, pain that felt like boiling lava radiated through my entire abdomen and left me feeling nauseous. Bowel movements were excruciating. Eating was unthinkable. Sipping water was all I could manage. I lay in bed as still as possible and tried not to move all day.

Taking six to eight ibuprofen a day soon stopped working, and I switched to the most potent over-the-counter painkiller available. It was only a matter of a few menstrual cycles until I had to take the maximum dosage of that just to be able to walk around and work like an average human being while menstruating, still feeling this curse churning in my abdomen and aching with every movement.

Menstruation. The gift of giving life. Having periods or becoming a mother was something I had no desire to do. I did not want this, and I did not ask for it. Yet here it was, whether I liked it or not. I looked around at the world and saw the environmental destruction, wars, poverty, political dramas, etc. Why would I want to bring more life here? This agony was all I knew about menstruation. I had no idea of the gifts it offered.

Pondering the doctor's advice, I decided that starting on birth control just a few years after the onset of menstruation didn't feel right to me. Tinkering with my hormones and body at such a young age seemed uncertain for longer-term outcomes in my health. I continued taking high doses of over-the-counter painkillers to get through the day. I had no idea that these painkillers were destroying my digestion and putting me at increased risk for a heart attack.

When I turned nineteen the relationship with my high school boyfriend ended. I managed to find house sharing opportunities and launched into multiple jobs to pay for my basic needs, my horse, and car loan.

By the time I was twenty two, I had chronic fatigue, eczema, irritable bowel syndrome, and killer periods that caused me to vomit repeatedly and have colon spasms as if I were giving birth on the first day of bleeding. I spent hours on the bathroom floor, cursing the universe and my existence as a woman. Though I had endured the radical symptoms of endometriosis since I was eighteen years old, my health continued to deteriorate as I slipped past any proper diagnosis or help due to the significant lack of awareness of the disease, misinformation, and total ignorance of my doctors at the time. I still believed I was just one of the unlucky women with severe menstrual cramps.

It takes an average of *eight to twelve years* for a woman to receive a diagnosis of endometriosis from the time symptoms first begin to appear. And symptoms are not light or easy to miss. During menstruation and often at times between periods, the symptoms range from debilitating cramps (said to be the equivalent of labor contractions) to headaches, nausea, vomiting, heavy bleeding, painful bowel movements, and pain during sex. It is estimated that 5-10% of women of reproductive age are affected by endometriosis. This comes to 190 million women globally.

## *What is Endometriosis?*

Endometriosis is a condition where tissue similar to the endometrial tissue in the lining of the uterus grows outside the uterus. It creates its own estrogen-like hormones, swells, and bleeds into the abdominal cavity every month.

It may cause severe pain, nausea, vomiting, cramps, extreme fatigue, adhesions, cysts, and other symptoms. For some women, it also causes them to bleed irregularly several times throughout the month and have pain at various times or daily. It can cause pain during sex.

Women with endometriosis may have all of these symptoms, or only a few. The root cause of endometriosis is still unknown, and while there are treatment options for symptoms, there is no definitive cure or guarantee that symptoms will be alleviated.

# The Unraveling

No one seemed to understand how bad my symptoms were and could not offer any reasonable advice. I finally got in to see a specialist, and he told me that I likely had endometriosis. It was the first time I heard anyone mention this disease. I was twenty two years old.

Telling the specialist I had an interest in trying herbal and alternative medicine first before taking any prescription drugs seemed to upset him. He threatened that if I did not go on birth control now, I would need a total hysterectomy by the time I was thirty, if not sooner. He very nearly shouted at me that if I wanted to drink some herbal tea, it would do nothing for me and leave me worse off than I already was. He insisted that the pill was all that could help me.

Leaving his office, I felt furious that I paid money to be yelled at and ridiculed for wanting to explore natural options. Looking back now, I can see the misinformation he had been taught and his frustration at my not accepting his only valid idea of health care.

Something within me held onto a solid sense that my body was trying to communicate with me on a deeper level. I sincerely felt that suppressing and overriding my body's system with drugs (painkillers and the pill) would only do more damage. The mere thought of undergoing a laparoscopy made my whole body ache and my stomach tighten up with pain that I couldn't see going through with it, especially when the chances of success were so slim. The success rate of laparoscopy for endometriosis was around 45% at the time. The odds of getting better were a mere coin toss.

And a hysterectomy? It's like the patriarchy and modern medicine had said, "We don't know what to do with this. It's dark and mysterious. It's misunderstood, under-researched and taboo. Let's just cut it out and throw it away."

The only other solution I heard about was that women have fewer symptoms after childbirth. However, that is a common myth. Many women have complications during pregnancy or symptoms that return after pregnancy. Many women who have endometriosis also have fertility challenges and are unable to get pregnant. I had no desire to be a mother in my young twenties, and there was no way I could see bringing in a child for the mere purpose of easing my pain.

Going against my doctor's advice, I decided to take the alternative and traditional medicine route. It was not an easy journey, and indeed, it was a path less taken at that time. But I was willing to do it.

To avoid vomiting, I stopped eating the day before my periods began. My body would dry heave, going through the motions anyway. Sometimes, I would go three days without eating, only drinking water or miso soup, and at times, my body would reject that too. I have spent many, many days on the bathroom floor, crouched over in the fetal position, trying to stop the sharp, stitching cramps, feeling too dizzy and nauseous to get up, fighting every symptom along the way.

Feeling betrayed by my own body, I felt cursed for being a woman. I cried, wanting to know what it was all for, and I felt fragile and helpless. I was the victim of this horrible thing called endometriosis. It was my enemy, and my body was the battleground. I didn't know I was waging war against myself.

Regardless, I marched on. What else was there to do? I found a new gynecologist who respected my choice to treat with natural, traditional medicine. I had many tests and examinations, ruling out any possibilities of tumors, fibroids, or other diseases. I even wore a heart monitor and had an EKG to test for heart disease due to all the heart palpitations and dizziness I was having.

At the same time, I began weekly acupuncture sessions. I found these sessions to be incredibly therapeutic and vital to my well-being. It was the first time I felt like a doctor was interested and sincerely cared about what I was going through.

My acupuncturist asked me more about my symptoms than I had ever thought about myself. I did not feel like I was being viewed merely as a body that needed repair. For the first time, someone was treating me as a whole being. He included my life holistically in my healing process.

# The ER

Exhausted as I lay on the hospital bed, I watched the IV drip slowly into my veins. I was a bit delirious but grateful for the relief, however minor. I could still feel the aching, nauseating, hot lava churning in my abdomen, but it was a bit distant now, as if held back by a wall that I could peer over.

At my request, my boyfriend at the time had driven me to the closest hospital that morning. I knew I was dehydrated and in trouble. I was just twenty three years young, and one year into my quest for health via natural remedies.

"You are so stoic" the nurse said as I gazed into her fair complexion. Her blue eyes seemed to beam out from behind her soft waves of blond hair and her face was sincere and kind.

"What is stoic?" I asked, my head spinning a bit and not entirely sure of what that word meant.

"You're strong. Most people wouldn't have endured that." She said with such determination and presence.

"Oh. Thank you," I replied, now closing my eyes, finally in at least a bit of peace in this newfound place of rest.

I had been through three days of vomiting, heavy bleeding, and excruciating pain, alternating from laying on the bathroom floor and my nearby bed. Unable to hold down water anymore, I had become dehydrated and realized I needed help.

Some hours later, a day later? I lost track of time but soon felt strong again, and my nausea subsided as they gave me anti-nausea and pain medications intravenously. Now, on day 4 or 5 of my period, I was in the clear and released from the hospital.

# Chinese Medicine

"**H**e's young, but don't let that sway you. He's known as the god of acupuncture around here, and he knows much more than I do."

My acupuncturist smiled warmly at me through his rosy round cheeks mirrored in the shape of his glasses and large brown eyes.

I listened to him intently. It had been just a week since my visit to the emergency room. He was a tall teddy bear of a man filled with such gentleness and kindness.

While my acupuncture sessions with him were creating changes and helping me in some ways, the trip to the ER was a wake-up call. I was at a plateau. If he felt he could treat me no further, I wanted to follow up with this other acupuncturist he recommended seeing.

∞∞∞∞

Upon my first meeting with Peter, I could see that, yes, he was young, maybe just a few years older than myself, but obviously, he was a well-educated and skilled physician of Traditional Chinese Medicine.

Standing there in awe, I watched as he strode around confidently in his office, filled with hundreds of jars of neatly arranged Chinese herbs, each labeled by name in

English, Latin, and Chinese. How did he hold all this knowledge? What life path led him here and revealed him to be so confident at such an early age?

I felt timid, shy, and inadequate. I didn't even know who I was anymore, let alone what I wanted to do with my life. And here he was, seemingly in his prime already. As intimidated as I felt internally, I sensed this was where I was supposed to be. I scheduled an appointment with him for a new patient intake.

The following week I found myself nervously squirming in the chair of his treatment room. The questions he was asking me were, well, embarrassing. I thought my previous acupuncturist was thorough, but apparently, that was just a warm-up for this experience.

Not only had he closely examined my tongue and asked me about the shape, color, and frequency of my bowel movements, but I was now bursting into tears as I described an instance of childhood sexual abuse from a non family member. I had gone from giggling about poo to opening up about some of the most vulnerable, scarred places of my childhood, and Peter was right there with me, compassionately present to it all.

He seemed different this time from our first meeting two weeks prior. He was vibrantly alive, intensely present, and unyielding in his inquiry to my well-being, yet soft and gentle. I felt raw and exposed. It seemed he could see everything within me, and it was all blurbing up like a volcano beyond my control.

As my weekly sessions went by, I began to expect and know that I would likely be sobbing in his office, spilling my guts out, and receiving an abundance of acceptance and nourishment.

Who was this man? I had never met anyone like him. He became a catalyst in my life.

Things began to get better very slowly. Like drops of water building up in an empty bowl, I began to see the benefits of my efforts as my periods improved. For one or two periods I had only one symptom. Then, the next, they would all return. It was not easy.

Feeling weak and defeated, I often felt desperate and wanted to quit, escape, or give up. Most months, I was so sick that it felt like I had died, and I had to get back up on my feet and pull myself together again and again. It was a horrible emotional roller coaster. I remember feeling like it was some sick, cosmic joke, a teaser, to be given a taste of good health, of heaven, and then to be thrown back into hell.

It took me a long time to release my emotional pain about the physical pain. It took me years to transition from seeing the disease as a curse to looking at it as a wake-up call from my body. I was neglecting my body's physical needs and many emotional needs, but I didn't even know it. The suppression of emotions and chronic neglect of my body were not the source cause of the disease, however, but this certainly was not helping.

Bucking up and pushing through these problems seemed normal to me. It's just what I learned to do. Taking the time to tend to my inner rhythms, nature's rhythms, and my needs and listening to my body's cues and cries for help seemed entirely unnatural.

## *Invitation - Body Awareness*

Are you aware of your body, your breathing, and energy levels throughout the day as you go through daily life?

Do you rest when tired?

Do you eat when you're hungry?

Are you on a schedule that supports your body's well-being?

Are you staying hydrated and drinking enough water?

Simply writing down the answers to these questions and acknowledging any areas with room for improvement is the first step toward ending the struggle of ignoring your body's cries for help.

# A Great Candidate

"**I** think you are a great candidate for this," Peter announced as he was preparing my prescription of Chinese herbs.

"Candidate?" I thought with surprise. "What do you mean, candidate? What are the requirements?"

"Well, it feels like a good match. I think you are a person who can take the most from this opportunity and get a lot out of it," he replied.

Peter handed me a brochure, a plain, cream-colored paper with simple black-lettered words, "The Liberty Experience." It described something about converting energies, uncovering blockages, creating the life you want, and contributing to your communities. I could barely hold myself together. How could I possibly have anything to contribute to an entire community?

The brochure went home with me, where I placed it on a stack of half-read books. It was in my 'deal with it some other time' pile.

Six months later, the very foundation of my life was crumbling before my eyes. I had been battling endometriosis for several years now, which was the first part of my life falling apart. The second part was my relationship.

We had known each other for three years before we had married and were deeply in love. He had opened my mind to so many things, many of which were very spiritual, including alternative healing, energy healing, reiki, Taoism, Buddhism, Hinduism, and acupuncture, the latter of which was the only thing successfully managing my endometriosis. He sang beautifully to me. We were both artists. We enjoyed long walks on the beach and exploring spirituality together. He was tender and gentle with me, and we seemed to click together naturally.

When I first met him, I energetically felt like my head (crown chakra, or energy center) opened up like a satellite and was receiving and sending information with him. I had lucid dreams with him, and he saw me one night while he was wide awake, floating above him in his bed, giggling. We had amazing experiences and love as I had never experienced with anyone before. I had no way of knowing what it would become.

Things began to escalate as soon as we were married. It was like an invisible switch had been flipped in him; he was a different man. It started with him shouting at me furiously in the car while driving. I was shocked, hurt, and confused by all of the verbal abuse he was unveiling. None of my previous partners had ever called me names like that or torn down my identity as a woman so badly.

One night, after he had finished slurring his aggressive rant in the car, he slammed the door and went inside while I sat there alone in the darkness in complete despair. I just wanted to die. For the first time since I was a teenager, I contemplated how to kill myself when suddenly I felt an energy appear near me, a presence. It felt dark and ominous. It wanted me to kill myself and eagerly waited for me to do so. I could feel this presence pushing at me, 'Yes! Do it"! It was so clear and startling that it shook me to my core. It shocked me out of my despair, and I shouted, "No!" I left the car and went inside, trying to shake off the experience.

What ensued over the following year of our short marriage was my begging him to see a counselor with me, which he did three times and then refused. My health continued to deteriorate, and I had long bouts of shallow breathing where I literally could not take a deep breath or take in sufficient oxygen.

The raging continued, even when I was sick with endometriosis. One afternoon, after vomiting and having painful cramps for hours, he screamed at me through the door for what felt like an eternity, finishing with, "You deserved to be left by all your past boyfriends. You are nothing, nobody, a selfish whore!"

The emotional pain and physical pain was overwhelming. I gasped for air frantically and finally screamed. There were no words. Just two bone-rattling, earth-shaking screams came out of me. It felt as though my lungs might fall out. It both terrified and amazed me. I did not know my body was capable of such expression. The words' primal scream' took on a whole new meaning for me.

It also frightened my at-the-time spouse. He stopped shouting immediately and began apologizing, telling me he only wanted me to feel how bad he was feeling, for me to feel the same kind of pain he felt. He said he hated it when I put physical barriers between us. He couldn't stand to have a closed door between us. At that moment, I finally began to realize how unsafe it was for me to be with him. But the whole reality of it had not yet sunk in. I was still holding on, longing for the 'us' we had before marriage, hoping he would get help and be himself again.

In the weeks that followed, his rage turned into pushing me around the house, breaking pottery and artwork I had made, and waking me up in the middle of the night to listen to his shouting about how unfair the world had been to him and how much he could fight back and 'show them.'

Several times, in a rage, he pushed me against a wall, held his fists right in my face, and shook them, shouting, "I am this close to punching you," with a long pause and glaring me in the eye, "This close!"

Fearing for my physical safety in my own home, I began sleeping alone in a separate room upstairs so that I could at least hear him approaching if he started to rage in the middle of the night. I was in a living hell.

The final day came when he threatened me with his latest prized purchase: a six-inch, three-pronged knife made in Afghanistan. As I pushed the bathroom door between myself and him, he held it to my face through the widening crack in the door and finally declared, "I am going to go upstairs and kill myself."

This moment was the end of the road for me. I would carry it no further and knew that I had completely lost any piece of the loving relationship I thought I had found. As soon as he reached the top of the stairs, I ran for the phone, locked myself in the bathroom once again, and called the police. I was done. I could handle no more.

I waited for what felt like hours but it was only minutes. He was storming through the house, screaming atrocities at me through the locked bathroom door, but I hardly listened. I could barely breathe, fearing he would kick the door in.

Not a moment too soon, a firm knock finally came to the front door in the middle of his screaming rant, the knock I had been waiting and praying for. He didn't hear it and continued screaming. Another knock came, this time louder, and he stopped. An eery silence fell over the house. He opened the door, and with a surprisingly calm, cool, collected voice, he said, "Hello, officer, how can I help you."

A man's voice responded, "Well, we received a call about a domestic dispute."

"I am just having a conversation with my wife," he snarled at the officers on our doorstep. I don't remember what followed, aside from a stream of tears as I collected a few of my things and called my dog to me. Within moments, the officers safely escorted me out of the house. I went to my father's home and stayed there until my new ex-spouse could find a place to go. We had been married just under one year.

In the weeks and indeed months that followed, I awoke with a heavy, desperate feeling in my body every morning. Was this really my life? How could this have happened to me?

Facing any judgments and fears I held about divorce, I

could not escape the currents I found myself caught in. While I thought of all my loving experiences with my ex in our first three years together and grieved deeply for the relationship, I never thought of returning to him. I had already given him more opportunities than anyone ever should. He had denied any help or counseling. His choice and his path were clear. So was mine, and we were going our separate ways. Even so, I sat in Peter's office the following week sobbing harder than ever.

"I just don't know how I will live without him," I said, surprising even myself with these words. But in that moment, it was the truth of how I felt. At the beginning of the relationship, there were so many positive experiences. It was so good, and my life had changed so much. I had felt incredibly loved, understood, and seen in a way no one had ever expressed to me before. And suddenly it had ended in a horrible nightmare.

Peter was entirely supportive and encouraging, but his words echoed past me as if in a dream. I could not begin to imagine how my life could go on in any positive way at all.

It was just two months before my twenty-fifth birthday, and I had already become a 'divorcee'. I had ended a toxic, abusive marriage that I never imagined I would be in. I felt no direction or passion for any type of career. And my health problems were at their all-time worst. I wanted to quit. I felt I was a frustrated victim of this thing I'd been given called Life. I was afraid of it. I didn't know how to live it.

Each morning, the same questions rang in my ears, "how is this my life? This can't be my life. I don't want this. How could this happen to me?" I felt ashamed of my life and wanted to hide.

I had no sense of freedom, except for a tiny window within my own Spirit and Soul, in that vast, open, eternal world, where I felt free to commune with Spirit, a glimmer of light, a mild remembrance where I felt for at least a fleeting moment that I truly was one with the entire Universe. That was all I felt I had, and I clung to it quietly.

And so began my real journey, what I now call my awakening. I had no way of knowing, seeing, or possibly imagining what beauty lay in the path before me. And it wasn't just a path. It was a full-on birthing into an entirely new reality and world to live and thrive in.

## *Journal*

May 17, 2000,

So, based on my acupuncturist's advice, I will start journaling again. We spoke a lot about my list of concerns possibly related to my health issues. I always feel guilty for talking about my problems to other people, like I'm dumping it off on them. But he said it was good and was glad I could share it with him. He was talking about listening to all parts of yourself, even the angry ones, because if I ignore them (which I have), they will act up even more to be heard. I'm sure I've been holding back, stuffing, and swallowing my issues to be strong for everyone, everyone but me. I think I need to let go.

I cried a lot during my treatment today, which surprised me. He said sometimes acupuncture moves energy and can affect emotions that have been 'hanging around.' Parts of me want to face those, and parts don't.

May 18, 2000,

It has been a very long time since I journaled. Writing every day is going to take some getting used to! Discovering old wounds that I thought had been taken care of has been weird. Before, I was apprehensive about exploring and releasing them, but now I feel ready, at least a bit more than I was yesterday. As a teenager, I wrote in my journal every night, lit a candle, and burned incense. I should get back into that ritual again. It always felt good!

May 23, 2000,

Well, today, my period is typical of this past year: vomiting, painful bowel movements, Horrible Cramps, etc. I don't think I can take this much longer. It has already been almost two years since I began acupuncture. I know it is helping, as some months I have fewer symptoms than others, but I don't know if it will heal all of my physical problems. I'm thrilled it is healing and moving all of my suppressed grief and emotional energy. I wasn't aware I was stuck in survival mode, probably since I was 16!

May 26, 2000,

Today, we left for our road trip to New Mexico. We were going down the freeway at sunset. I was watching cars pass by in the other direction. The sound of them passing became like a woman's whisper. It startled me. I'd never heard anything like it before. I listened closer.

"Perseverance." I heard it several times. A little freaked out, I thought, "Right, whatever!" But I didn't forget it. Perseverance. What's the big deal? I know how to persevere. I've made it this far already, haven't I? What does perseverance mean anyway?

*Perseverance: (according to Webster) - to persist in an undertaking despite counter influences, opposition, or discouragement.*

June 7, 2000,

On the drive home from Cascadia National Forest, I looked down at the river nestled deep down in the earth, cradled by rocks, ferns, trees, roots, and soft, spongy moss. I felt this primal urge, a longing, to slip into the water like a river otter and return home. Then I realized that's what I'm doing. I'm returning home to a deeper part of myself, leaving behind this old life I have created that doesn't honor my soul.

June 9, 2000 "Grasping,"

I've thought of this analogy before, of feeling like a drowning woman, desperately grasping at other people or things, food, movies, alcohol, whatever, to save myself from this deep pain. A while back, I realized I needed to sit with the feeling of grasping when it came up, and I found that by relaxing, I could "float" and no longer drown in the emotion.

*The Tibetan Book of Living and Dying* connected for me that the grasping is ego or my shadow self. I start to grasp when I forget who I am and how connected we all are. When I remember, I can see that I am not a desperate drowning woman who is insufficient. That's my false identity, my ego. The more I open to my true self and wisdom, the less I will grasp.

∞∞∞

# a Tree

*I sat in a hammock under a tree, watching her branches blow sweetly in the summer breeze.*

*My hammock swayed, and for a stunning eternity of a few moments, I became the movement of the branches;*

*I became the tree in a state of exquisite ecstasy.*

∞ ∞ ∞

# A Spontaneous Meditation

T he incense burned sweetly as I listened to the
music, riding on the energy of it and allowing
myself to let go completely. I closed my eyes
and saw running energy lines forming into sacred
geometrical shapes. Soon, I was flying over them, or
they were flying past me, as I entered the center.
Pyramids, flowers, swirls, and intricate patterns of
perfection permeated my being.

With massive speed and precision, I flew through a
rotating, flowing, giant torus, a ring-shaped doughnut
of circles rotating on an axis and appearing as all the
colors of the Universe. The sound of its movements
consumed me, like a thousand swords, their blades
hissing against the sharpness of each one flying against
the blade of the other.

Arriving on the other side of the torus, I came to a rapid
halt. Now facing a beautiful stage, silk curtains drew
open, revealing a giant, life-size thangka, a Tibetan
scroll painting, with a Goddess at its center. She blessed
me with an exquisite gaze of total bliss in a breathless
moment of silence.

Time, movement, and thought ceased to exist.

I am the stillness. I am the I AM. I am face to face with
the infinite, and the infinite is me!

# A Fresh Start

Feeling like a complete failure in romantic relationships of any kind after my divorce, I took a vow of celibacy. I had never gone more than a few months at a time without being in a relationship, and I knew I needed to get to know myself, just as myself. I was going to figure out where I was going wrong in my life, and I was going to do it without causing more pain to myself or others for as long as it would take.

Support continued for me through my family and my acupuncturist. I formed friendships with some motherly women in my qigong class. We met weekly and discussed what we read in *The Invitation* by Oriah Mountain Dreamer. The book is based on her famous poem, which I first read years ago when I was 21. I discovered it while house-sitting for an artist, and I found the poem hanging on the wall of her studio. It brought me to tears. I read it repeatedly and cried with relief every time I read it. Someone 'out there' understood something I had felt inside myself my entire life but could never put into words.

My life began to take on a new meaning. And as Oriah Mountain Dreamer eloquently wrote in her poem The Invitation, *"I want to know if you can sit with pain, mine or your own, without moving to hide it or fade it or fix it... I want to know if you will stand in the center of the fire with me and not shrink back,"* it became my personal practice to sit with my pain, and others, and face the inner fires that dwelt there.

Renting a house just down the road from my father's place, I moved into a three-bedroom ranch-style home with a huge picture window overlooking the surrounding grass fields and the beautiful Oregon Cascade and Coastal Mountain Ranges. In the middle of the valley, with no surrounding buildings or homes, I could see the horizons to both the east and west.

Every day, I watched the rising and setting sun. It was my piece of Heaven, a masterpiece. My sacred healing retreat, and I had it all to myself. In this space, I had a newly opened mind. I was ready and willing for my life to begin anew.

Within the first few days of moving in, I did a simple ceremony for myself by lighting a candle and gently playing my brass singing bowl. At sunset, just before dark, I could see cool, white clouds spilling over the mountain range on the Western horizon, following the slopes and valleys of the Earth like liquid silver. I breathed in the stillness and quiet serenity.

Prayerfully, I called in the Ascended Masters, Saints, Angelic Beings, all the powers of Heaven, and all that was good to enter this space for my highest healing and for all who entered. It was officially my sanctuary.

I had never lived alone before, not completely alone anyway. I usually rented a bedroom or had a shared living arrangement. This house was the perfect place for me to decompress.

It took several months for me to stop hearing my ex-spouse's demeaning, criticizing voice in my head. I internally heard him scream at me if I left my dirty socks next to my shoes, even for a moment.

Now, in the safety of my new home, I left them out on display in a corner. I purposefully set my purse and coat down in a chair rather than in the closet as he had required. I left a wet towel on the bathroom floor. All of these little things would have triggered his rage in the past, and now they triggered only my memories of him shouting at me. I noticed my emotions. I listened to how I felt. And I waited patiently for his voice inside my head to fade away.

# Seeking Joy

Every morning, I could barely look at myself in the mirror, and when I did, I did not like what I saw. In the first weeks after leaving my ex, I contemplated the deep anguish I was in, and I remembered a time when I felt inexplicable joy as a child. I would smile and play with my reflection in the mirror, even practicing for my first kiss! I loved myself, and I loved my life. How did I lose this joy? How did it escape me? How is it that I was ever blessed enough to receive this kind of joy in the first place?

The joy I am speaking of is not the kind of joy you get from hearing a good song on the radio, watching a great movie, eating your favorite food, or even on a first date. It's a joy that is entirely, absurdly ecstatic; where all of life is alive, where every breath is bliss, where you notice when you fall out of ecstasy immediately because you have become so accustomed to experiencing it as a normal state. Though I had experienced all this before as a child and remembered it mentally, I could not remember what it felt like in my body, heart, and soul. I believed it was truly lost.

Contemplating how this joy first came upon me in my early childhood, I realized it was when I was at least under five. I had a spiritual experience that stayed with me like no other childhood memory I can conjure up.

My family was Catholic, and my Mother read me a bedtime story called *Jesus and I*. It was a beautiful little book with illustrations of Jesus standing beside a child through all their daily activities, helping them to do good and to resist harming others. I believed every word in the book and wholeheartedly knew that Jesus was my pal. What a great friend to have in life!

One day, a few weeks away from Easter, my sister was coloring in a huge, two-foot-length coloring book she had received as a gift. It was a coloring book on the life of Jesus. I had yet to learn of his crucifixion, and the picture I saw my sister coloring was of Jesus on the cross. When I asked her what it was, she said it was Jesus when he died. I was horrified. I asked my Mother about it, and she told me the story of how they whipped him, placed a wreath of thorns on his head, and hung him on the cross.

My whole world went gray as I fell into a deep depression. My friend, my hero, was tortured and dead. It was all I could think about every minute of every day. I had a deep, empty ache in my stomach that would not leave me. I loved to draw pictures, but from then on, all I could draw were the images in my mind of Jesus being whipped.

My father was away on a business trip, and my Mother faced the task and frustrations of raising two children alone. He was to return in a few days, and we were all anxious to see him. The day before his return, I sat in our playroom with a bottle of glue, and in my pain and frustration, I squeezed the entire contents of the bottle out onto the carpet.

Watching it soak into the carpeting and dry in a transparent, hardened blob, I knew exactly what I was doing. It was an outward expression of what I felt inside.

My Mother found me and naturally was quite upset. She sent me to my room to take a nap. I loved taking naps, so this felt fine for me. I fell asleep on my bed facing the window. In a dream, I saw Jesus. I knew it was a dream because I was sleeping, but it felt more real than life. Jesus filled my entire room with bright white light, and his body appeared to me as shimmering silver and pastel colors of light, like soft flames. He kissed me on the cheek and told me that he had complete faith and trust in me and that everything would be alright.

Laying on my bed, I awoke, looking directly at the sun shining through the window. It seemed strangely dim and yellow compared to the light I had just been in.

Exuberantly overwhelmed with joy, I could not contain myself. Jesus was alive and with me, for real, in my everyday life! I skipped and smiled everywhere we went. I remember running gleefully through the parking lot when we met my father at the airport. Every moment was bliss.

Later on, when I was around ten years old, the subject of seeing Jesus came up, and I told my Mother I saw Jesus when I was younger. To my surprise, she said, "Yes, I know!" She then told me her side of the story and even showed me an article she had written about it that was published in a Catholic editorial.

She remembered when I asked about the coloring book my sister was using and how she told me the story of his crucifixion. In retrospect, she was not sure why she had told me the details of his torture, as, of course, it would be disturbing to me as a child. But that is what happened. She remembered the pile of glue in the carpet (which may still be there to this day,) and she remembered sending me to my room for a nap. She was ironing clothes and watching television when I awoke.

She said I came bounding into the room with a smile on my face stretching from ear to ear and exclaimed to her, "Mommy, I saw Jesus!"

"That's nice, Sara, go play," she said at first.

"No, Mommy, I saw Jesus! He showed me his hands, his feet, and his side where they hurt him with a spear. He's okay now, everything's alright!"

Now she listened. My Mother had not told me about when they struck a spear in his side. I continued smiling from ear to ear, telling her that Jesus was okay and there was nothing to be sad about now.

Looking back on this memory and reflecting, I do not know how long I stayed in this state of joy, but it was purely the most ecstatic state of living I had ever experienced up to that point in my life. And now, in my early twenties, that joy was utterly lost to me.

Perhaps it faded when my first-grade teacher insisted that Jesus was not actually with me, and I couldn't speak to him directly. Maybe I lost the joy during my parent's divorce when I was thirteen. I am not sure when the joy left me, but I was certain now, during my divorce and ill health, that this joy was completely absent.

In an act of something I never really imagined I would do, I attended a fundamentalist Christian service. I sat uncomfortably through the ceremony of shouting and tears, testimonials, and invitations to 'come to Jesus' and be reborn. Afterward, I approached the minister. I told him of my current circumstances and asked him to pray for Jesus to fill my life with joy again.

He was a nice man, full of conviction and spiritual intensity. He prayed for me, I thanked him, and I left. Nothing felt new or different. I let it go, thinking I was a bit of a desperate fool, and continued on, placing one small step in front of the other, facing each day as best I could.

# The Gold Stars

"**P**romise me you'll do this." Peter pressed a sheet of gold star stickers into my hand, his kind, blue eyes intensely looking, searching determinedly into mine.

"Promise," he insisted.

"Okay, I promise," I sheepishly smiled and finally agreed. I resisted it and felt it was a silly, frivolous idea.

But Peter was known for his kind intensity and ability to help others heal. I trusted him. Still struggling with shallow breathing and barely able to take a single deep breath throughout my entire day, Peter had come up with a solution. I was to take the whole page of gold star stickers, just like the ones I used to get in grade school on my tests if I got an 'A,' and stick them all around my home, where I would see them multiple times throughout the day. Each time I saw a gold star, I was to take a deep breath as deeply as I could manage.

Not liking to be a procrastinator, I went straight home and began peeling off the little stars and sticking them throughout my house: on the corner of my calendar, the back of my phone, my closet doors, a few kitchen cabinets, the bathroom mirror, and the back door to the house that I left through every morning on my way to work. My home was now glammed out with shimmering, shiny gold stars, and I struggled each time I saw one to breathe in deeply and let go.

At first, it was simply challenging. Then, it became annoying. But I knew Peter would not back down, and I had made a promise to him. So, I continued for weeks and weeks. It slowly became easier, and within a few months, I loved my golden stars. They were my stars of victory, as I breathed happily, freely, fully, and regularly for the first time in a very long time.

To this day, I still react to seeing a gold star with a deep breath. It's ingrained in me! The gold stars have taken on a new meaning. They symbolize my triumph over a life that went from barely breathing and barely existing to living passionately, loving my beautiful self, and discovering the equally beautiful beings in many people around me.

# Initiation into Breath

"**I** know a great breathing technique that I think might help you. Would you be willing to come in for a session and try it?"

I considered Peter's latest invitation. *Where and how did he come up with all of this stuff?*

By this time, my acupuncture sessions had become somewhat cathartic. I could hardly walk into his treatment room without bursting into tears before either of us could speak. It was as if I had been sitting on a volcano of emotional pain my whole life without really knowing it. And now, in his calm, supportive presence, the tears erupted and finally started to flow.

I thought about his offer to teach me a breathing technique. It sounded ridiculous. Breathing! I am already doing it. It's something we all do automatically. What's the big deal about breathing? Everybody breathes! I looked at him, watching me enthusiastically, still waiting for my response. My thoughts continued to swirl. *Well, breathing is harmless. I may as well try it.*

"Alright. I'll do it," I annoyingly agreed.

Later that week, slightly put off and feeling that I was wasting my time, I showed up for my first Rebirthing Breathwork session.

After Peter's careful instruction about the breathing rhythm, I lay stretched out on the treatment table covered with a soft, warm blanket and began breathing. Deep inhale, relaxed exhale, deep inhale, relaxed exhale, one right after the other. I felt terrified. Why was it so hard to just breathe while someone watched me?

Deep inhale, letting go on the exhale, pulling in the next deep inhale. I began to feel light as air. Tingles began to vibrate in what felt like every cell of my body as I inhaled and exhaled. Peter continued guiding my breath along. Leaning close next to my ear, he began to speak affirmations to me softly as I breathed. "You are safe. You are whole and complete. You are perfect."

Things started to feel completely surreal. My lungs fought against taking deep breaths, and my throat tightened.

"Push through the resistance. Keep breathing. Deep inhales, you can do it!" Peter encouraged me. It was as if he knew exactly how I was feeling.

A few breaths and a few affirmations later, I noticed tears were rolling down my cheeks. When did that start? What in the world is happening here? My breathing was taking off like a bird in flight. Connected breaths now seemed like the easiest, most natural thing to do.

And then it happened; a deep wave of grief washed over me. It was like a tsunami of sadness that consumed and crushed every corner of my soul. A memory came with it.

Around age three, I stood on the beach with my family, screaming and crying that they should not go near the ocean. I was certain a tidal wave was coming that would wash them out to sea, leaving me there alone without them. The fear and the grief were overwhelming. Why was that fear so natural for me? Was it a past life trauma? Was it simply something I saw in a movie during my childhood? Where did that fear and grief come from? The tears streamed down my face. Impulsively, I stopped breathing. It hurt so much. Too much.

"Breathe, keep going, breathe right through this," he beckoned me. It was as though I stood on the edge of a cliff, and he was asking me to leap. I struggled to breathe. I continued to cry. Finally, the breaths took over again and carried me through the chasm of emotional pain. I breathed, breathed, and breathed, and slowly, softly, a deep peace overcame me.

All was well. It was a peace I had never felt and didn't know was possible. I was immaculately serene. I felt peace in every cell of my body, mind, and emotions. Even the air around me felt softer and more calm.

Continuing to breathe, several more waves of sadness came over me, each followed by a deep state of tranquility that grew stronger and stronger. My whole body was buzzing by now. It was an electric vibration emanating from the every fiber of my being. The peacefulness was exquisite.

Upon completion, I opened my eyes. I was amazed by what I had experienced. And much to my astonishment, I noticed two and a half hours had passed. What in the world just happened? How was it that in my twenty five years of living, I didn't know of this before? Prana (life force) is real! Prana is amazing!

We spoke briefly about my experience, which gave me time to integrate. I was astounded. How often can I do this? How do I learn more? When I left the treatment room, my body was transformed, still buzzing, and the atmosphere felt charged with electricity. Everything, *everything*, was alive and humming with energy.

*So this is what prana is,* I thought in this altered state. In Hinduism, prana means breath, a life-giving force, a universal energy that flows in currents in and around the body and throughout all of existence itself.

At that moment, I knew I had to learn more. I knew I had found my calling, and my life would never be the same. For all of my life, everyone had asked me what I wanted to be when I grew up, and I never knew until that day. Breathwork was what had been missing.

Something gloriously Divine had opened up in my life in a very real and practical way. I decided to find a professional breathwork training. I went home and searched online to find a school or a teacher, but none seemed to call to me. So, I continued my sessions with Peter and trusted that the right path would unfold.

### Invitation - Stickers

Whether you use stickers of gold stars, unicorns, or bunny rabbits, etc., this invitation is to choose a sheet of stickers and put them up around your living space to remind you to take a deep breath as you go about your day.

# An Education

"**I** still think you are a great candidate for this," Peter stated. "Do you still have the brochure?"

I remembered the plain, cream-colored paper with simple black-lettered words, *The Liberty Experience.* It was a weekend intensive organized and created by Matt Garrigan.

It seemed Peter was constantly pushing me toward the edge. I hated group activities. What on Earth could this be about? I pondered to myself that he was the person who introduced me to Rebirthing Breathwork, yoga, and qigong. I could take a look at it. *The Liberty Experience.* Maybe it could surprise me and be fun.

"Alright, I'll go," I could not quite believe the words as I said them.

Peter had not advised or led me anywhere I had yet regretted, so I decided to take a leap of faith and trust his invitation. And this felt like a big one. It was going to cost a lot of money for me at that time. It also required several days of my time and was located out of town.

To this day, I am so grateful that I said yes. It turned out I was a great candidate for this kind of 'training.' I was eager to learn. I was driven by a life of pain, and I was ready for liberation. I was seeking joy and had no clue where to find it or how. I was open and willing to receive.

It was May of 2002. I went into this event feeling that I could trust no one, feeling insecure, on guard, and apprehensive. It was a simple sort of training based on experiential learning through games and exercises. Still, it took many of those participating to their deepest, darkest fears, vulnerabilities, insecurities, and heartaches. Three and a half days later, I left with more than fifty new friends and deep, vulnerable, emotionally intimate connections that would change my life forever. It seemed to me we all left the training like shining champions who had just conquered death itself.

On the final day of the Liberty Experience, I once again sat in a circle with all the other participants. Tears streamed down my face as the final process had been for me, more of an energetic experience in which I felt all of the garbage, shame, burdens, fears, resistance, and pain that had accumulated over my lifetime release from my body energetically. I felt complete in my divine life essence, power, endless creative possibilities, love, and my*self* in the highest imaginable meaning of that. My body was buzzing and vibrating at a frequency I didn't know I could attain outside of a Rebirth. I sensed that we all were living in this new vibration.

The energy in the room was so potent it was palpable. As a group we sat in silence, swimming in our newfound radiance. I breathed in, vibrating in this new experience of myself and my personal power, my love, *my life,* owning it for perhaps the first time since I was a young child. And within the freshness of this sacred moment, I was transported back to my experience as a small child with Jesus when he appeared to me in my dream and kissed me on the cheek. Joy exploded through my body and Spirit in what seemed like a lightning bolt of energy. All I could do was breathe it in and receive.

The following weeks were total bliss for me. Everything was playful. Everything was enjoyable and delightful. Even looking in the mirror, I once again felt like a child smiling, playing, and loving myself unabashedly. My plea, my call, my prayer to access that JOY I had felt so lost and distant from, was fully answered, turned on, and alive in me again.

Looking back on this time of my life, I can sincerely describe it as my awakening. I was hatched from my egg and born into a new, vibrant, exciting life filled with beautiful, endless possibilities. I had a new understanding of how my thoughts and feelings shaped my reality and were either limiting or liberating myself.

The following day after I completed the training, I began my period, and for the first time in my life, I had no painful symptoms at all.

I was in perfect peace yet filled with incredible aliveness. I felt the vibration of all of life, the hum of creation, the infinite Presence singing in the very air that I breathed. I had stepped into a new reality. Throughout the Liberty Experience training, I cried oceans of tears and released tons of fear, negativity, and blockages that I didn't even know lay buried deep inside.

When I thought I couldn't shed another tear, I shed a thousand more. I believe I cleared up so much negative mental and emotional energy that I was in an altered state, one that my body was undeniably responding quite happily to. This, along with the continued acupuncture, Chinese herbs, and life changes I had made transformed my body and I had no symptoms of disease.

Does this mean endometriosis is psychosomatic? No. Women all around the globe have been told that their debilitating endometriosis symptoms are all in their heads and denied medical treatment. This is wrong. One could contemplate the possibility that all diseases are ultimately psychosomatic, but even so, being informed of available therapies and approaches should be accessible to anyone seeking health.

Quickly after attending the Liberty Experience, I continued my training with Matt by completing all the remaining courses he offered. I would go on to volunteer and assist with his events for the next four years until Matt went on a sabbatical in 2005.

Finding an abundance of support and new ideas that permanently transformed the quality of my life, I uncovered enormous amounts of harmful, unconscious beliefs and identities I was unknowingly clinging to that were affecting my health, relationships, self-esteem, career, and virtually every aspect of my life.

Matt's courses taught me simple and practical tools I still use daily to transcend my self-limiting beliefs and behaviors. His classes were based on the element of experience, not just intellectual understanding.

I learned to live clearly and purposefully during

my four years of education and service. It was an invaluable resource, offering fundamental skills essential to functioning and effectively contributing to my community. It empowered me to grow toward my fullest potential each day.

Life became a powerful, omnipotent, omnipresent energy, a miraculous, wondrous gift. I learned that life didn't just happen to me; I am Life. I had a choice in how I wanted to be with it. I learned to create profound and miraculous peace in my relationships with my family and friends. I actualized my physical healing numerous times.

Experiencing greater clarity and various states of sheer joy, bliss, and serenity, increased my self-trust; my trust in my ability to respond to life events. The skills I learned were simple yet profound. They permeated into every aspect of my life.

Through my work with Matt, I found the courage to challenge myself, extend my career goals, and nurture my dreams into existence. I gained expanded feelings of incredible openness and unity within myself and with others. It gave me an increased depth of my spirituality.

I have done more things, shared my life, and expressed my love and enthusiasm in ways I never imagined possible. My experience of life became fearlessly inspiring, divine, and delicious!

I still have moments where I may feel overwhelmed, powerless, or experience upsets. But I now know that I can consciously use them as opportunities to strengthen my confidence and gain more profound self-awareness.

In sharing this with you, I hope you will be inspired to experience Matt's work for yourself or to start exploring and finding the right teacher for you on your path. I can not tell you what your experience would be like, as we each bring our unique personality into the world. There are as many perceptions of life as there are people. No two people are the same!

## Invitation - Experience

Experience is the ultimate way of learning, growth, and evolution. While reading a well-written book may give you an experience and offer changes to your life, hands-on experiential learning is different. I encourage you to get out there and find the people walking their talk, demonstrating their greatness, and lifting others. Sometimes, we need to sit close to the fire to warm our bodies, find those burning brightly, learn from them, and ignite our inner fire.

The invitation is to participate in a course or training focused on personal development, integrity, authenticity, and unlocking your unlimited potential.

Find a community that awakens you. Find the teachings and experiences that will ignite your spark. Take every opportunity to learn and grow as much as you can.

Discovering the true beauty, power, love, and creative potential within yourself is the greatest gift you can give yourself and the world. If you are interested in Matt's work, check out www.MattGarigan.com

# Integrity

Integrity is one of many core concepts I learned during my education with Matt. It's not that I didn't value or have any integrity before I enrolled in his curriculum; it's just that I didn't fully understand the vital importance and power of consciously living in my integrity daily. One might ask, what exactly does that mean?

Have you noticed that the people with a high sense of integrity are the ones who are out there accomplishing extraordinary things and enthusiastically enjoying their work? Integrity is one of the core pillars I now stand on, whereas before, it was almost an afterthought. It didn't have the front-row seat it deserved in my attention, choices, and actions.

Webster defines integrity as - *an unimpaired condition, soundness, the quality or state of being complete and undivided; incorruptibility.*

How does your integrity affect health? Integrity is the quality or state of being complete and undivided. When experiencing my integrity, I am centered and undivided at one focal point: my purpose. I am a stand for something new to show up in the world, not out of arrogance, self-righteousness, or egotistical endeavors. I take action out of love, compassion, and the understanding that what I do or don't do affects not only myself but also others. I know that we are all united, and when one benefits, the whole of humanity benefits as well.

When I have integrity, I know myself, my true self, my deepest inner nature. I know that I will walk the talk and can be relied on to take action. I know the purpose of my actions. I know my presence matters. I have a high sense of self-worth. I stand in my wholeness and vital role in the fabric of life. I am clear enough in my mind to be open to greater energies and wisdom.

To have integrity is to have a strong sense of inner trust and to be willing to let old past creations die and give way to the new. It is to know and live from the truth that transformation is a gateway into a new and greater sense of life. When I cultivate integrity, I am taking a stand for my well-being. I am in such complete abundance that it overflows, extending with compassion for the well-being of others also.

Many people believe that they don't matter and that the Universe would not miss a beat if they weren't exactly where they are right now. It's the feeling of being invisible, unimportant, disconnected, isolated, less than deserving, unworthy, incapable, inadequate, and so on. These limiting, self-sabotaging perceptions must be dissolved to create a new, empowered self-image. This can be done through consciousness work, inner inquiry, breathwork, etc. It requires the willingness to take a deep, honest, humble look at oneself and be open to uncovering what may lie suppressed in emotions and the psyche.

Integrity is incorruptible. Incorruptibility is not rigid and unmoving. Life is constantly changing. It is a flow. Integrity is the essence of Life and nature itself. It is the perfect harmony between defined material form and undefined, fluid, flexible energy. To have integrity is to be familiar with, comfortable with, and welcoming of transformation, changing the old material form into something new.

Just as winter gives way to spring, I had to release old identities of being not important, weak, unworthy, ashamed, diseased, and disconnected from life to create the space for health, vitality, vibrancy, joy, and aliveness to occur within myself.

There is a certain quality of maturity that comes with cultivating Integrity. I could no longer point the finger and blame. I could no longer complain and recreate myself as the victim. I could no longer lie even in small ways to myself or others because I knew that to do so would close off a piece of myself from life every time.

This new sense of integrity was not a heavy burden or load. On the contrary, it became an incredibly light and freeing experience. It fostered a maturing that did not kill off the youthfulness, wonder, enticement, enchantment, and discovery of my magical inner child. This maturing is not a closing to life; it is an opening to Eternal Inner Youth, the very essence of one's self.

Cultivating integrity is crucial to health and well-being. It is a significant contributing factor to the well-being of physical existence. It isn't easy to be relaxed and stress-free in the body when you don't know or trust yourself.

It is nearly impossible to value or love yourself when you don't trust who you are and what you say, do, or do not do. Without self-trust and self-love, life is full of confusion, fear, pain, and loss.

I am enthusiastically grateful for the people who have taught and demonstrated the true meaning of Integrity. Strengthening my integrity saves my life every day that I practice it. My integrity restores my health and inner balance. It has restored my self-worth, productivity, and passion for life.

## The Integrity of Nature

Nature is a perfect demonstration of integrity. Incorruptibly, the law of gravity is constantly in place, holding your house and things to the ground. Whether you think of it or not, all these physical things are still there when you wake in the morning.

The trees grow in the sunlight and absorb what nutrients and water they need. They release oxygen for all to breathe. Bears do not eat more berries than their fill. The grass grows, and the bees pollinate. Everyone and everything has its place of giving and receiving. Nature is an intricate balance of harmony; a delicate web of life.

Humanity is a part of this web, too. Yet we are not in integrity. We take more than we need at great expense to others. We have raped the Earth of her trees and oil, polluted her waters and skies, drugged her body - lands with chemicals and altered genetics. By consuming and wasting more than our fill, we are out of integrity with nature. No wonder we are sick and depressed. It is time for us to live in a way that aligns with all of life and Mother Earth.

Every moment of every day, we are surrounded by the unthinkable beauty of nature. And it is ours to be a part of, participate in with peace and harmony, and witness.

My body yearns to live in the light of day and rest in the dark of night, bathe in the full moon's luminous beauty as she illuminates the secrets of the heavens, dance under a sea of stars, and gaze into the infinite vast Universe. I know that living in cities far off and disconnected from the gifts of nature is part of my disease.

Menstruation, my 'moon time', is like a gauge telling me when I am off course. When I have strayed too far from the rhythms of nature, my natural rhythms, the rhythms of my body, my womb lets me know.

Our Mother pulses with a perfect rhythm in the cycles of life. She wraps us in diverse ecosystems of mountains and streams, deserts and beaches, prairies and wetlands. We live in a garden of the heavens. We can be in reverence, respect, and gratitude for it, or we can continue to destroy it. Either way, ultimately, I believe balance and harmony will prevail, with or without us.

## Invitation - the Natural World

Write your thoughts about the following questions, and contemplate or meditate on them. Notice how you feel about the natural world and your place in it.

Considering your physical symptoms and disease, how might they relate to the state of our Earth?

How much time do you spend in nature, away from artificial lighting and electromagnetic fields?

Which of your habits or lifestyle choices are not sustainable or in harmony with nature? How can you change this? Are you willing to make the needed changes?

Spend some time in nature to the best of your current capacity. Contemplate and observe the rhythms of nature. Feel and consider the rhythms of nature in your own body.

# Imagination

## a Most Powerful Ally

I had become friends with my disease. I was discovering it, inside and out. I was getting educated, surrounding myself with lots of support, and was willing to have this whole experience full-blown. I was doing deep inner inquiry. I was committed. Now what?

First, I had to accept the idea that my body could heal. Some of my symptoms returned in the following months after the Liberty Experience. It was hard to face, but I now had a new experience of what was possible. I had to be willing and desiring to experience a fully healthy, alive body. I had to be ready to heal with no reason or medical explanation at all.

Second, I had to begin to imagine myself wholly healed. I had to forget the memories of ill health. What does it mean to do this? I'm not talking about doing a visualization once or twice. I needed to consistently and permanently change my self-image and how I viewed my body, life, and health. At first, imagining myself menstruating pain-free was more challenging to do than I realized. Since I had only one period that was pain-free without taking medications, I needed to develop a new identity and let go of the old. I had to begin to see myself and imagine what it would be like, what it would feel like, to be totally healthy every month. I had to envision, feel, and think as if I had my period and felt great!

We can embody whatever qualities we desire by consciously and attentively choosing to do so. Putting on a new identity or quality is like putting on a new pair of shoes. It is that simple! Just like new shoes that may need to be broken in and worn for a while before they become comfortable, it takes a while to get comfortable in a new self-image. We must keep re-choosing to 'wear' the new image every day until it becomes integrated as a natural way to be. Qualities of being are not magical gifts bestowed upon a few worthy and withheld from the rest. They are to be cultivated from within. All we need to do is decide to be it.

Most people have this process backward. People tend to think that first, they have to acquire something, and then when they have it, they will be able to do it and become it. But the truth is that energy follows thought. Imagination is the combination of thinking, visualizing, feeling, and flowing of energy. We can be whatever we want to be in our imagination. This is not just child's play. Our bodies are listening in on everything we imagine. And our bodies respond.

As human beings, when we intend to achieve a goal, vision, or dream, we must first *become* the desired result. We become it by thinking, feeling, visioning, and imagining that we are already there. This affects our personal energy, ability to respond, and choices, which moves us into the second phase; *do it!* The third phase is a natural progression in that we will eventually *have* it.

As we progress in our healing processes, we must, at some point, release old perceptions of ourselves as damaged or diseased. We must stop ruminating on that which we believe we can not change. We must stop recreating the unwanted experience or condition repeatedly in our minds. Even if it is still happening in the body, we can decide in our minds to let it go. It is a circumstance or condition. It is not *who we are.*

We can be willing to surrender disease and perceived limitations to something bigger than the tiny little picture we see ourselves as. We can be ready to expand ourselves out larger than the disease and beyond the body.

The mindset to play with is that the disease does not have you. It has not taken a hold on you. You have taken a hold on it. It's crucial to *play* with this idea and not use it to beat yourself up or make yourself wrong. Make it as light, fun, and open to miracles as possible!

The essence of healing is to be willing to have the disease without building up resistance to it, yet also release it, even if only through imagination.

Negative thinking and imagining directly impact all aspects of life, including others around us. Cultivating trust in our ability to have seniority over our imaginings is like working a new muscle.

Perhaps you have never thought of taking authority over what you imagine. If you don't believe you have authority over your imagination, over what you dwell upon in your mind, then who does? Who else is in charge?

Always imagining the worst-case scenario is the misuse of power to Imagine. Instead, we can imagine and dwell upon *what we do want* in our lives and in the world. We can spend time in silence to imagine and feel the peace, love, and wisdom we want to see manifest in our health, life, and world. We can imagine that which is life-supporting and sustaining. This is the very seat of the creative self. Imagination is at the heart of all things.

When you are imagining, you are putting your life-force energy into action. Imagination is creation itself. Be willing to experience it all. This is your Greatness.

## *Invitation - Be, Do, and Have*

What qualities of being would you like to experience more of? Joy, gratitude, humility, inspiration, empowerment, full aliveness, energy, enthusiasm, vitality, humor, playfulness, ecstasy?

Make a list of 100 things you would like to be, do, or have.

After making your list, imagine yourself there now as if all else had simply fallen in place. You are the lead actor on the stage of your life. In which direction are you leading the play in your imaginings?

# It is a Gift to be a Woman

Hot tears streamed down my burning cheeks as I gasped for air. What began as a journaling process had turned into a spontaneous Rebirthing Breathwork session for me.

"It is a gift to be a woman." This was the first affirmation ever given to me, and it was given to me by Peter, a man. And it felt like a lie. What did he know about being a woman?

I thought of all the pain and bloating I had with menstruation, and ensuing paranoia as I walked through my high school hallways, terrified that my heavy blood flow would seep out of carefully arranged pads and tampons. It was a constant battle, hiding the red river that gushed through my legs, which left me feeling dizzy, disoriented, and isolated in a world of pain.

My mind turned to all the jokes, harassment, unwanted advances, and flirtations by intimidating, older school boys and sometimes grown men. As a young, quiet, shy girl, I carried the burden of unwanted attention, unwanted advances, and unwanted physical contact.

Didn't they see me? Couldn't they see who I was much further beyond this body? Could they not relate to me as a human being, with feelings, thoughts, and emotions? Was this all I was to them? A sex object?

*It is a gift to be a woman.* Hah! It is a curse.

"Bitch. Cunt. Seductress. Manipulative. Evil. Eve. Only good for sex. Here to please others. Worthless." I continued to scribble out the words, shocked by the hateful thoughts coming to my mind as I breathed connectedly through the searing pain I felt in my heart, in my body and in my womb.

All of this garbage. All of this negativity and hatred of the feminine. All of it contained in the cells of my body, imprinted from a society and culture lost in the throws of objectification of women, the patriarchy, the glorification of male dominance, and aggression. These lies continued to surface to my conscious awareness with each breath, as I felt and witnessed the many years of suppressed pain and soul wounding begin to unravel.

The next memory to surface was the story of Adam and Eve, which I had learned from the nuns teaching at my Catholic grade school. I learned that because Eve had picked the apple and tempted Adam to taste it, they were cast out of the Garden of Eden, and as punishment to her and all of humanity, childbearing became painful.

I was about seven years old when I learned that. I was horrified. I was being punished. Me. In my female body. I would never be right in the eyes of God.

"Scum of the Earth, toiling in pain. Unworthy. Outcast. Guilty." The final words dropped like bombs on the now five sheets of paper, filled and exploding with the weight of years of shame.

My pain began to release as I finished. My pen fell to the floor. I lay down, breathing in a deeply connected rhythm as I felt the anger turn into grief, a deep sadness, and a longing for all the years that were lost in a nightmare of self-hatred, fear, worthlessness, and rejection.

I was, and always had been, a sacred, Divine WOMAN. The tears of realization streamed down my cheeks now. Finally, I had a taste of the sweetness of my femininity, of my own inner sacred woman.

What did that even mean; sacred woman? If it is not a curse, then what does it mean that it is a gift? I still could not see this in my mind.

By the young age of twenty five, I had already endured years of debilitating cramps, hours of vomiting and dry heaving, painful bowel movements and spasms, clots, and heavy bleeding, all of which left me writhing on the bathroom floor, cursing being a woman and begging to know "why me"? With all of this happening right here in my body, how could I embrace the idea that it is a gift to be a woman? I knew I needed some good role models if I was going to heal from this disease.

I began studying and learning about the various goddesses from Greek, Roman, and Pagan traditions. I started a small book club with other women who had similar spiritual beliefs and interests. I reached out to my friends and sisters and began meeting with them weekly to talk, share, and give each other feedback, encouragement, and support.

In reaching out to the women around me, I found strong, unending, steady reserves of sisterhood. I connected with drumming and ecstatic dance communities. I started to unlock the fear: what if I look stupid? What if I do something wrong? What if I'm not safe to be fully expressive in my body? By banishing these mistaken thoughts fed to me all my life, I kept choosing Her, my free, liberated sacred woman, my innermost Divine self.

Delving deeper into studying world religions was something I was always afraid to do as I was raised Catholic, and it was discouraged. But I found deep spiritual truths emanating from all cultures of the world. I found spiritual ecstasy in Rumi. Profound truths in the Tao te Ching. Bhakti (devotion) and love for the Divine in Hinduism.

Opening my heart and soul to what called to me, I discovered the bliss of singing devotional kirtan, hiking in the mountains, and soaking naked in natural hot springs. I began celebrating my life. I started feeling alive again despite my circumstances and symptoms. In every spare chance I could take, I slipped away into moments of what fed and nourished my soul.

This is my wish for you: that you celebrate your life and your body in whatever means of expression that is healthy, safe, consenting, beautiful, and abundant for you.

## *Invitation - Gender Ideas*

Schedule some time to be alone and be truly present with yourself. Write out every negative thought, every belief, every derogatory, name-calling, nasty comment or joke you can ever remember hearing about being female or male; pick one to do first and then come back and do the other. Fill in as many pages as you need. Write whatever comes to mind without judgment. Writing it all out and letting it all go is wonderfully liberating. Know that now, you can choose to believe it or not.

What are your beliefs about being a woman or a man?

What jokes, ideas, and thoughts have you heard about women/men?

How did you feel when you heard them?

Which ideas did you identify with?

Do you believe it is a gift to be a woman?

Is it a gift to be a man?

Why or why not?

What were your mother's ideas about her female body? What were her ideas about women?

What were your father's ideas about his body? What were his ideas about women?

How do you feel about your female (or male) body?

How does your culture portray women and our place in the world?

How does your culture portray men and their place in the world?

# Breathwork Psychedelics

## *The Woman in the Road*

Over the following months, I continued to receive breathwork sessions with Peter every chance I could. I was also expanding my search for healing modalities and information that could help me heal from endometriosis. This landed me at the Mind, Body, Spirit Expo in Portland, Oregon. A friend starting her hypnotherapy practice would be there offering mini-sessions and she invited me to stop by.

I meandered through the rows of booths and treatment spaces; crystals, essential oils, energy work, and other healing modalities I had never heard of splayed out in a packed sea of people meandering through the expo. Psychics, massage therapists, it seemed to all be there, but I saw no one offering breathwork.

However, I kept circling back to one man's booth. He was older than me and smaller in stature than my towering six feet of height. His space consisted of a massage table, lights for color therapy, and crystals, so many crystals! There were large, seventy pound crystals under the massage table on a copper grid, hooked up to two copper handles to be held by the person on the table. But each time I passed, there was no person there receiving treatment, just his kind smile and hello, which I shyly slipped away from.

Returning to my pickup in the parking garage, I sat down, ready to leave. I was not too fond of big cities, and I was eager to return to the calm, open pace of the countryside. My hands were on the wheel, ready to start the engine, but I paused. A mild churning was building up in my stomach.

This man's booth kept gnawing at me. What was the work he was doing? I didn't understand it. But I felt so curious.

The 'old me' would have retreated and left, tossing it off as nothing. But that is not what I was here to do anymore. I was here for growth. I was here for a breakthrough. I was here for a change. And I knew it required getting uncomfortable at times. And in that moment, I knew if I left without going through the uncomfortableness of finding out what might happen in that booth, I would be cheating myself. I could not leave without going back and seeing what this man was about.

I quickly paid for more parking. How much time would this take? Whatever, max the meter out. I raced back inside, gliding past all the other booths and people inviting me in. My mind was set on where I was going.

Finding his booth again, I walked directly up to him this time and smiled.

"Hi!" I very nearly shouted at him with nervous enthusiasm. "So what is it that you do here?"

He had a twinkle in his eye that was pleasing, enchanting, and almost star-like. He smiled warmly. Intently present and very grounded, he calmly said, "Well, this is a place just to breathe, receive, and feel."

I glanced around his booth. *Soul Time,* it said in bright colors with a geometric wheel of colors beneath it and sacred geometry in vibrant colors laid out on the table. The massage table looked comfortable, and the crystals beneath it were out of this world beautiful.

"Okay, I'd like to try it. I'm Sara," I said, shaking his hand.

"I'm Brian," he replied happily. His hands were strong but warm, gentle, and soft.

We discussed the details of his fees and exchanged a few words to get to know each other. He explained that the treatment involved laying on the table and connecting with the energy of the crystals and that he sometimes used his hands to help the energy move. He asked if I would be comfortable with that. I gave my consent, and the treatment began.

Lying on the table, I clasped the copper handles with curiosity as he placed them in my hands, explaining that they were connected via copper wire to the larger crystals and that the handles themselves were filled with smaller quartz crystals. Each handle also had a small quartz point attached to the end.

He invited me to relax and breathe. He closed his eyes and sang some sort of invocation in a language I did not understand. Was it Hebrew? I had no idea, but it was obvious he did it with great intent and meaning. It felt powerful.

He then instructed me to take deep breaths; one leading right into the next and just feeling, breathing, and receiving.

"Wait, like, connected breathing?" I asked.

"Yes," he replied.

"Oh! Okay, I can do that!" I replied, wondering how that would feel in an expo loaded with people and spectators, some of whom were already gathering to watch. I quietly decided to myself, *well, I'll go for it and find out.*

I began breathing connectedly with Brian standing by my side, continuing to speak gently and holding his hands over me. The familiar buzzing and tingling of my few previous breathwork sessions began; however, this time, it came on more quickly and with more intensity. The copper handles seemed to be buzzing in my hands. A rush of energy went to my head and out my crown. My feet opened up with tingles as well. I could feel a crowd gathering around and hear comments and whispers. I breathed on.

Brian's hands were warm now, laying gently on my abdomen or just below my clavicle. The warmth penetrated my body, seemingly reaching into my very organs. Old feelings of shame and unworthiness surfaced, and I felt a lump of sadness welling up in my throat.

Swoosh! Brian made several sweeping motions down over my body and out my feet as my whole body lit up with more tingles, lighter, free, and alive. It was like an energy bath with crystals and breath. Time passed, but I had no idea how long. An hour? Two? My breath became more effortless, flowing, gentler, and connected, like the gentle waves of a lake lapping onshore.

Floating light as a feather, I felt Brian standing beside me, calm and quiet. I slowly rolled my head to my right, stretching my arms a bit, and spontaneously opened my eyes. I gazed out into the crowd of onlookers who were dispersing now. Their spectacle was over, and all seemed to lose interest in it, except for one woman who stopped, turned, and looked straight into my eyes.

"Nila?" I asked incredulously.

"Sara?" She replied with equal disbelief.

Nila and I had just recently met in Portland weeks before at the Liberty Experience. She walked over as if in a trance, and my joy was overwhelming at this synchronicity on top of the bliss of just completing another breathing session.

Unable to sit up just yet, I lay there washed in an energetic field of delight in Brian's presence, feeling the purity of him and his beautiful energy. It was like Nila was naturally drawn in, and all three of us just beamed, gazing into each other's eyes in a bliss-filled silence, smiling. Laughter broke out, and either Nila introduced herself or I did her. It was like a dream. Brian and Nila both had bright, piercing blue eyes, and I felt as if a true, spiritual family surrounded me.

Brian, it turned out, lived in southern Oregon but regularly traveled the entire length of the state and on up into Washington. He would be passing by my small hometown within a few weeks. Wanting to do more sessions with him but unable to afford it, I agreed to host an event for him in my home with friends, happy to receive another breathwork session as a trade. Of course, Nila wanted to attend as well. I sent out the invites, and within weeks, five friends, some local and some from Portland, were gathered in my living room, the sanctuary that was my home.

At the start of our little gathering, Brian gave a simple but sweet introduction and answered some questions. Everyone found their place of choice comfortably on the floor with their mats, pillows, and blankets, some laying on copper grids surrounded by Brian's gorgeous collection of massive crystals connected with the now familiar, terminated quartz copper handles.

He sang his invocation and guided us all into the breathing rhythm. Brian invited everyone to sit and hold space if they didn't feel called to start breathing yet. One of my friends, Rhea, sat beside me, watching me breathe.

Some time into the session, both Brian and Rhea were sitting near me. Rhea began singing softly, toning and sounding in some language made up as she went along. It sounded almost Hawaiian to me. I felt so safe and soothed in the presence of them both.

A vision in my mind's eye slowly came into view as I continued breathing; I was lying under a roughly built shelter on a warm, tropical beach next to a small fire on a woven mat. She was a medicine woman singing prayers and chanting over me. I was apparently near death, but I felt blissful and serene. It was as though I were in both places at once: my living room and this hut on the beach.

Suddenly, I felt extremely cold, unbelievably cold. Then,

quite unexpectedly and seemingly out of the blue, I heard someone scream, a terrible, loud, blood-curdling scream.

*Whoa, they are really going for it,* I thought to myself.

A few more breaths went by, and I heard two more of the earth-shaking, primal screams.

The next breath came, and I realized it was me. I was screaming! Why was this coming from me? I momentarily forced my eyes open just in time to see Rhea's face contort in tears as she went into a spontaneous Rebirthing of her own, and lay down on her mat.

In the next breath, I left. My living room was gone. Everyone there was gone, even Brian.

Lying directly in the middle of a dirt road, I soon discovered chaos erupting around me. People were panicking and running in every direction, some were being slaughtered right before me by swordsmen on horseback. Where was I? I looked at grass-roofed huts burning in a tropical setting.

It was the middle of a raid, an attack, or some kind of war. I was alone, lying on the dirt road naked, and I was giving birth.

A total sense of terror, indignity, fear, panic, loss, and anger washed over me all at once. I was not sure if I was miscarrying or giving birth, but I feared I was physically unable to complete the birth. I did not want to have this baby here amidst this horror. I did not want to bring life into such existence.

At the same time, I so very much wanted this child. I wanted to live and be its mother. The shock was all-consuming. I was in a state of stasis. Complete stasis, unable to choose in either direction. Do I birth this baby or not? Somehow, it was clear to me that I had the power to make that decision. But I couldn't. I was suspended in indecision, torn between the love for my child and the horror of the world to which I would be bringing it.

Continuing to breathe connectedly, I became increasingly present in my body, assessing the situation. I noticed a sharp pain in my left side and looked down at my abdomen.

Someone had stabbed me with a knife and left it there.

Now, feeling utterly hopeless, I knew I couldn't complete the birth. I tried so hard, but I knew I was dying, and so was my child if they hadn't already. I breathed in total agony and emotional turmoil. Who had done this to me? Where was the father? Where was the rest of my family?

I struggled horrifically until, strangely, I began to feel at peace with it. A Divine Presence washed over me; it was an effortless surrender to something greater than myself. It felt like a deep healing was beginning to occur. I felt compassion and forgiveness for myself and those battling around me. This feeling of deep peace grew in its warm embrace. I then floated outside of my body, observing the woman (me) who was trying to give birth, and I stayed with her until I sensed she was at peace. I breathed, and the peace continued to expand as

I moved further and further away from the situation.

Suddenly, yet softly, I felt the presence of the Divine Mother. Mary appeared larger than life in her flowing pastel pink and blue robes. Taking me into her arms, I continued breathing in Her peace, compassion, and healing. It was all I could do. My body began to feel warm again. I stayed in this peaceful state for what felt like quite a long time, but in Rebirthing, you never know, nor is time relevant; time ceases to exist.

Slowly coming out of my experience, I was now aware that I lay on the floor where I had started my session, discovering that I was curled up in a fetal position under a large, warm blanket.

The more time passed, the more shaken I felt about my experience. At the beginning of my session, I knew I was in a completely open, relaxed, receptive state of being. As always, I had no idea what was coming, but I did not expect this. It was the last thing on my mind. It is humbling how life (or consciousness) can throw those little curves at you!

## *Journal*

November 17, 2002,
Wow. I have always said giving birth would be better than endometriosis because at least then there would be a reward and an ending to it! It always felt like my body was trying to give birth to an unborn child, like there was a baby in me that was dead, that I never gave birth to. I never told anyone how I felt because I thought it was too weird. No wonder I have felt so strongly about not wanting to have children!

November 18, 2002,
I felt inadequate (in the past life experience) because I couldn't complete the birth. I felt helpless and powerless completely. I felt angry at the world for being in the state it was in. Perhaps this carried over and created my birth trauma of leaving my body at birth, the tremendous fear of I can't do it, being stuck, and having to be pulled out by forceps.

November 22, 2002,
I felt exhausted all day today. Yesterday too. I took the day off from work. I've been 'resting in the arms of the Lord,' so to speak. I took a nap or two today. It feels like a dream, and I can't wake up completely, just partially. I know a lot is going on for me energetically. It must be what I need, but I'm feeling challenged right now. I want to know more about that past life. Where was I? How did all of that happen? Who was my mate? Why was there a war?

I am so thankful I was able to talk to my friend today. He said knowing the details of that life may or may not help the energy move and to let it go in my mind. It may go beyond a past life into something deeper, something primordial, and there's no need to control it with my mind or put limits, boxes, and definitions around it.

Another one of my friends told me, quite adamantly and several times, to release the woman in the road, to hand her over to God/Universe, and that I don't need to figure it all out. It's shocking how much I don't want to do that. Something in me wants to hang onto this, tooth and nail, to the bitter end. I didn't realize until now how strongly I believe I have to take care of everything myself. It's like somewhere in me, I've believed I have to do it alone; not even God can help me.

I'm still learning to let people in. It's lovely to have all this support; I feel blessed and grateful; so many unique, extraordinary, loving individuals offering their gifts to others.

November 28, 2002,
I did another Rebirthing today. I was slightly afraid to breathe, not knowing what would come up. It turned out to be incredibly peaceful despite my fears! It was exactly what I needed. I feel like I released, handed over, and let go of "the woman on the road." As I was breathing, I felt something heavy in my lower belly. I felt pregnant. It felt like the child I was unable to give birth to. I kept breathing, and I let it go. I felt that life's presence with me. It was the first time I realized I wasn't alone in that experience. We'd gone through all that together and healed it together. I let it go to be its own free soul. I felt it leaving my aura. It was beautiful. It was like we had been clinging to each other and the trauma like we were both stuck in our fear.

I kept breathing and had a vivid visual experience. I still felt pregnant, but this time, I gave birth, and the baby was me. Facing me, it immediately grew and became just as I am now, but it embodied only all of the higher qualities. Smiling at myself, I felt something beyond words. All of the virtues she/I had, and all that I've ever aspired to be, have always been with me, right inside of me. All this time, I had been the one suppressing it. It's alive in me now. How sweet is that?! I also told my Rebirther about how I had always felt like I was carrying around an unborn child and that I was too afraid to tell anyone because of what they might think of me. It was the first time I told anyone, ever. He was very understanding and said precisely everything I needed to hear. Smooth. My breathing session was smooth.

# Conscious Breathing

## Rebirthing Breathwork

**M**any people assume they already know how to breathe because we do it naturally, right? Breathing is so simple that it's true potential and power are often underestimated. Breathing is the most basic contributing factor to your aliveness. Your body will survive for days without food or water, but give yourself less than five minutes without air, and you will die.

Conscious Breathing (also known as Rebirthing Breathwork) is a powerful and simple tool that has the potential to permanently transform the quality of your health, energy, and aliveness. Conscious Breathing utilizes a simple technique called connected breathing. To breathe connectedly means to merge each inhale with each exhale; there is no hesitation or holding in between.

Connected Breathing is our natural breathing pattern. Babies and animals breathe connectedly all the time.

As we grow and experience a vast multitude of life situations, we develop inhibited breathing patterns. Various traumas, ideas, and experiences influence us to begin to control or unconsciously inhibit our natural breathing rhythm. This causes tension, blocked energy, suppressed emotions, and pain to accumulate in our bodies on a cellular level.

Completing ten *individual* sessions with a trained Rebirther / breathing guide is recommended. Within these ten breathing sessions, most people will develop the confidence, security, and ability to practice connected breathing successfully on their own.

In the first sessions, many people may feel that they are over breathing or will have symptoms of hyperventilation; temporary cramping of muscles, intense emotions, and various sensations. This is caused by inhibited breathing patterns of either withholding the breath or pushing and forcing it. Once the breathing mechanism is healed and balanced in a free flowing state, these symptoms fade away and rarely occur. The attentive guidance of a Breathworker in one to one sessions is crucial to assist the breather in healing their inhibited breathing habits.

By healing our own inhibited breathing patterns, we heal your body's most basic energy system. Many forms of bodywork and meditation focus on the breath because it is fundamental to our body's healthy functioning. Healing the breath heals the entire body-mind-spirit from the inside out. Conscious breathing is a gift, a tool available for use and enjoyment no matter where we are.

Free-flowing, uninhibited breathing is contagious! Have you ever noticed yourself catching or passing a yawn to someone else? By healing your breathing pattern, you naturally influence others to do the same, creating a soothing, calming effect on the people surrounding you. Breathing freely and liberally in the presence of others creates safety for others to do the same.

It is natural to experience strong emotional releases, memories, or various physical sensations during Rebirthing Breathwork sessions. This is a normal part of the process. Our bodies are like giant containers of information. Experiences, traumas, various sensations, ideas, and memories are stored in our bodies on a cellular level. We keep these suppressed in our bodies by controlling our breath.

You can experiment with this on your own. Notice your breathing the next time you are angry, sad, stressed, or upset. Connected Breathing allows the suppressed energy to move through the body as needed, rise to the surface of your consciousness, and be released.

To hold in a suppressed emotion or past trauma is much more damaging to yourself and your body than it is to let it out. The focus of connected breathing is to access the energy, or prana, in the breath, inducing states of deep relaxation and bliss. In this process, any emotional blockages and experiences that are not completely integrated can come to the surface to be re-experienced and released. By doing the connected breath you are signaling to every cell of your body that now is the time, and now it is safe, to allow these stored memories to rise for the purpose of being let go. This creates the opening for you to experience your natural states of being: JOY, BLISS, and SERENITY.

## Why is it Called Rebirthing?

Conscious Energy Breathing is also commonly known

as Rebirthing since many people remember and heal the trauma of their birth through the connected breathing technique. Rebirthing Breathwork does not involve any practices of simulating the womb or restricting the body or breath. It is simply lying down and breathing freely in a connected rhythm, with the skillful guidance of a well trained Rebirther.

In the late nineteenth century, the medical field established that babies don't feel pain. Babies were handled by most medical staff without consideration for sensitivity or pain and even operated on without anesthesia up until the mid-1980s. These practices changed in 1985 when Jill R. Lawson discovered that her baby had open heart surgery without any anesthesia other than a muscle relaxant. She forged a movement in the medical industry, and by 1987, the understanding that babies are sensitive and feel pain became the norm again.

However, it is still commonly thought that babies are not aware and will have no memory of what is occurring around them or during their birth. Authors and early pioneers in Rebirthing Breathwork have well-documented people's spontaneous recollections of their birth, even down to the details of what was said in the room and how others felt. They were later able to verify it with family members.

Consider that birth is our first experience of the outer world, our first direct contact with people. The transition from the womb's warm, cozy, protected environment to the external world is our first experience of significant change and may have often been traumatic. This is a reasonable basis for the typical fear of change that many people struggle with.

There is wisdom in a woman's body and communication between her and the fetus. A ripening needs to happen, and the all-powerful love hormone, oxytocin, is at its peak when the baby is ready to be born. Induction overrides this natural process and begins a domino effect of further medical interventions.

Birth is the moment of taking your first breath, transitioning from 'breathing' amniotic fluid into your lungs to breathing air. Birth is your first experience of separation from your mother. All you knew before birth was complete and total oneness with her all of the time and it is quite possible that you were very conscious of her presence, emotions, and thoughts while in the womb.

There may have been dramatic temperature changes going from the warm womb to a cold hospital room, contact with rough surfaces, bright lights, deafening loud voices, and an extreme sense of urgency and drama in the delivery room. These are just a few possible challenges many of us may have faced at birth. A fantastic resource for understanding birth trauma and gentle birth is Fredrick LeBoyer's book *Birth Without Violence*.

## *Primordial Identities and Beliefs*

As conscious, living beings, we likely made primal, preverbal decisions about life, the world, and ourselves at birth. Some possible fundamental beliefs stemming from birth trauma are:

I am a burden.
I cause pain.
I'm not wanted.
I can't hide.
I'm too big.
I cause problems.
Change is hard.
I'm not strong enough.
I can't make it on my own.
Living is painful.
Life hurts.
Love hurts.

Babies are excruciatingly sensitive to the emotional states of those around them. They have not yet developed the hardening and dulling effects of emotional suppression. They are fresh, pure Spirit. If you hold a newborn baby in your arms you will likely experience the tenderness and softness in every fiber of their being.

You were once this soft and tender too, and my guess is somewhere inside you, there remains a spark of this memory. Babies can't help but be entirely empathic. They can feel each one of your emotions: your joy and your pain. Experiment with this. Do you feel uncomfortable holding a newborn baby? What is that discomfort? You may be able to suppress it, avoid it, or pretend it's not there, but a baby or young child will not. In this way, our youth are our greatest healers.

When we take all of this into account, we can begin to

understand the depth of the brutality and cruelty with which we have historically 'welcomed' each new life onto our planet. The majority of people do not feel safe in the world. Many people are fighting an illusionary phantom they believe is out there, ready to inevitably destroy them.

I believe birth trauma is a significant contributing factor to this primal, insecure, uneasy feeling about inhabiting a physical body on this Earth. Remember that all experiences, traumas, and memories, until dealt with consciously, are stored in your body on a cellular level. Ending the violence and trauma of birth on a global scale may be one of the most influential and practical steps to take toward a peaceful, enlightened world civilization. There is already a rapidly growing movement toward more conscious birthing practices that support the child and mother together through certified midwives supporting in-home births or birthing centers specific to gentle birthing practices.

## A Note to Mothers

I have heard from many mothers who experience unresolved trauma during their birthing process. The most important thing you can know is that it was not your fault. You did your best within a society and system that is not fully aware of birth trauma and its impacts.

And the good news is that birth trauma can be healed. You survived it, your child(ren) survived it, and we are resilient beings! Learning about birth trauma, talking about it at a developmentally appropriate age, and learning Rebirthing Breathwork are just some of the ways you can begin to heal.

## *Invitation - Your Birth*

Take a few moments to write out any details you know about the circumstances of your birth.

Who was present?
What were the family dynamics at the time of your birth?
Where were you born?
What stories have you heard from family members around your birth?
How did this impact you?

Many ideas, fears, identities, and primal emotions can be developed prenatally or at the time of conception.

Were you a planned baby or a surprise?
Were you a wanted or unwanted pregnancy?
Did you have older siblings who were jealous?
Were there financial stresses in your family about providing for a new member; you? What were your parent's emotions and attitudes about the pregnancy, your existence like?
Did they want a boy or a girl?

Even if you have no details or information from others about your birth, you can begin to explore your birth by sitting quietly and doing some inner exploration.

How do you feel in your body when you think about

your birth?
What emotions surface?

Write everything that comes to mind without judging
it.

This is an exploration of consciousness.

# A Master Teacher

*Leonard D. Orr*

Three years after my initial decision to heal the endometriosis, my symptoms began to disappear steadily, as my new normal, one by one. I had started a daily practice of meditation, yoga, and qigong. I continued to receive acupuncture and Chinese herbs and remained involved in the courses with Matt. I sought breathwork sessions from Brian and Peter whenever I could.

I can not even begin to describe the transformations I was going through; they were numerous and incredible. It was and still is as if great doors to the core of my being have been opened up, allowing all of me to be brought into the light; all of my unexpressed love and joy, as well as all the pain and sadness. All the emotions and mental content I previously didn't even know were there continued rising to the surface of my consciousness. I was completely unaware I had been hiding from myself for so long. I now only had mild cramping with my menstruation and no longer needed to take Chinese herbs. My body just did not need them anymore.

I would have occasional mild cramps or maybe a heavier flow one month more than the other, but it was the first time in my life I had ever experienced consistent, pain-free menstruation without any drugs or treatments. Menstruation felt good to me, like a warm internal massage. I was ecstatic! At times, I was still afraid that my symptoms might return. My fear was so intense that it took me over six months to accept that my body had healed!

Several months had passed since my first Liberty Experience with Matt, but the memory of him saying something about an 'unconscious death wish' during the weekend still rang in my mind. As soon as I heard him say those words, I was shocked. I immediately knew that this is what I had been struggling with my entire adult life.

Wanting to learn more about this subconscious death wish, I scheduled a phone consultation with Matt and asked where I could learn more because I felt that I had one. I also shared with him about my breathwork experiences and asked if he knew where to get trained in this as a career.

"You need to get in touch with Leonard Orr. Go online and look him up. You want to find Leonard Orr." Matt's words sounded cathartic, almost prophetic. Tingles went through my body as he spoke.

You can imagine my surprise when, the next day, I looked Leonard up online and found that not only had he coined the term *unconscious death urge* and spent 40 years of his life studying it, but that he was also the discoverer and founder of the modern-day breathwork movement. And he was still alive, right here in the USA giving trainings year-round!

Delighted to be able to go straight to the source, I called the phone number on the website for the Rebirthing center. In my mind, I imagined a university full of students and teachers, a full-time schedule of classes and activities, a library, and a bookstore. My heart pounded with excitement as the phone rang.

Finally, an answer, "Hello, this is Rebirth International, so-and-so speaking."

I didn't quite catch the name, but he sounded like the classic brainiac, and I was sure he could answer all my questions. I inquired about a 9-day training and potential arrival dates for when I could start. Were meals included? Where was the lodging located? What city should I get my flight into? How could I get from the airport to the training center? What was included in the training sessions, etc?

We spoke for some time, and my confidence grew that this was the right place for me to be. He offered to send me their latest newsletter so I could read up and get more information on the trainings and center. I gave him my mailing address.

"Thank you. What was your name again?" I asked him politely. He was my first contact with the university, and I looked forward to meeting him.

"Leonard Orr," he responded. I sat there in a moment of stunned silence.

"Excuse me?" I asked incredulously; it escaped my lips as soon as I took a breath.

"LEONARD ORR," he said, this time with what I perceived as a bit of irritation.

"Oh! Oh my goodness, thank you, I didn't realize it was you I was speaking to! Thank you, Mr. Orr. I will be in touch!" I hung up the phone quickly, my mind in a whirlwind of anticipation.

When Leonard's Newsletter, *the Conscious Connection*, arrived in the mail, I poured over it. Yes. This was the right place for me. However, the 9-day training was only three weeks away, and I did not have a dime for the tuition money: $1,008.00 plus airfare. I called the training center again, this time knowing that I was speaking with Leonard.

When I inquired about a discount or partial work trade, as he had mentioned that those are often available, he responded that it would be better if I could pay full price as he needed to cover my lodging costs and be able to pay his trainers. He had a new lead trainer arriving from Australia on the first day of my training. The price was already very reasonable at $1,008 for nine days, including lodging and meals. I considered this and felt he was right; it was already a great deal.

"I'll see what money I can come up with and try to make it happen," I decided.

"Wonderful; I look forward to meeting you," Leonard replied.

We finished speaking, and I hung up the phone.

*I look forward to meeting you.* His words stuck like cement in my mind. He sounded confident I would be there, yet I felt unsure I could make it; nine days of Rebirthing and seminars, professional trainers, consultations with Leonard himself, the founder of the entire movement. I had to make this work.

Fortunately, as I was still participating in Matt's trainings, I knew how to set a goal, put together a plan, and stay in integrity with it. I immediately emailed all my contacts, letting them know what I was doing. I asked for ideas and support.

Three weeks did not seem like much time for me to raise over $1,000.00 plus airfare. I was working a minimum wage job at just $7 per hour. And I was still needing to frequently rest with my menstruation a week out of every month. But I was committed. I simply had to do this for my heart and soul.

Immediately, I began selling extra stuff I didn't need. I plunged myself into working extra hours and doing odd jobs such as house sitting, pet sitting, and cleaning. I said yes to every opportunity for work that came my way. I helped a friend move and sold a few of my original paintings. The following week, I purchased my plane tickets. Now, I had to make this work!

In a race against time, I continued the extra odd jobs to make enough money. Just a few days before my departure date, I went to the bank with a pile of checks and cash in hand. I hadn't stopped to total it all up until that moment with the bank teller. It came to the exact amount of money I needed to raise to pay my training fee; $1,008.00 exactly, right down to the last penny. It was miraculous, and I loved it!

Soon I would be on my way to Virginia for my 9-day training. It was January 2003. What a way to start the New Year. I had been preparing for this for weeks. However, I felt my entire life had somehow prepared me for this moment.

As I drove home from work, just a few nights before my journey would begin, I thought of Leonard and his guru, Herakhan Babaji, whom he wrote about and spoke so frequently. The idea of a guru was foreign to me but I read a lot about Babaji in Leonard's newsletter.

Herakhan Babaji, also known as Haidakhan Babaji, was said to be an incarnation of Shiva. Leonard shared that being in His presence was like being with God in a human body; He knew all of everyone's thoughts, feelings, past histories, and futures. He called people to Him from all over the world and many miracles were reported in His presence. I had no experience with a guru before and didn't understand the relationship. However, I had read that if you ask Babaji for a blessing, he will give you one.

So, relaxed and driving down the highway that day, I pondered this and asked, "Babaji, will you give me your blessing"?

Within seconds of thinking this, and much to my surprise, I felt the space in the center of my head, directly behind my eyes, open up and fill with a soft, loving presence. It was like a golden inner glow that was comforting and soothing and, at the same time, powerful. I breathed this in and uttered a thank you, still unconvinced about what was happening. But something had changed for me, and I knew it was for the better.

∞∞∞

The next day, my new friend and breathworker Brian was traveling through the valley past my country abode and I had invited him for an evening workshop. This gathering was smaller, with just three of my local friends returning for another session with him.

Feeling confident and easy about breathing, now that I had released the woman in the road and the unborn child, I felt completely relaxed about having another session again.

Brian was so fun and comforting to be around. This time, I made sure to help him unload the boxes of heavy crystals weighing down his small car. He hung his color therapy, geometric stars in my window, and soft colors diffused by the soft hues of winter light spilled into my living room, transforming it into a magical breathing space.

That evening, Brian led us all into the breath as he so beautifully did. I entered the breathing rhythm and later in the session, an intense sadness overcame me. Dark, heavy, and ominous, it hung over me like a giant iceberg with no end in sight. I hesitated, sensing that all the emotional pain I was feeling was only the tip of it. It was so huge that it scared me.

The few other people breathing in the room were already coming out of their experience, sitting up and chatting quietly. I knew I could continue with my experience, but I stopped the breathing rhythm when all this sadness overcame me. I was unwilling to go there, terrified that it would consume me. I did not feel well but forced myself out of the breathing rhythm. An ache took over my heart and head. No matter, I would stop here. I was not going there today!

The next day, even though I was not on my period, all of my symptoms were present. I had fatigue, cramps, nausea, and pain in my entire pelvic region. Stopping the breathing process last night had not done me good.

## *Journal*

January 7, 2003,
Until the breathing session I did yesterday, I never realized how grief–stricken my soul has been. It felt like I was touching the tip of an iceberg. It felt so huge that it scared me. I never imagined I would say this about anything in my growth process, but it feels so deeply rooted in me that I don't know who I will be once I embrace that grief fully and let it all go.

It feels like my deep sadness is where all my "maturity" has always stemmed from. I've always been praised for being so mature for my age. It always felt like my stronghold, something steady and grounded. What if I never come out of it? What if I come out of it high as a kite and have no grounding whatsoever?

One thing's for sure: I don't want to be alone when I face this. I want to be with sweet loved ones who will be with me through this. Suppressing it is taxing on my body. I feel horrible. I don't want to practice breathing on my own anymore. I don't even want to do another session. I feel so scared. And here I am, preparing to leave for a nine-day Rebirthing training with Leonard Orr!

# Meeting Leonard

## the 9-Day Training

**W**ith an unexpected dread weighing on my heart, screaming at me not to go after my previous breathwork session, I chose to stay with my commitment. I packed my bag and left for my first Rebirthing Breathwork training with Leonard Orr on January 17, 2003.

It was a comfortable four-hour flight across the country, landing in D.C. where I caught a small, 12-seater airplane to Charlottesville. It was the closest flight I could get to Leonard's center, located on the outskirts of the small, charming town of Staunton, Virginia.

Walking out onto the tarmac with the other passengers, I heard a few of them joking about the size of the airplane and whether we would indeed all fit in it or not! With a field of butterflies now collecting in my stomach, I climbed up the steps and into the plane.

Upon entering, I could barely stand up straight without bumping my head. My seat was in the very back of the small plane. I have never been prone to claustrophobia, but this was reaching new limits. Butterflies still churning, we soon took off for our short flight to Charlottesville. There was plenty of turbulence, to the point that I was searching for a puke bag to no avail and gripping my stomach, praying for my life to continue past this day. Indeed, we did arrive just fine, and I thankfully stepped off the airplane. I decided this was a new experience not to be repeated unless critically necessary!

Arrangements had been made for Leonard's wife at the time, Isabelle, to pick me up at the tiny airport. I wandered around a bit, waiting for her arrival. Not having met her before, I didn't know how we would recognize each other, but it seemed easy enough in such a small airport. I was strolling through a domed-shaped room, enjoying the acoustics, when a beautiful, angelic woman who smiled at me graciously entered the dome.

"Sara?" she asked with a slight French accent.

Stunned, I could barely speak as I looked into her eyes, gazing at me soft as a doe but intent with energy and a radiant aliveness.

"Yes, you are Isabelle?" I asked, barely able to hide my disbelief. She was so young and beautiful, a vision, like an angel. She looked at me, perhaps a little taken back by my gaping jaw and expression. I was completely enamored and in awe of the energy about her.

"Yes," she responded matter of factly.

We greeted each other and waited for Leonard's new lead trainer, Kim, to arrive from Australia. Her flight came in synchronistically just after mine, and we met her at the same dome-shaped entrance of the small airport. She had a strong stature, long blondish brown hair with golden highlights, and deep blue eyes. She struck me as a determined, strong, confident woman who had just set out on a new adventure of her own, no doubt. She was warm and friendly. I was very excited to meet her and eager to gain every ounce of wisdom I could glean from her years of experience as a professional Breathworker.

We rode together in a van, chatting and getting to know each other, as Isabelle drove us to a small Bread and Breakfast where we would be lodging for the first few nights. We met with the other trainee, Ross, who had arrived from Canada a few days prior. Isabelle showed me to my room, which was a beautiful Victorian suite with a full clawfoot bathtub and comfortable amenities. Leonard was to arrive soon to greet us all.

It has been said that meeting Leonard will change your life forever and open you up to an entirely new and different, if not surreal, reality. So, I was nervous and unsure of what to expect.

Our small group had gathered together in waiting, standing in the lounge of the Bed and Breakfast. I felt an awkward anticipation hovering in the air. However, when Leonard walked quickly into the room, standing straight and tall, with a sense of purpose and strong attention, it felt like a small party breaking out with warmth and greetings.

An inexplicable, giddy, kind of childish joy washed over me. His eyes were beaming with light, but present energy, and an easy smile spread gently across his face.

Leonard's gaze caught mine, and I could not for the life of me, stop smiling. I was beaming like a child at her own birthday party. He walked directly over to me, smiling and seemingly amused at my excitement and joy.

"Welcome," he said as he placed both hands on my shoulders and kissed me on the cheek.

"Oh!" I said in surprise. He laughed and then kissed my other cheek.

"Oh!" I said again, now slightly blushing as the others were chuckling in the room. I had never received a European greeting before and quickly learned it was Leonard's favorite way of greeting women.

He addressed our small group and then took some time to chat with me. I asked him some questions and expressed my interest in the Unconscious Death urge and his ideas about Physical Immortality. He was pleased and said I would do well here in the nine days. Leonard left the bed and breakfast, returning to his ranch just a short distance away on the edges of town, leaving us trainees and our new trainer for our first night together.

Kim wasted no time; we were to bathe first and return for individual breathwork sessions. Still carrying some of the symptoms of endometriosis that had surfaced from my last session and the iceberg of overwhelming grief, I was unnerved to learn that we would be breathing so soon. But I came for this, so I took a leap of faith and dived in.

Hardly able to relax in my bath, I speedily got dressed and prepared for the sessions. We met a half hour later in Kim's room as it had the most floor space for us to lay down and breathe. I felt like we were kids at a slumber party. Since both Ross and I had previous experience with breathwork sessions, we could sit in on each other's sessions and watch the other breathing as Kim demonstrated how to guide sessions.

Surprisingly, my session was relatively calm; some tingles, peacefulness, and easy connected breathing integrated at the end. I felt incredibly safe and accepted by my new friends. Something magical happens when you complete a breath session with a person; it's like an energetic connection is made that is purely Divine. There are no words to describe it, but what a sweet first night of the training we all shared.

Isabelle returned briefly, bringing us a warm, home-cooked meal of lentil soup and vegetables, which we heartily enjoyed while still sitting on the floor of Kim's bedroom. It was a cozy and homelike atmosphere.

This would become our daily schedule: morning bath, breathe, lunch, and an afternoon visit with Leonard to discuss our sessions and offer a teaching. Our evenings were filled with a special seminar from Kim or Michael, another local professional Breathworker. The schedule was full, and each day felt intensely emotional, healing, blissful, and transformational.

We were to finish each night with at least a twenty minute long soak in our bathtubs. I had to admit that with a beautiful ensuite and clawfoot tub, I wasn't complaining. However, even though I had spent many years as a teen showering twice per day, washing my hair in the mornings to set my curls, and again in the evenings spending way too much time in the bathtub to clean the dirt and grime from a day's work at the stable, it felt odd to me to soak in a tub twice per day. I always had that swimmy, just bathed feeling and I worried if my skin would get dry. What would people think of me if they knew I bathed this much?

Stepping out of my bath and drying myself off, I lazily put on my bathrobe. Wrapping my hair in a towel to let it air dry, I meandered around my bedroom suite, taking a closer look at my surroundings. A framed, black and white picture of the bedroom hung on the wall. Strange, I thought. I read the inscription below it and saw mention of the room's purported haunting. Wait, *haunting?*

Looking closer at the picture, I could see a faint image of a young girl standing near the bed. A ghost known to haunt this very room? *Geesh, that really puts a damper on things, doesn't it,* I thought to myself. *It's likely some made up story put on by the management.*

Brushing it off, I went to bed. I wanted to have a good night's sleep. The next day we would trade sessions again, and the following day we were to spend an entire day outside with a fire, fasting on liquids for our day of fire purification in a one-day vision quest. We were all, no doubt, on quite the adventurous ride together in consciousness.

## *Journal*

January 17, 2003,
My first session here was light, gentle, and relaxing. It felt like I was building trust in my surroundings. I had flown across the country all day and just met Leonard, his wife, my trainer, and another fellow trainee who

had been there for a few weeks. I was exhausted, but it felt so good. I had such a warm welcome from everybody. Even though I didn't relax entirely in my session, it was still wonderful and just what I needed. If only people could be welcomed this way everywhere they traveled!

January 18, 2003,
My second session was releasing the trauma blocked in my cells from the one-time sexual abuse I experienced at a very young age. It re-opened all the anger, hurt, fear, and sadness, as well as my survival instincts kicking in. It shook me to the core. I was never able to scream, breathe, or speak during that trauma, so WOW, was there a lot I had to say. I didn't know all of that was in me. I'm not alone with that anymore. I went through it with two angels by my side! (Both the trainer and fellow trainee were with me during this session.)

# Fire Vision Quest

"**Y**ou look like G.I. Jane," Leonard said, laughing as I stepped outside. I felt slightly self-conscious as I stood as tall as the men, dressed in my newly donned army print suit with my long brown hair flowing down to my waist.

It was 15 degrees Fahrenheit outside, and the ground was frozen solid. I had just been inside the house with Isabelle, who had helped me get into one of Leonard's ski suits. It was the day of our fire vision quest, and it was just too cold to be outside in our regular clothes, but none of us visitors from out of town were prepared for that.

The only ski suit remaining to choose from was a full body, green and brown, army print camouflage suit that zipped up my torso and closed warmly around my neck. Kim and Ross had already taken the other fashion options. Blushing a little at Leonard's comment and the other's laughter, I laughed too at the sight I must have been, but I was prepared for the elements and ready to go.

We walked around his home and down a small hill in his back pasture. He motioned to two shelters, each about the size of a horse stall, some thirty feet apart. They were *dhunis*, a covered, sacred fire pit consisting of a roof and four sides. The walls were enclosed about halfway up, leaving the top open for fresh air. Inside each shelter was a pea gravel floor and a fire pit dug in at the center. Kim and Ross were shown to their dhunis for the day, and Leonard walked me around to the other side of the house where mine was, in the horse pasture.

I had volunteered to take that one since I was the most comfortable of our group around horses. I looked across the field to see five of them. Four white horses and one black stood cozily snuggled up under a lean-to out of the wind: Breezy, Spunky, Artex, Vayu, and Dancer, the black one who belonged to Heike Strombach, Leonard's longtime friend and lead trainer from Germany.

Sighing, I felt a bit more relaxed around the horses and fire. Aside from the below freezing weather, I felt right at home.

We had all bathed in the morning, as was part of the training protocol and skipped breakfast. It was our day of fasting. I had never done a liquids only fast before. Isabelle had plenty of fresh juices ready for us in the house anytime we wanted.

Eyeing the cold, blue sky and my breath dispersing in the icy air, I sat down on the camping mat provided and built my fire. I was to spend the whole day here. I shifted uneasily, wondering what to do for an entire day in the cold next to a fire. Leonard had instructed us not to write or journal, read, sing, or do anything. We were to sit quietly and rest with the fire.

The wind bellowed through the opened walls, swirling the smoke in my face. It didn't matter where I sat or stood; the smoke found me. Growing tired of dancing around the smoke and flames, I laid down on the camping mat next to the fire. The cold, blue winter sky infused the air with a crisp freshness against the backdrop of naked trees and homes in the distance. It was peaceful here.

Sipping on a delicious large cup of apple carrot ginger juice that Isabelle had given me, I shifted around on the camping mat, getting more comfortable. The mat and my extra padding of clothes provided just enough cushion for me to lay on the ground comfortably. There was certainly no extra fluff here. After a while, my arm grew tired, supporting my head as I lay down. I looked around and found a block of wood to use as a pillow. How ascetic of me! It didn't occur to me to go to the house and ask for any creature comforts. I was content to lay by the fire and gaze into the flames, keeping warm out of the wind.

Sounds of the frozen ground crunching beneath feet and snorting breath occasionally approached as the horses circled my dhuni, peeking in with relative curiosity. I said hello and blew my breath into their nostrils as they came to say hi in the same way horses would greet each other. They didn't stay long, probably disappointed that although I smelled of carrots and apples, I had none to share.

The day lulled on in quiet solitude and crackles of the fire. I dozed in and out of sleep, flowing in and out of the liminal space between waking and dreaming consciousness, at times being roused by a gust of wind or sounds of the fire. I enjoyed tending to it, adding wood as it burned low, feeling the sting of just how cold it was outside, and gaining the relief of a more vigorous blaze emitting heat from its flames.

Around what I imagined to be lunchtime, I took one bathroom break at the house and got some water. I watched smoke curling from the other two dhunis and wondered how my friends were faring with this.

I continued to fall in and out of sleep as I moved around in increasing discomfort with my wood 'pillow' and the growing cold. However, I felt more energized and clean each time I woke up.

The sky was growing dimmer, and the sun was starting to set. I could hear the horses munching on hay as Leonard or Isabelle had been out to feed them dinner. Just as I felt I would need to go to the house to warm up, Leonard appeared, leaning over the dhuni.

"How is it going here?" he asked, studying my fire and the space around it. I sensed he was somehow reading the energy.

"Great!" I proclaimed.

"Good," he replied. "Would you like to stay the night in the dhuni or return to town?"

I leaped to my feet. "Oh, I'll go back now, thank you!"

"How do you feel?" Leonard asked, smiling in a kind of Cheshire cat grin.

I stepped out of the dhuni and paused, checking in with myself as I stood outside.

"I feel lighter," I replied, pleasantly surprised by it. "Even the air around me feels lighter and softer."

"That's good. Very good." Leonard smiled. And off we

went to gather the others and head back to our lodging.

It was the last night we were to stay at the bed and breakfast. Since Kim would be staying in town for quite some time working as Leonard's lead trainer, she had found a house and already signed the lease, giving us access to it the next day. I was grateful to be moving out from my 'haunted' room and hoped I wouldn't be meeting the ghost during my last night there.

Thankfully, I didn't, but I did wake up feeling terribly nauseous and like I might not make it out of bed. Was it from the fasting? The fire? Or sleeping on this old, overly soft mattress?

Well past sunrise, I managed to pull myself out of bed almost a half hour later than planned and nibbled on some hazelnuts I had kept in my room. I didn't feel like I could stand up, but I managed to crawl to the bath and plopped myself in for the recommended twenty minute minimum. I felt a little bit better, and packed up my small bag of clothes and personal items, and made it downstairs for breakfast.

Thereafter, we soon arrived at the steps of Kim's new home: a charming, historic, two-story brick house.

"It's my gingerbread house," she beamed. "Now I just need to find my gingerbread man!"

We laughed as we carried our things inside. Kim had such a joyful, warm nature about her, and although at times I had a terrible time understanding what she said with her beautiful Australian accent and differing expressions, we got along marvelously. I was increasingly aware of just how sheltered a life I had lived.

Kim unlocked the front door, and we stepped inside. The house was clean and spacious, with plenty of natural lighting. A large fireplace greeted us to the right of the front door; the living room opened into a kitchen, dining area, and a half-bath in the back. The bedrooms and a full bath were upstairs. It would make a lovely training center.

The house was unfurnished, and no one had had time to bring any items or beds aside from a few dishes to cook with and some camping mats, pillows, and blankets provided by Isabelle. Kim and I slept in the living room next to the fireplace, per Leonard's recommendation of fire purification, and Ross settled into one of the rooms upstairs.

After a short time of sorting out our suitcases and sleeping areas, we gathered for the day's breathwork session in the living room. As I was still feeling slightly nauseous, Kim and Ross invited me to go first.

Kim was giving more instruction now to us as trainees on how to guide sessions, when to say something and when to remain quiet, and the fine art of following our intuition while the rebirthee was breathing.

Laying on the mat with Kim sitting on one side of me and Ross on the other, it took some work and effort for me to get into the connected rhythm this time, but soon, my breath took off on its own.

"Let the breath breathe you, that's it!" Kim encouraged me.

The familiar buzzing and tingling sensations began as usual. A wave of sadness came over me. I soon realized it was not really a wave but more like a heavy, dense cloud. It was the iceberg I had so tremendously feared in my last session at home before coming to Virginia.

It was different somehow this time, though; I felt sadness but also tenderness. It was an entirely new feeling that I had never remembered before. It came with the sensation that it was okay to feel that tenderness without any edge to it; there were no barriers in this cloud now permeating me.

It was incredibly gentle, soft, and subtle, yet massive, like a giant cloud lifting or evaporating from my body and aura. Yes, that was it. It was a floating cloud of grief. It tickled me oh so sweetly as it floated away.

"Breathe," she gently whispered as my breaths slowed and faded into the cloudiness.

Placing my attention back on my breath, I pulled on the inhale, and relaxed on the exhale. My thoughts began to move. I don't have to feel sad anymore, at least not sadness like that. It truly was that iceberg that I was afraid to confront alone.

Riding my breath through just a strand of awareness as I floated in this now blissful sensation, my breath was light and easy, and my whole body was full of tingles from my crown to my toes. The tingles gently dissolved into a simple, pure feeling of being the light. A pleasurable, earthly heaviness filled my feet and legs, moving up my body into the center of my mind. My eyes spontaneously opened on their own.

It was as if I was opening my eyes for the first time. I felt the freshness of a newborn baby, looking around at my surroundings for the first time. I felt like a Princess, a perfectly divine female, born of the Earth herself. Kim and Ross, whom I now felt totally at home with, smiled gently at me, welcoming me back from my truly delicious ride.

I could have never imagined feeling so fulfilled and joyful in any profession or practice! Later that day, in our meeting with Leonard, I asked about certification. I knew we would receive a certificate of completion for the 9-day professional training we were in, but I wanted to have a more precise definition of what it meant to be certified.

Leonard's response was a brief history of the certification game he had played with the first Rebirthers back in the 70s. His take on certification was that it is a money-making game, and the only one who could certify or de-certify me was God, the client, and myself.

I took that to heart, so when he opened up the certification process years later of reporting with write-ups from 3 clients on their first ten sessions, I didn't take it seriously, and I didn't do it, even though I had far exceeded the qualifications. I deeply valued his original concept of 'certification autonomy' and viewing certification as a game, as there are many, many people in the world doing subpar work who are certified.

Almost a full decade later though, I would begin to

see certification as a structure for building high-quality communities and improving the quality of Rebirthing Breathwork offered professionally around the globe.

## *Journal*

January 21, 2003,
Remember when I said I was afraid to feel all that grief because I didn't know what would remain of me or if I'd ever come out of it if I did?

Well, that was the purest, sweetest, most Divine cleansing of my soul I've ever experienced. I don't have to be sad like that anymore, even though many more layers of this may be uncovered. Beautiful! Immensely Beautiful!

# Birth of a Breathing Guide

The next day, Kim declared we were ready; it was time for us to guide a session on our own, with her taking a back seat and supporting only as needed. I was nervous to take the wheel and guide a session for Ross, but he was sweet, smiling, and reassuring me that he felt he was in good hands. I guided him into the breathing rhythm as I had heard Kim doing for us all week. I also borrowed a few phrases I had heard my friend Brian use, just breathe and feel, that's it. You're doing great.

Ross's connected breathing was so open, free, and strong. I was amazed by how little resistance there seemed to be in his breathing. I didn't say much during the session, as there seemed to be no need to until I saw pain begin contorting in his face and hands. He had tetany, the cramping of muscles that commonly occurs for beginners in breathwork but usually subsides after the first ten sessions as the breathing mechanism begins to heal. Ross had catapulted into an experience and an intense one, no doubt at that.

Gently taking his hand and placing my other hand on his forehead, I encouraged him, "You're doing ok, Ross. Just keep breathing. Let the breath carry you right through this".

He sputtered and gasped, releasing some painful groans and trying to move from side to side, but it seemed as if something held him in place. His breaths became even more robust and fluid now. I could hear a different quality of power in it. The breath truly was breathing him as the kundalini (pure life energy) washed through his body, releasing whatever memory he was reliving.

Continuing to focus solely on him and offering a reassuring hand or comment, I tried to follow my intuition on what would be best to do. A few times, Kim nodded in approval. I was grateful she was there.

Ross's breathing was more relaxed now, but I could still see signs of tingling and buzzing in the muscles of his face, body, and hands. I waited patiently for the breath to do its work. He was doing fantastic, staying with the breath the whole time through, aside from that first onset of tetany. More time passed, and his breath transformed yet again: smoother, effortless, peaceful, full of aliveness and energy, yet tranquil. The air in the room seemed lighter, clearer, and fresher. It had an electric, bright quality to it.

An atmosphere of complete and total transcendence permeated through Ross, the room, and myself. It felt very blissful and easy. He soon popped open his eyes. Moving his arms and legs a bit, rubbing his face, he slowly sat up in amazement.

"I was burned at the stake," he said. I calmly listened and held space for him with such honor, grateful to hear the insights he shared.

Had I not had my rebirth experience of 'the woman on the road' just months prior, I would not have been prepared to hear a client talk about being burned at the stake in a past life. But Leonard said that as we clear things in our own consciousness and energy body, it allows others to heal similar issues. That's why he recommended that we support each other as Breathworkers and breathe with as many experienced Rebirthers as possible.

Ross finished his sharing, and we all gave each other hugs. We decided to take a short break before starting my session. It was his turn to lead a breathwork session and hold space for me.

Once again, I laid down on the camping mat I was using for my sessions. Leonard had said not to share the mats we were breathing on but to each use our own to avoid Emotional Energy Pollution, the energy that spins off of other people's auras and can be absorbed by objects, materials, and other people in contact with them.

Getting comfy and wondering what kind of theme park ride I would be going on this time, I laid back and smiled up at Ross, sitting next to me, gazing at me with such kind intent.

I entered into 'breath land' and continued with the rhythm patiently until I felt the breath take off on its own. I soon became nauseous and felt a headache come on. Something was squeezing and pushing at my feet. I soon realized I was lying in the fetal position somehow. My feet began to hurt, really hurt! Like they were stuck and something was pulling on them. My ankles were hurting, and my legs felt prickly.

Feeling a hungry, cold ball form in my stomach, I breathed right into it, and it melted away. That felt very good! But it still wasn't complete, even though I wanted it to be.

I rolled onto my back and began to get drifty, like dreaming. But it was like I was choosing to go or stay, to be born or not. I couldn't decide. I felt a neutral emotion, paralyzed, immobile, indecisive, and lost in a foggy haze of thought. I drifted further into nothingness.

Bam! Someone, something, or God pushed me back into my body. I had a body? I had lost all awareness or reference to that.

Warmth filled my forehead. It was all I could feel, as if the rest of me was not there. It rushed down, filling my body with a huge rush, so much so that it made me dizzy. There was my body!

My third eye, the space of the forehead, between the eyebrows, felt open and charged with energy. Then I felt very, very connected. I've never felt so in my body before. It was unbelievable, but there I was, experiencing it. I became aware of the room. I felt a very silent angelic energy around me. Ross had been there with me the whole time, an hour? Two? Three? The atmosphere in the room, my body, and both he and Kim felt blissful; sweet, gentle, bliss.

Slowly, I sat up and stretched, feeling more in my body and connected to my physicality than I had ever experienced in my life. Kim explained that I had had a breath suspension. I had completely stopped breathing for a time and re-experienced my birth.

Confused, I pondered, "Really? That was my birth?"

It was as if I could not hold a mental concept of birth. It was like it had just been a series of random sensations and experiences. Yet, as I mulled over what had happened, yes, it made total sense that it was my birth.

That evening, we met with Leonard, and I shared my rebirthing experiences. He said the cloud lifting of grief I felt during my previous session was the experience of being in the womb. And the grief was my desire to be back in the womb, in the floating, spacious, cozy, safe, timeless, carefree womb. He shared that traumatic births cause the baby to grow up, right on into adulthood, with an unconscious desire and longing to return to that state of existence since it was such a blissful state. It manifests as a deep, inexplicable, longing desire to return home. If someone has a traumatic birth, the external world out there may feel painful and threatening.

This made a lot of sense to me; no wonder I felt like a baby at the end of my session, opening my eyes for the first time. I then shared a memory that surfaced of being in a yoga class and doing prep work for headstands. I never liked being upside-down, at all. Actually, I had never really done anything that required me to be even remotely upside-down. In the yoga class, I was feeling nervous, anxious, and irritable. I did not want to do it. I decided to go for it anyway to see what would happen.

So, I did the exercises in class, got dizzy, and felt angry, almost rageful. When I got home, I threw my yoga mat across the room and started crying. At the same time,

I felt bewildered because I had no idea where it was all coming from.

The next memory that surfaced was when I was five. My sister, myself, and our friend next door were all swimming in our backyard pool. I didn't know how to swim, so I had one of those circular lifesavers around my waist. As I was playing in the pool, I got flipped over somehow. I was unable to push it off over my hips and I couldn't flip myself back over either. My sister and friend thought I was performing a trick. They didn't know I was drowning upside-down! I don't remember how I got out of the pool, but I woke up laying in the grass with my mother standing over me. I felt very dizzy and angry.

Leonard said these traumas were manifestations of my body memories from being held upside down at birth before taking my first breath. I was reliving part of my birth trauma; the experience of being held upside-down and struggling to take my first breath.

∞∞∞

The next day we enjoyed a brisk walk outside with Leonard upon his afternoon arrival. Being around him always felt exciting and unique. I never knew what thoughts or feedback would be coming from him. He was astoundingly connected to his energy and to others.

We finished our time with Leonard, having shared more about our day's session and asking him many questions.

He stood next to me at the dining room table we now had for our daily meetings.

"Good work today. That's a lot of progress," he finished with a smile, as he stood next to me at the dining room table we now had for our daily meetings.

Standing to face him, I exclaimed, "Leonard, thank you so much!" and hugged him. As soon as I leaned in with my arms around him, I was shocked to feel a pillar of light and energy where his body should have been that sent me back a bit. I may have fallen over had I not been holding onto him. He looked at me surprised and smiled, patted me on the back, and stepped away.

"Oh, Leonard does not usually give hugs. He is very sensitive to the energy and energy pollution of others," Isabelle offered in explanation. Later on I would learn that this was a part of his healing process as he was coming out of a very long sabbatical.

However in that moment I was slightly horrified, I realized hugging Leonard Orr was not the norm. So that's why he preferred the European greeting of a kiss on each cheek. But Leonard seemed alright that I had hugged him, so I excused myself and considered myself lucky.

Our group disbanded for some downtime to tend to personal needs, and we began the nightly process of negotiating in what order we would all get our bath. With three people present and one bathtub, it took some planning to ensure the hot water did not run out.

This time, we agreed Kim would bathe first; it had been a long day, perhaps a longer one for her. I rested downstairs by the fire and later took my bath. Returning to my camp mat, I snuggled down under the blankets. Kim and I talked and giggled like school girls. Ross was upstairs, settling in for the night and burning some sweetly smelling incense.

The next day was our last full day together. I quietly dreaded that thought a bit. I felt as though I could stay in this community and energy forever. But I knew I would soon be on my way and launching my breathwork practice back home in Oregon. I had a journal filled with workshop notes, experiences, and wonderful new friends to call on for continued support. And yet, I would surely miss everyone terribly.

# *Breath Release*

It was as though a cyclone was ripping through my body; my lungs, my breath, and the entire room around me buzzed with torrential dynamic energy. I gripped the blanket beneath me, pressing my knuckles into the mat.

Michael, a local Rebirther who had been joining us to give seminars, was giving me my last session before my departure. I had been falling asleep in my session, so much so that he had me get up on my hands and knees to keep myself awake with the task of holding myself up.

Moments ago, I could hardly breathe as I choked and struggled to gasp even the tiniest bit of air. But now, my breath moved in and out of me smoothly, rhythmically, fast, and free like an eagle soaring through the skies. It was as though breath was literally making love to me!

I thought I knew what it meant for the breath to breathe me. I had the experience so many times before of my breath taking off on its own, but this time, it was completely and utterly different. The power was unimaginable.

In breath, out breath, in breath, out. Breath penetrated me with no will or control of my own. All I could do was witness, surrender, and be filled with ecstatic pleasure as I had never known before. I anchored my hands and knees to the floor.

With no choice but to ride these waves, I entered into the eye of the storm; it was ecstasy. Every cell of my body, every particle, atom, rotating neutron, and the very air around me was bathed in fluid energy and love.

The room fell quiet, all but for my breath. My in-breath and out-breath were the same. There was no separation. There was no inhale or exhale, just one fluid flow of breath.

Michael, Kim, and Ross sat nearby in reverent silence, witnessing and holding space for what was occurring. Did they know? Could they feel the ecstasy I was in? What were they thinking and feeling? Did it even matter? Either way, I didn't mind. In the presence of this power, those were fleeting, meaningless thoughts lost in the wave of my pure Being. I entered into a stillness and silence that is utterly indescribable.

Upon completion, I was so blissed out in my body that I could not move. I lay on the floor, snuggled up in blankets like a baby. Someone brought me a bowl of warm soup. Michael's face shone at me with a gentle smile, "You had your breath release; reliving the moment of your first breath taken at birth."

For certain, I felt reborn. I was renewed. It was the initiation I should have had at birth, the first sacred breath in this divine, ecstatic body of sacred spiritual love on Earth. It is here for all of us.

The breath release is our birthright. It was meant for all of us as our first breath on Earth and to be with us through every footstep taken on this sacred ground. And now I embodied it.

∞ ∞ ∞

"You are going to make a very good Rebirther. I just know it. I really feel and sense it when people are going to do well with this." Isabelle smiled sweetly at me with such warmth in her radiant eyes. I had just said my final goodbyes to Leonard, Kim, and Ross.

I felt tremendous love and respect for each of them, especially Isabelle. Her presence, patience, kindness, and warmth were prominent in the way she brought us food every day and offered us so much support. As an addition to our breathwork training, she taught us Aarti, a ceremony of devotional songs and offerings of light to Babaji the Divine, and introduced us a little more to Leonard's guru and hers, Herakhan Babaji, every day.

Isabelle's presence was like magic to me. How was I to leave these people who felt like such angels? But her words encouraged me. And surely I would be back soon, yes, as soon as possible.

## *Journal*

January 28, 2003,
I feel very sad sitting here, despite my enthusiasm to return home and share what I've learned with my family and friends. I was just dropped off at the airport, and I'm waiting for my flight. I know I will be back again. I already can't wait to return and see what growth my friends have been through. Living and

breathing with them so closely for the past nine days has developed a bond that feels completely priceless!

An angel is working here at the airport, an older lady working as a janitor. She's spreading cheer and good energy. She woke me up from my sadness and reminded me how easy it is these days to get around and travel. What a blessing it truly is!

January 30, 2003,
Life feels so different! So Alive! Between flights the other day in a huge airport, I felt bombarded with energy: people whirling by in a mad rush, children crying at their mothers, TVs blaring, and noisy announcements repeating over the intercom. It felt like a different planet from where I had been the last nine days! Very overwhelming! What a madhouse our society is!

Yesterday, I fasted, resting by my fireplace. This morning, I rebirthed myself in the bathtub. I breathed gently and began laughing, much to my surprise (and delight!) My hands felt tingly, and I began splashing, kicking, and playing like a little kid with no restrictions. I just couldn't help myself. I realized I hadn't splashed in the bath like this since I was a kid. I hadn't allowed myself the freedom to enjoy the water.

When and how did I ever get so serious? And thank goodness I'm getting back to playing! I loved it, and it moved so much energy!


February 9, 2003,
I spoke with Mom today about remembering my birth. It was amazing. I was so afraid she wouldn't understand

and think I was crazy, but she listened to everything I had to say and was very open to it all.

She said she remembered that my birth took about five hours and that during the labor, my heartbeat went flat on the monitor. She felt terrified, but after some time, it started back up again. She didn't like how roughly the doctors handled me, and she did not like that they had used forceps to pull me out and held me upside down by my ankles.

It was a very healing conversation for me. I had no doubts about the validity of my Rebirthing experiences, but sharing them with her was even more validating and absolute magic.

February 17, 2003,
I did a breathing session at my friend's house tonight. I suddenly felt my Great Grandpa with me. (He passed when I was fourteen.) I just felt his presence with me.

It was very lovely and soothing. I remember when I was around seven, and we were all eating out at a restaurant, having a big family reunion for Thanksgiving. I had gotten ill in the ladies' restroom and vomited all over my new dress! I especially remembered being back at my great-grandparent's house, lying on a bed and resting in their guest room.

He had come into the room to check on me and sat beside me in a chair by the bed. He didn't say much to me; he just sat there, simply Being with me. It was exactly what I needed. I didn't feel like talking but didn't want to be alone. It was like he had a magical presence about him and was here with me again during my Rebirthing session today.

I continued breathing and enjoyed feeling this connection. I coughed a lot, laughed a little, and cried some. It was very different. It always amazes me how different each session is. I kept hearing footsteps coming from down the hall, and it felt like someone was standing at my feet, someone very loving, strong, and wise. I thought of Jesus, angels, and guides and decided it didn't matter that I didn't know who it was because I felt an ecstatic, beautiful, healing energy flowing through me in a very gentle and subtle way.

It took a long time for me to come out of my session. I lay in an "x" with my arms and legs out. I felt amazing healing energy in my hands and arms, unlike the usual buzzing sensations I had felt before. I felt like whispering words, sweet, beautiful names, though I didn't know who or what they were; I just knew they were something very sacred. I asked my friend later, and she said no one was walking through the hallway, not even her cat! I feel very blessed and grateful for this experience.

# Elemental Purification

## The Complete Healing System - Keys to Relaxation

ealing with the elements is based on earth, air, water, fire, mind, and loving community. They are founded on the practices of the immortal Yogis of India and all cultures and traditions of the world. This was truly a lifelong passion and study for Leonard.

Healing with the elements is natural. Our bodies are made of earth, air, water, and fire organized together by creative intelligence. Our physical manifestation would not exist without each one of these elements. The elements are like the natural laws, agreements, providing the structures and prerequisites for having a body here on Earth.

### Earth

Healing with the element of *earth* incorporates anything to do with this physical matter, the basics being:

*Exercise* -having a regular, well-balanced exercise routine. This can be more simple to practice than you might think. For example, walking is a natural tranquilizer that promotes the release of endorphins and is low-stress on the body. I like to use the stairs instead of elevators, drive into town, park my car, and walk to each location I need to go to that day.

I have found yoga fundamental to my healing and relationship with my body, as it incorporates breath, slow movements, and good stretches. It naturally connects me with my inner energy flows.

*Nutrition -starting with a basic vegetarian diet.* "You are what you eat" is something to consider. The horrors of slaughterhouses, the effects of animal products on the body, and the spiritual, humanitarian, and environmental ethics of a vegetarian diet are all very well known today.

Some of the greatest minds in our recorded history were vegetarian: the Greek philosopher Pythagoras, Albert Einstein, St.Francis, George Bernard Shaw, Mahatma Gandhi, Leonardo da Vinci, Thomas Jefferson, Ben Franklin, Henry Ford, Vincent Van Gogh, Mark Twain, Ralph Waldo Emerson, and Henry David Thoreau were just a few of the people who openly announced their stand for vegetarianism.

*Fasting* - Fasting is a potent tool that cleanses the blood and gives the body a rest. It takes energy to digest food constantly. Food is not your only source of sustenance & energy! Before fasting on your own, it is helpful to get educated about it.

*Career* -this means doing the work you love, or bringing your love to the work you do. This is also known as Karma Yoga, which is service, making your surroundings & environment beautiful for yourself and others. Your career is the physical expression of your divinity on an interactive human-to-human level. How do you bring your ideas, talents, and love for life into the physical world?

*Being in Nature* - Spending time outside, gardening, hiking, camping, etc. This includes your relationship with animals and the natural world. What is your relationship like with the Earth? Are you conscious that the earth is a living, collective awareness? Do you feel a connection to the Earth?

Everything that manifests has consciousness: the trees, the ground, animals, forests, rivers, etc. Are you in touch with that energy? The moon and the pulling of the tides, the seasons, the Earth's tilt, and the sun's rays -all affect your physical body. All are happening in your body, too.

You are a microcosm of the macrocosm. Your body is very in tune with nature's rhythms. It is all too common that we spend most of our lives living and breathing, stuck in boxes, dark, non-natural environments, isolating ourselves from the healing power of our natural environment: NATURE!

## *Air; the Breath*

Healing with the element air is mastering Conscious Energy Breathing/Rebirthing Breathwork. This means learning to breathe the prana, life-force energy, and allowing it to flow through the body in its natural state as we were intended to.

Rebirthing Breathwork is always done in individual sessions by a well trained breathing guide. Leonard considered the initiation into the power of the breath to be absolutely sacred, and he felt that it was vital to provide a safe and private space for this initiation.

The goals of Rebirthing Breathwork, as he developed it, can only be achieved with the attention and skill available in an individual session with a skilled Rebirther breathing guide.

## *Mind*

*"The mind & the breath are the king & queen of human consciousness. What spirit thinks about, it becomes."* ~ *Leonard D. Orr*

The mind is like the active, creative, directive, yang, male principle. The breath is like the receptive, yin, female principle. Breath is the substance or void that gives life to the creative mind. What you think about and breathe into, you give life to.

Healing the mind means healing the quality of thoughts and ideas about yourself, life, the world, humanity, and belief systems. This means watching your thoughts, consciously choosing to dwell on life-sustaining ideas, and using affirmations.

Affirmations are much more than repeated statements of wishful thinking. When we begin affirming a new truth for ourselves, it feels like a lie because our old beliefs are so deeply developed. Affirming the new truth without addressing any of the underlying sabotaging belief systems can quickly turn this process into nothing more than denial.

When you state an affirmation, for example, "I love and accept who I am," listen to any emotional reaction you feel in your body or hear in your mind and write it down. One emotional reaction might be, "No, I don't; I ate all that food I know was bad for me." Repeat the affirmation again, and write down the next emotion that bubbles up to the surface. Continue this process until you have no more emotional responses or only the same response again and again.

Now go back and create a new affirmation for each negative emotional reaction. In this example, the new affirmation might be, "I love and accept myself regardless of what I eat. I enjoy loving myself by eating healthy foods." Always take the painful, negative thought and turn it into its polar opposite; the very best, ecstatic outcome you can imagine and would want to have in your life!

Keep working with the same affirmations until you are completely cleared of negative emotional responses. You will know the new affirmations have become your personal truth when you can look in the mirror without squirming or flinching and say it, and mean it with all your heart.

This process may take days, weeks, months, or even years. Staying with it through all the negative thoughts and feelings is essential. It takes a leap of faith and trust to know that, eventually, one day, the affirmation will feel natural to you. Keep working with them, writing them down, speaking them out loud to yourself in front of the mirror, and even saying them when talking to friends. Say your positive life affirmations until you can say them with a smile. Then you will know it is true and you will remember them like you know your name!

These are tools to help us uncover unconscious identities and belief systems at the root of our self-limitation. This is mastering our imagination. It is the power to visualize, feel, and sense the energy of a new version of ourselves or something we wish to create.

Our thoughts qualify the life force energy of the breath. What we think, feel, and believe, we breathe into being. What quality of thoughts do you add to the receptive breath - universal life-force energy?

## *Mantra*

Healing with the mind also includes the use of mantras. The word mantra comes from Sanskrit, the oldest written language in recorded history. It has been used for thousands of years by millions of people throughout human history and continues to this day. The literal meaning of mantra is 'a tool for the mind.'

Beyond mere recitation of affirmations, traditional mantras are the names of God, a divine frequency encoded with a quality or aspect of creation that heals and cleanses our mind and energy. Mantras invite a higher power or consciousness and energy to take place within and around us. Mantras, repeated internally or out loud, create a vibrational state that transcends the mind and acts as a bridge between our egoic selves and a higher power within us.

Om Namaha Shivaiya is the Hindu mantra I learned

from Leonard. Shiva is the Hindu Deity known as the God of Destruction and Transformation. He is the Lord of the Cosmic Dance, often depicted in a circle of flames known as the Nataraj. He is the Dance of Bliss, the dance in which the entire universe is created, maintained, and dissolved in the eternal process of rebirth and renewal. A cobra snake coils around his waist, representing kundalini or Shakti, the Divine essence in all things. He is posed on one foot, displaying perfect balance amidst the fire of transformation. The small dwarf-like figure he stands upon represents mastery over ignorance, subduing the deluded ego that has suffered and cried for the liberation of enlightenment.

As long as we remain ignorant, we suffer. Shiva is the power to transform our suffering. Shiva is the great destroyer that brings relief from our disillusions and lifts us to liberation. Shiva is the power to transform anything.

Om Namaha Shivayia means I bow to the Lord within me. I take refuge in God, in the eternal, unchanging, omnipresent essence of Life.

This is also the definition of Om Namaha Shivaiya I learned from Leonard;

Om - Infinite Being

Namaha – Infinite Manifestation

Shivaiya – Infinite Intelligence

Often, this mantra immediately erases any fears I may be ruminating upon. It is a direct way to quiet and focus my thoughts on the omnipresence of divinity.

Om Namaha Shivaiya. This is you. You are an Infinite Being, Infinite Manifestation, and Infinite Intelligence. You don't need to work at connecting to God/Source/ Spirit/Universe anymore because the need to connect indicates separation. You are already a spark of the Eternal Life Substance. You couldn't possibly be made of anything else.

Om Namaha Shivaiya. I AM Infinite Being, Infinite Manifestation, and Infinite Intelligence. There is nothing that exists outside of you or me. This is the concept Jesus presented when he said, 'The Father and I are one.' There is nothing I need to learn, acquire, attain, or search for. I only need to accept the truth of who I am and who we are.

Meditating upon this can be infinite joy. Since I am an *infinite being*, I never end. I will never die. I may change, leave this body, or go elsewhere, but I can not destroy the divine spark of my soul, my deepest inner self, my infinite being. Since I am a part of infinite manifestation, I have infinite creations to play with. This is playing in the world of creative imagination. Since I am a part of infinite intelligence, it's possible that there is nothing beyond my ability to know. I only need to practice this consciously. I only need to remember my natural divinity.

Meditating upon these concepts helps us erase illusions of separation, isolation, pain, fear, etc., while at the same time maintaining our unique personality and expression of Life/God. By recognizing each other's divinity, we support each other's life, health, and eternal happiness.

In modern terms, mantras are done with any religious or nonreligious connotation. A high-quality thought can become a personal mantra and be as simple as repeating 'this moment, right here, right now,' or 'I am peace, I am love.' It is entirely up to your personal preference and imagination.

## *Water*

Healing with water includes staying hydrated (drinking plenty of good quality water) and bathing twice daily, preferably before sunrise and after sunset. I feel that nothing can be as refreshing and revitalizing as a shower or bath after a long day of work.

What is it exactly that is so good about being in the water? Why does it work so well? Your body is anywhere from 60 to 78%, depending on your age, gender, and health. And your body was formed for 9 months in the water! The healing effects of water are profound and amazing. Warm water opens and cleanses the chakras. Cold water closes and cleanses the chakras. *Chakra* is a Sanskrit word, the literal translation meaning wheel. There are seven main chakras along the body, which are the structure of your energy body and aura. Swimming in large bodies of water, oceans, streams, or lakes is also recommended. Always practice water safety while doing this, of course!

Try it yourself. I recommend practicing bathing twice per day for at least one week and noticing how you feel. Then you can decide if you want to continue. What would happen if you did? Try it for one month and then two. Go home and bathe for twenty minutes or more. Focus on your energy field, physical body, inner energy, and outer energy. What changes do you notice in your body after a long soak? Go for a walk afterward and pay attention to any changes in how your body feels.

## *Fire*

Healing with fire means sitting with an open flame. Fire is an element that exists in your body, in your body heat and the spark in your eyes. A person with a lot of passion can also be said to have a lot of fire or a fiery disposition.

I felt great the first time I spent a day with the fire. It was very relaxing, and after a few hours, I noticed something about it felt very soft. The air around me, the energy in my body, and the energy outside my body felt very soft and light. Leonard taught that sitting with fire burns away the heavy material, or information, in the energy body such as depression, rage and hopelessness, etc.

Fire has been used all over the world by all cultures of humanity in many rituals and traditions. Its healing effects are ancient and deeply rooted in our collective consciousness. Fire ceremonies, vision quests, and other traditions are rewarding topics to study and practice.

If fire can reduce the wood into smoke and ashes then imagine what fire can do to the heavy energies accumulated in your aura/energy body.

## *Loving Community*

Participating, receiving, and contributing to a loving community is elemental to our healing and well-being. A caring community is a supportive environment. It is a source of encouragement, nurturing, fellowship, learning, and sharing. A loving community will also challenge you to grow and call you forth out of helplessness, lack, low self-esteem, etc., and into your greatness. A loving community is composed of individuals willing to be with you in your emotions and hard times yet promote your ability and capacity to manage them.

Being in a loving community means you get to experience your presence and impact on others. It can be a concrete way to experience that you do matter and are a vital part of the whole. Community is like the backbone of humanity. Each individual is an integral part of the structure. Each individual is supported by and supports the other individuals.

More people are on the planet now than ever at any other time in recorded history. There is an abundance of loving communities to participate in. Notice if you think or feel you have nothing to offer a community or aren't good enough to participate. Notice if you think or feel no communities are good enough for you to participate in. Both of these are anti-life thoughts that keep people isolated, alone, and cut off from the love and life that is so abundantly surrounding us.

There is also a balance between having time alone and spending time in the community. Time alone is imperative for rest, clearing one's energy, and integrating your life experiences. Experiment with how much time alone and time in the community you need for your optimum balance. It's my observation that many of us overindulge in one or the other.

## My Experiences with the Practices

I have been applying Leonard's ideas and practices since I first heard of them in December of 2002. I did, however, have some resistance to using the purification practices that I needed to push through. I thought I knew how to breathe properly because I'd done a few breathwork sessions. I thought fasting would make me sick, be a miserable experience, and eventually kill me. I thought bathing twice per day would be a waste of water and bad for my skin. I thought I would not have time or the resources to sit with fire. And finally, what would people think about me if they knew I did all this?

Using the practices daily has yet to prove one of my resistances as true. They were thoughts crossing my mind, and I was ignoring the fact that I hadn't yet physically experienced these practices for any length of time to feel how they worked. I thought they weren't necessary and I resisted giving them a good, sincere, honest chance.

Applying each one of these practices to my everyday life sent my energy through the roof, and using just one was enough for me to notice a change. I recommend practicing one at a time until it becomes a habitual part of your natural flow and routine.

It is wonderful experimenting with these practices. I have creative ideas and inspiration flowing through me almost nonstop. I can choose when to open it up or take a rest. Inspiration is not some magical outside force that just randomly happens to me. I AM an inspiration. I AM Alive. Most of the time, my body feels completely relaxed. I can feel soft energy flows opening up and moving in my heart, stomach, and legs. I feel areas softening and warming in gentle currents through my entire body. This is a far cry from the chronic fatigue I used to carry.

I found I needed less sleep, and popping out of bed like a daisy in the mornings became my new norm. My old routine took thirty minutes to wake up and drag myself out from under the covers. I also stopped catching colds or flu as often as I used to. Many people who utilize breathwork as a daily routine may find that they have fewer and less severe colds.

## Invitation - 30 Days of Healing

We are made of the elements. All forms of healing happen through the elements. Pick one of the above practices and commit to doing it daily for thirty days. The idea here is to explore and experience how you feel doing the practice vs. any ideas you might have about what doing the practice would be like. We can think about something for days, but doing it is an entirely different education.

What are your resistances to trying these practices?

Are you willing to look beyond them?

Are you ready to step out of the intellectual world of mental indulgence and step into experience?

After the 30-day time period is complete, notice any changes in your body, emotions, or mind. You can reassess if you'd like to continue the practice, stop the practice, add on another one, or go back to your usual routine. The important thing is to have fun exploring the elements and how they affect your awareness and physical being.

# Returning to Oregon

U pon returning home to Oregon, I immediately set up my practice in a space from my home. My only prior experience in being self-employed was giving horseback riding lessons to some kids at a local horse stable, so I relied heavily on the concepts of Leonard's Prosperity Consciousness Seminar.

To build more experience for myself as a Breathworker, I gave three or four people ten sessions for trades at no charge. This built some momentum that led me to rent a healing space from a local yoga studio. I soon had a small clientele that grew by word of mouth. I continued taking clients and friends through ten sessions if they were interested. For others, I gave whatever number of sessions they desired. I gave a beautiful couple ten sessions each and taught them to rebirth each other. I also began to give sessions and build a clientele in Portland at Nila's home office. I paid her a percentage of the sessions, and she let me sleep overnight in her healing room where I gave rebirthing sessions during the day.

To further support my physical healing of endometriosis, I launched deeply into nutrition, herbs, yoga, qigong, and everything I could continue to find to keep me on my path of healing. After coming across Nancy Appleton, Ph.D., and her work on the harmful effects of sugar, I decided to kick the habit.

Simultaneously, I also decided to stop ingesting milk

and cheese products, as it is theorized that the estrogen in dairy products can negatively impact human health and endometriosis specifically. Naively, I had no idea how hard it would be to stop eating dairy products and sugar simultaneously.

Within a week of stopping both sugar and dairy, I woke up one morning intensely craving a cheesecake, and not just a slice of it, but to eat the whole thing. I had been without sugar for several weeks already and was trying to appease the cheese cravings with vegan cheeses, which at that time meant choosing from two different brands of bland, dry almond cheese. It wasn't working for me.

Moving through my morning routine, I prepared my breakfast. All I could think of was what local places sold cheesecake. I tracked through the list in my mind and landed on the nearest grocery store to my house. I could be there in ten minutes.

The cravings increased and I feared I might go. I looked down at my hands and realized I already had my keys in hand and was walking through the kitchen toward the back door of the house. Stopping myself at the countertop, I placed the keys down. I grasped the edge of the countertop as the cravings were now screaming at me. *Just eat the cake!*

Several breaths later and still gripping the countertop as hard as I could, my knuckles began turning white. I noticed I was in a spontaneous Rebirthing session. I stood at the countertop, breathing for I don't know how long until I felt calm and *the feed me cheesecake now* storm had passed. I finally left the counter, trusting myself to stay home and not get in the car to purchase the cake. I later learned that sugar is as addictive as cocaine, and casein fragments found in cheeses, called casomorphins, are a compound that attaches to the same brain receptors as heroin. Rebirthing helped me overcome the food addictions.

∞∞∞

Springtime was exploding in Oregon, with verdant green fields, blooms of cherry trees, and flowering plums. I felt a new vibrancy and enthusiasm so I was exceptionally excited to hear that in a few weeks, Leonard and Isabelle would be traveling out to the West Coast for the first time in many years, offering workshops and seminars. I invited them at the last minute to host an evening lecture in Corvallis.

Leonard and Isabelle arrived at my home sanctuary in their van, chock full of books and travel items. He unloaded their bed from the back of the van and set it up in my living room in front of the wood stove. I asked if it would be good enough access to the fire for his energy purification practices, and he happily said yes. It was the best he had had yet on his road trip across the USA.

That night after the lecture, Leonard fell asleep in the bathtub, with the water flowing at a slow trickle through the night. I woke to find all of my bath towels on the floor as he was cleaning it up, an occurrence I would later learn that Leonard was famous for with many of his organizers.

## *Journal*

April 26, 2003,
Looking back now at my history of endometriosis, I feel nothing but a complete sense of gratitude, love, and compassion for what my body went through. It was healing my spirit.

I feel a funny mix of anxiety, enticement, and wonder when I think of where my life will go next. And yet, at the same time, I feel a deep sense of calm and peacefulness, rooted and growing within me. Thank you, Life, for all that you have taught me!

May 23, 2003,
I used to be shy with my voice; I feared speaking out. Now, I will take my voice with me everywhere I go to carry the true essence of my prayers for all sentient beings, for liberation and peace!

# Rebirthers Convention

In July 2003, I returned to Virginia, just as I had hoped to after the 9-day training. Every year Leonard hosted a 3-week Rebirther's Convention for newcomers to breathwork and old-timers alike. It was an excellent opportunity to meet highly experienced breathworkers and attend their seminars and trade sessions. People came in from all over the world.

This year, it was located in the woods of Afton, Virginia, in a two-story cabin with a fully stocked kitchen, metaphysical library, and individual rooms to trade breathwork sessions in. The cabin smelled of incense, patchouli, and awesome home-cooked meals by Alfredo, a long-time Italian Rebirther who attended every year.

Everyone was in hot pursuit of the one bathroom with a deep clawfoot tub for giving water sessions or rebirthing themselves in their morning and evening baths. But there were also individual baths dispersed outside in the forest, with a few tankless water heaters that kept the warm water flowing. It seemed that at any given time of day, someone, somewhere (anywhere really), was getting a breathwork session, participating in a seminar, crying, or laughing. It was a buzz of high energy and spiritual activity I had never experienced before.

Some people had paid to stay in the rooms of the cabin, while I, like many others, camped outdoors. Virginia in July was nothing like the fresh winter I had just experienced months prior. It was hot, and my clothes stuck to my back in an eternal bath of humidity.

Several other Rebirthers and I managed to get some relief from the heat by swimming in a nearby pond until one of the Rebirthers told us there are poisonous snakes in Virginia, and they can swim. That was the last of swimming in ponds for me!

The mosquitos were thick, and one night, I absentmindedly left my tent door partially open. A cricket or giant insect of some kind found its way into my tent to terrorize me through the entire night. I was also having intense nightmares and difficulty sleeping. I shared this with Alfredo, who advised that after my evening bath, I go straight to bed and not socialize. He said I was processing the emotional energy pollution of the other people present there. I tested his advice, and to my surprise, it worked. I slept like a baby every following night.

It was still a real challenge with the discomforts of a hot, humid forest with poisonous snakes and walking back and forth to my tent in the dark. But the breathwork sessions and friendships that formed made it worth every minor inconvenience.

Glenn and Barbara Smyly were there offering their Alivening Workshops. Dan Brulé was there, with his wild curls of hair bouncing as he scribbled away passionately on a flip chart, drawing diagrams of mental representations of what occurs in a breathing cycle. Heike was there giving what seemed like a constant stream of sessions.

Another Rebirther who had lost 100 pounds and ended his drug addiction was giving Personal Law Seminars. Accents and languages from around the globe flitted and fluttered around the grounds of the Convention. It was like a strange sort of heaven for me.

It was here that I received my first breathwork session while breathing entirely through the nose. Alfredo taught me this and corrected a few of my breathing habits, showing me how powerful nose breathing is. A woman from France who had been raised by two Rebirthers and grew up exchanging sessions with her siblings also gave me a session while breathing entirely through the nose. She taught me how easy it is to allow emotions to move through nose breathing. Her presence was like that of a fairy: light, pure, totally intuitive, and tuned in. Kim and Michael from my fist 9 Day Training were also there, planning to start a One Year Seminar hosted at the cabin in Afton. The experience was pure gold.

Towards the end of the three weeks, many of us planned to drive to Washington, D.C., to see Mata Amritanandamayi, lovingly known as Amma, the hugging saint of India. I decided to go as well and see what she was all about. I had no context for it and was curious about her.

We arrived at a large, stately hotel in the middle of D.C. and waited the entire day for our turn to make the procession down the aisle to receive our blessing from Amma. First, there was a talk, then bhajans (devotional singing), and finally, people began to take their turns, one by one, approaching Amma for a hug.

We had been sitting inside the lecture hall and taking breaks out in the lobby throughout the day, where we were chatting up a security guard. My friends were attempting to explain the magic of Amma to him, but he was laughing it off. "Go and get a hug from her!" My friends encouraged him.

Finally, around 10 pm it was our turn to go. Kneeling in a row, one in front of the other, we crept towards the seat of Amma. Leonard and Isabelle were several people ahead of me. I had no idea of what to expect and remained in open curiosity. Watching Leonard receive her hug certainly looked like joyful bliss.

It was my turn at last after what had felt like an eternity. One of her supporters led me gently up the steps, and in a single moment, I was suddenly face to face with her. She wrapped her arms around me, smiling radiant with joy, and sang gently into my ear, "Ma, ma, ma," she repeated over and over as she rocked me from side to side. Holding her felt like holding a soft, airy pillow of light. And then the moment was complete. She released me into the arms of another supporter, and I was back in line, following my friends back to our seats.

Upon leaving, everyone seemed to be in bliss. I felt like it was nice but nothing significant. Glancing over my shoulder as we were leaving, I saw the security guard stumble out of the room. Several of my friends went to him, but he could say nothing. He was sobbing in what looked like tears of joy and relief.

∞∞∞

I departed from Virginia early the next morning, and leaped back into activities at home in Oregon. A few days later, I sat in the classroom during Matt's third course, *Awakened Potential.* A fresh summer breeze gently blew through the opened windows as he spoke in the front of the room. Every word he uttered seemed to strike a cord within me effortlessly and easily.

With my breath flowing smoothly almost constantly now, I felt soft and clear. My mind was uncluttered. My heart was open and present. It had been over a month since my hug with Amma, and I was definitely feeling a significant change. It was like she had placed a tiny seed into my heart, and it slowly bloomed over time, offering its fragrance like the sweetest flower in the warmth of the sun. The energy was soft, nourishing, and pure. What a gentle and welcomed surprise.

## *Journal*

August 1, 2003

I am having my holy, sacred moon cycle today. That's right, not my period, or on the rag, as I used to say with disgust, but my Holy, Sacred, Moon Cycle!

I am twenty six years old, and for the first time in my life, I am experiencing month after month of pain-free menstrual flows. Now, when I am on my moontime, I often feel completely blissed out and exuberantly happy! I never imagined until now that having my period could feel good! It's my time to rest and nurture my body as I relish my deep feminine nature. It's my time to embrace the deep, melancholic moods that often accompany my moons. There's a power and strength in the quiet reflection of this time. I feel my body goes into an altered state, and I have many insights.

My moon is sacred. It is sacred to be a woman. It is a gift. I lovingly give my blood back to the Earth from which my body has been made. There is an abundant flow of life coursing through my body, and I happily share the creative energy I have received because I have been given more than enough. I am in abundance. To me, menstruation is about letting go, surrendering my hold on the creative process, and trusting the flow of life. I release the old manifestations, and I open to receive the new. I am constantly present, neither clinging to the past nor grasping for the future. I Am here right now, and there is nowhere else I'd rather be.

# Home in Virginia

L eonard and Isabelle invited me to house sit at their home in the autumn of 2003. He was coming out of many years of being on a sabbatical, stating what he identified as his senility process. Leonard had been diagnosed and recovered from several terminal diseases, including heart disease, Alzheimer and cancer, the latter of which he was still managing as it came and left. He and Isabelle would be going to Europe and India that fall, and invited me to come house sit for him at his home, which was also the heart of the international nonprofit.

The timing was good for me. I was in the throws of emotional healing from past traumas and it was like the floodgates were opened. I also had a friend from Matt's trainings looking for a place to stay while he was between housing that winter, so he could house-sit for me at least part of the time while I was gone, and potentially stay as a housemate when I returned. I found myself once again on a flight to the East Coast.

∞∞∞

Exiting the baggage claim area at the Dulles International Airport in Washington, D.C., I stepped into the warm, humid air tinged with a crisp hint of autumn already on its way. I had traveled the entire day from my home sanctuary in the Oregon countryside to the East Coast, where I would be house-sitting and working for Leonard and Isabelle for at least three months, maybe more. The autumn leaves already showed bright oranges, yellows, and golden hues. I wondered if I would need to wait long before Leonard arrived to pick me up from the airport.

To my surprise, I found Leonard quickly and easily as he stood quietly, leaning over the edge of the guard rail, watching the mass of people fluttering to and fro. He turned to me and smiled. I was relieved and tired, and I had hoped not to be waiting long. My period had started two days prior, and although I had no symptoms of endometriosis as a norm now, I still had some discomfort at times which made me uneasy, fearing that the symptoms could return.

He greeted me with the usual kiss on both cheeks and a big grin, eyes shining like something magical was happening in every otherwise normal moment. We walked to his van and began the drive to his home in Virginia. My heart was full of nervous excitement.

"Do you have a mala?" Leonard asked me as he drove, pulling a prayer mala out of his pocket.

"Yes!" I replied. I was wearing a mala that Peter had given me after one of his recent trips to India. It was made out of rudraksha seeds, from the Rudraksha tree. A prayer mala has 108 beads on it and is used for the repetition of mantras and meditation. I had asked Peter about Hinduism, as I was curious but confused by the many aspects of it, and I was also interested in agnihotra, a sacred fire ceremony of offering rice and ghee in a special copper fire pit. Peter had given me the mala and initiated me into the practice earlier that year.

"I do japa mantra every day, multiple times per day," Leonard explained. "My favorite mantra is the mantra Babaji taught, which as you know, is Om Namaha Shivaiya. Om is infinite being, Namaha is infinite manifestation, and Shivaiya is infinite intelligence. You can do a round of Om Namaha Shivaiya on your mala now."

Leonard had already begun to repeat the mantra quietly on his mala as he passed one bead onto the next with his right hand, holding each bead with his thumb, middle finger, and ring finger, just as Peter had shown me before. We rode in silence as we did the mantra together.

"Good," he said upon our completion. "Now I like to use the mantra in various ways, as Babaji instructed me. When fasting, I like to use the mantra, 'Om Namaha Shivaiya is sustaining me now.' Go ahead and do a round of that now."

I began the round on my mala, trying on the mantra and feeling it. It was a pleasant, comforting thought to repeat in my mind.

After some time, we began small talk, and Leonard paused.

"I am more in tune with my feminine energy than most men," he commented. "And over the years, I have developed a sensitivity to the smell of menstruation." He smiled gently.

Mortified, I became increasingly aware of my body odor

after the long day of travel and cram-packed flight.

"Oh," I stammered awkwardly as I squirmed in my seat. Leonard smiled and rolled down the automatic windows of the van. After what was for me, some moments of uncomfortable silence and inner reflection about healing my relationship with menstruation, I decided that everything was okay and I had nothing to feel ashamed about. Leonard soon picked up with a happy note in a small conversation.

We pulled into a hilly neighborhood, the houses increasingly farther apart, until we arrived at a gentle downward-sloping hillside, his home resting at the highest point. It was nothing grand, a humble, white, ranch-style house with a teal blue accent and double entry doors. It was familiar to me this time, as I had visited his home before during my one-day fire vision quest in the 9-day training.

We stepped out of the truck, and Leonard walked me to the side of the house where a camp trailer sat, ready for me to sleep comfortably in. He showed me around, informing me of little details about the camper and my use of it. Isabelle had set out a pitcher of water, a glass, and a bowl of dates and almonds for me to snack on.

We walked a short distance down the hill to the entrance to the basement, where a patio space with double doors opened up into a large room. The walls and cement flooring were painted in the same beige color and making it feel like a yogi's cave.

"Heike, my lead trainer from Germany, just completed painting the basement and building out these rooms.

It's ready for you and a nice place to stay if you like," Leonard commented with satisfaction at the completion of such a large project.

There was an on-demand propane water heater and one of the large stock tanks used as baths, just like we used at the Rebirthing convention over the summer. It was just the right size for me to curl up in the fetal position to get all 6 feet of myself submerged for warm water rebirthing, which I would be doing on my own here both morning and evening.

In the back of the basement 'cave,' there were two more rooms, one set up with a picture of Babaji and a small wooden bench bed. Leonard did not keep mattresses around, even in his training center, as they absorb the emotional energy pollution of sleep, or rebirthing sessions, over time.

Settling in quickly before nightfall, I decided to sleep in the camper but utilized the luxuriously deep bath and spaciousness of the basement. I unpacked only the necessities from my suitcase. The warm bath felt terrific that night. Later on, Isabelle brought me a warm bowl of lentils and rice. I lit a candle and fell fast asleep.

10 am rolled around quietly the following day, and after my morning bath, I came to the front door, holding a blank notebook and pen in hand. I knocked. Butterflies whirled and did backflips in my stomach. I had done countless house-sitting jobs, caring for people's homes, gardens, horses, goats, chickens, cats, dogs, and various animals. But this was different. I would be single-handedly caring for Leonard Orr's house and the headquarters of his organization. We had

a few days before their departure to Europe, which was just enough time for Leonard and Isabelle to show me around and get the whole routine in place.

Isabelle opened the door and smiled. I took a deep breath and relaxed, embracing her in a gentle hug. It was so good to be back in Virginia with them! I stepped inside their home, this time taking a deeper look around beyond the entryway.

A dining table filled with papers and work was the first space that greeted us. Boxes of unopened mail and books decorated the wood floors. Isabelle's miele vacuum lay stretched out across the floor, and she apologized for the mess. I assured her I had no judgments.

A small fire was quietly smoldering in the fireplace in the living room, where Leonard and Isabelle's wooden platform bed sat with camp mats, pillows, and a few blankets. It was a surprise to see their sleeping arrangements, but it made sense, given Leonard's clear aura and resulting sensitivity to energy. His commitment to fire purification was impressive.

Leonard, I could hear, was still in his bath, just draining it.

"Om Namaha Shivaiya!" I heard him shout loudly as he turned on the shower. He advised always taking a cool shower, as cold as one could stand it, after the bath.

Isabelle led me to the small kitchen off to the left of the entryway. I knew she was a raw foodist, but I was still surprised that the kitchen had no stove. There were just countertops, a sink, a workspace, and a refrigerator.

A small portable electric burner, toaster oven, and rice cooker sat out on one of the counters for cooking other people's meals.

Isabelle prepared Leonard's breakfast of fresh raw juice and sprouted grain bread, toasted and topped with tahini and fruit-only jam. She invited me to make some for myself also, so I set out preparing it while she cleared a space at the table. Leonard came out of his bath, and we all sat together for breakfast.

Upon completion, we started work immediately, discussing the daily chores and weekly tasks that needed tending to. I scribbled notes in my notebook as reminders. It was a huge undertaking: the care of three horses, three dogs, and a cat, answering phone calls, checking voicemails, returning calls, retrieving mail from the mailbox and post office box, managing their banking, checkbooks, and bills, mowing their large front yard and back. We hadn't even touched on managing the bookstore and fulfillment of the book orders.

I noticed the phone was ringing nonstop as it interrupted our conversations and activities throughout the day. There was a wide range of people calling for more information about rebirthing, trainings, sales calls, the daily call from Kim and Michael regarding the training center and upcoming events, and even a person who had called in amazement to have found him and his phone number, as they thought Leonard had died over a decade ago.

Leonard chuckled but also seemed annoyed. "When I went into my senility crisis, I lost contact with everyone. Most people just assumed I had died and didn't bother to check up on me. I was like I had a complete blockage to any outside help," he explained.

At the time, it shocked me that people would assume he was dead, but Leonard said it is part of the senility process.

He led me through the living room to a hallway. His bathroom was directly in front of us, with Isabelle's studio space and own bathroom off to the right. The bookstore and his office were to our left. Isabelle was already in the bookstore room, typing and making calls. I could feel the hustle and bustle one would have before leaving for a long trip overseas.

A bookcase stretched the entire length of the hallway on the way to his office. It was Leonard's personal library of books; a collection of esoteric topics and near-impossible to find texts that were only sold in India. It was perhaps one of the most comprehensive libraries on physical immortality one could find on the planet.

Leonard smiled when he saw me gaping and gushing over the book titles, "You are welcome to read any of them while we are away for our travels," he offered.

"Thank you," I replied, sensing what a challenge it might be to balance work and rest during my stay.

We entered his office, and I was immediately overwhelmed. Stacks of papers, boxes of mail, opened letters, and half-written responses lay piled up and strewn about every workspace available. Photos of Babaji, Sri yantras, malas, crystals, and other religious Hindu artifacts lay scattered about the seeming chaos.

Om Namaha Shivaiya, written in both English and Sanskrit, covered almost every visible note, article, or newsletter Leonard had written. Photos of Babaji and Om Namaha Shivaiya adorned the walls and tops of file cabinets.

"I've been mostly nonfunctional for the past ten years," Leonard commented. "I'm just now recovering from my senility process. There are still boxes here that I haven't unpacked since I lived in Chico, California," he sheepishly smiled at me.

Nodding in understanding and approval, I listened intently. No matter how many house-sitting jobs I had done, it always felt intimate for people to let me into their homes and show me around the private side of their lives. He was riding the top of the wave of a significant, global movement while still managing his personal life and healing.

We finished our work that day with Leonard showing me where the electric horse fence charger was in the garage and how to use his electric lawn mower. It was slow going, mowing his huge yard with it, but it did a good job. Rummaging through a pile of tools, to my surprise, Leonard pulled out two large sickles and handed one to me.

"Come with me," he said, smiling.

We walked out into the horse pasture, and he began hacking away at a large patch of vining greenery.

"This is honeysuckle. It's invasive and takes over the pasture. You can come out here and do this anytime you need to," Leonard said as he took a few more amazingly fierce whacks at the vines.

"Anytime I need to?" I asked, a bit confused.

"It's good rage management," he chuckled as he paused to smile at me, then continued working away. "Just watch that you don't hit your feet and legs," he added with a wink.

# Emotions are Energy

Simply put, emotions are biochemicals and energy running through the body. Happy, sad, angry, etc., are just adjectives describing the energy sensations we feel in a body. Of course, we all commonly agree on events and circumstances that will initiate certain feelings, but for our purposes here, let's bring this down to its most basic, physical-interpersonal level.

Avoiding emotions is cheating yourself of experiencing your aliveness. I found that suppressing unwanted emotions was my unconscious fear of growth and change, a refusal to let my life's energy flow out of an attachment to some belief or protection. The irony is that suppressing emotions causes more stuckness and pain. Like floodwaters are blocked behind a dam, emotions will eventually break loose in one way or another, most often as physical pain and disease.

Through Rebirthing Breathwork and utilizing all the elements, Leonard taught the process of allowing blocked, suppressed energy to flow. The complete healing system allows oneself to feel safe enough to relax deeper into the subconscious, unwanted, rejected feelings and come out the other side in a state of equilibrium, harmony, and our natural state of joy. These suppressed energies are areas where our life force becomes trapped and held hostage by shame and denial.

Let's look at rage, for example. Rage is not a popular

emotion in the self-improvement business. However, unresolved rage that is suppressed often turns into depression, relationship problems, self-sabotage, and so on. Anger is an emotion many people avoid, deny, judge as wrong, or even declare it evil. Anger is such an enormous energy when it moves through the body, and frequently, people have not learned how to be with it and use it in a healthy way.

Stereotypically, little girls are supposed to be cute, pretty, and cry, but anger is not appealing or okay. Boys are often denied any feelings of sensitivity and nurturing, but displaying anger is considered as 'manning up' and being strong, leaving it as the only real display of emotion socially acceptable for men to experience.

But emotions can not be bad or wrong. To believe you're bad and wrong for having a particular emotion is a shame-based belief system that basically says you have no right to be human, and there's no room or acceptance for you here as you are. Anger is a human emotion. When you begin to take judgment off of emotions, look behind them, and see their purpose, you will start to access a new level of emotional intelligence.

This requires owning your emotions and not letting them spill all over others and do damage to the people around you. It requires inner inquiry and finding avenues to move the emotional energy through your system safely and responsibly. Leonard's use of the scythe and honeysuckle vines is a good example. Chopping wood with an ax, taking a brisk walk, primal screaming somewhere alone, getting access to a punching bag, and taking it into a breathing session are all good examples of letting the energy move so that you don't stay there, stuck in the emotion perpetually festering and rotting from the inside out.

Anger is so essential. It shows us where we need to honor our boundaries and agreements or if others have been overstepping our boundaries. When I'm feeling intense anger, I harness or honor it by asking myself, 'What line has been crossed? What do I need to advocate for? What am I suppressing? What do I need for my serenity to be restored? What boundaries do I need to establish within myself or with another?

Many people are afraid to let themselves feel emotions and pain because they believe if they do, the pain won't ever go away. Leonard's definition of fear was the belief that the pain would never go away; that pain is the effort of clinging to a negative belief. It is resistance to full aliveness!

Liberation begins on the inside in your inner world. A part of you is observing your thoughts, emotions, energy, and presence. That part of you expands out into and beyond infinity. As a *being*, you are limitless, just as you are right now.

For example, no matter how overcome you are with the feeling of sadness, you can not *be* sadness itself. You might say, "I am sad," as if that's all there is to you. You may experience yourself as wholly absorbed into the identity of 'sad.' But there is a part of you that is present to the energy of 'sad.' There is a part of you that is aware, your pure *beingness*, that is there to witness the energy and sensations of your body. This observer is you, *your Presence*. This is your ability to observe without attachment because your Presence is the part of you that is non-tarnishable and untouchable by any event, circumstance, person, outcome, or experience. Some may call this the Soul or the Higher Self.

It is helpful to begin the practice of observing your emotions, your thoughts, and your body sensations. Be aware that there is a 'you' that is watching everything that happens in your life, every moment of every day. It is the same you that was there when you were born and is still here today, witnessing, breathing, moving, exploring, and living. Your Presence is always there to catch you beneath your lowest lows and your highest highs. Rebirthing Breathwork is masterful at accessing, moving, and integrating suppressed emotional material safely and effectively.

## *Invitation - Observe and Define your Emotional States*

Often, I've discovered that I was so caught up in a negative belief about life, myself, my health, other people, etc., that the thought of even questioning it never crossed my mind. At times, I found myself not wanting to admit how angry or how hurt I was because I thought that having those feelings meant I was a bad person and, therefore, I would be unwanted. I had an image or idea that if I did not appear happy and have it all together, I would not be accepted, leading to "I would not be loved." What self-images do you have about yourself?

I discovered that by being honest with myself and in my relationships about what was truly going on for me, I created the freedom and safety for others to be just as open and vulnerable as I was. Pure honesty, gentleness, and kindness towards yourself and others creates pure magic.

Take a moment and close your eyes. Remember a time in your life when you felt extremely happy - maybe even exuberantly joyful! Dwell on that feeling. Now, observe and define where you feel it in your body. How does it feel? Is it warm or cool? Light or heavy? What color is it? Write these responses down.

Repeat this process with other emotions - anger, sadness, fear, etc. Begin to distinguish yourself from the sensations you feel in your body and simply observe what you feel.

By doing this, you are beginning to become aware of your energy body. Remember, you have emotions; you are not your emotions, and they are simply energy running through your body experienced in a certain way, often with a story or identity attached.

The next step is to have an 'emotion party.' For example, an 'anger' party. Most people have never done a thorough inventory of all the things they are still angry about in life. Write out your own 'anger list' of everything you are angry about in your life: the world, money, past relationships, your parents, etc. The core purpose is to safely and responsibly express all of the emotional energies you feel and experience in your body. Suppression leads to disease.

Are there words you did not express?

What did you really feel at the time but did not say?

Write it all down to let it go. Writing can help to move the energetic fingerprints or memories out of your thoughts and out of the cells of your body.

The main point is to let the energy move. This process is for YOU! Now pair this list with a Rebirthing Breathwork session or safe physical activity.

This process can also be done with any emotions. It's even fun to do with happy, ecstatic emotions! I suggest going through all of your most common emotional states with this process, one at a time. You can have your own 'happy party,' 'sad party,' and 'fear party.' What you discover in this process will be uniquely and entirely yours. The idea is to establish trust within yourself around all of the emotions present in the human experience.

# An Alternate Reality

The next day, Leonard and I went to run a few errands in town. He introduced me to the bank tellers at the multiple banks he utilized in town, and we sorted out which accounts were his personal income, which was for his nonprofit organization, which he paid bills from, and other details. I quickly realized that my notebook of scribbles was to be my bible while they were traveling overseas in remote locations and unavailable to communicate via phone or email.

We stopped for lunch at a small local deli that served organic, vegetarian meals. I couldn't quite grasp why, but I felt nervous and self-conscious around Leonard. It was like he could see right through me. He was so present. Maybe the most present person I had ever engaged with. We sat at the table discussing further details of work to be done while they were traveling, and Leonard asked me some questions about my background and upbringing. He loved that I grew up taking a bath almost every night and then sat in front of the fire to comb and dry my hair. I was raised practicing elemental purification without knowing it.

Our food soon arrived, but I began to feel slightly disoriented. Thinking perhaps I just needed to eat after such a busy morning, I picked up my sandwich to take a bite.

Suddenly, I felt a rush of tingles in my mouth, starting

in my tongue, then my cheeks, gums, and lips. My whole mouth quickly became numb, as if I had received a shot of novocaine. I set my sandwich down in a near panic, unsure what to do. Leonard glanced at me with detached curiosity as he chewed his first bite.

"Is there something wrong with your sandwich?" he asked undisturbed.

"No, no. It's ok," I somehow managed to stammer out. The numbness did not fade. It was becoming even more intense. I took a few deep breaths.

"Leonard, I feel like I just had a shot of novocaine," I mumbled nervously.

"What?" He looked at me like he had misheard me. Maybe he had. I could hardly tell if what I was saying was audible.

"I feel like I just had a shot of novocaine in my mouth," I desperately tried to say more clearly.

He was gazing intently at me and breaking into a smile. "Far out," he laughed and continued eating his lunch.

He seemed unconcerned, and I had no idea what to do except to breathe and take some sips of water. Strangely, the fact that he didn't seem to carry one iota of alarm about my predicament both annoyed me and calmed me.

A few deep breaths later, the numbness gave way to tingling, and I cautiously took a bite of my sandwich. I tried to get a few more nibbles but found I had lost my appetite. I asked for a take-out box, and we left.

Having finished all our errands in town, we drove back to his ranch. I didn't remember much of what he said on the car ride home; I was so preoccupied with the tingles and sensations in my mouth and wondering what on Earth was happening to me that I really could not pay much attention. It finally dawned on me that I had had my wisdom teeth removed earlier that summer, along with a massive dose of novocaine. Perhaps I was healing the physical trauma to my body from that?

After my bath that night, my appetite returned, and I seemed to have cleared out the novocaine. I enjoyed my leftovers from lunch and began to wonder what exactly I had gotten myself into by stepping into Leonard's *alternate reality*, as others had described before.

∞∞∞

The days flew by, and my notebook was filled with instructions and reminders. Each day, my anxiety seemed to peak and then strangely release into relaxation and trust. Working so closely with Leonard was nerve-wracking and blissful, although I couldn't quite grasp why.

With just a few days remaining before their departure, I met with Leonard earlier than most mornings. He had invited me to join him on his morning walk directly after his bath and before breakfast with his dog Hanuman. Hanuman, named after the Hindu god of the wind, was a beautiful, semi-long-haired white dog with beaming black eyes and a cute black nose.

"Hanuman is not an ordinary dog," Leonard explained. He can sense people's death urges and respond to them if they get too close to him. It's good to be cautious with him."

Nodding with understanding, I watched them walking together up the hill as I followed closely alongside them. Hanuman seemed to be in a world of his own. He appeared happy but did not seek much attention or affection from others. I had already met him and petted him several times before. Leonard was pleased that he had allowed me to be close to him and seemed to like me.

We continued up the hill towards his mailbox, passing it to walk a bit further beyond the bend in the road. The trees smelled of a fragrant mustiness that set in with the autumn leaves turning. I gazed up at the blue sky and squinted with glee as the sun shone down upon us.

"I like to do my breathing exercises every morning while walking Hanuman. So, I always start with twenty connected breaths through my nose, then twenty connected breaths through my nose with the mouth open. I like to do alternate nostril breathing on my way down the hill before picking up the mail. If you can manage to do this every day, or even twice per day, it can support you while we're away. But don't worry about it if you miss a few days. You're going to be quite busy." And with that, he chuckled and flashed a mischievous smile my way.

After our walk, we stood in Leonard's kitchen, preparing breakfast together in our now-familiar routine of toast with tahini and jam. Suddenly, he stopped.

"So I have a question for you," Leonard said abruptly. He stood directly opposite me with his full attention and gaze directed my way. "How has it been for you to have me processing your energy?"

A flush of blood ran to my cheeks which were now blushing like they hadn't since I was a young school girl. From the energy I could feel in the room and something beyond what I could even verbalize, I suddenly became aware that Leonard was finely in tune with all of my anxieties ebbing and flowing, and oddly releasing. I couldn't quite understand what had been happening with me all week, but now I understood.

Leonard could intimately read me like a skilled pianist reading a sheet of music: what I was feeling, where I was blocked and stuck, when I broke through and broke free from an emotional blockage, all while I unconsciously went through the motions! I took a moment to integrate this new awareness as he patiently waited, totally present and fully energized.

"Well, it's been beautiful, really," I realized as I said it.

As uncomfortable as the week had been at times, it was also fascinating and astoundingly beautiful. I was no longer processing my thoughts and feelings alone. It was as though a gentle current was helping me release insecurities, disharmonious beliefs, and limited ways of being. It swept me up and showed me where the whirlpools were that I commonly would get stuck in and then carried me around to the side of it rather than falling in the hole again.

Leonard broke out with tremendous joy and energy, which surprised me.

"Good," he clapped his hands and jumped back into making breakfast. He seemed almost relieved by my response, as though I had just entered the next level of abundance and magic we could create together. He stopped and turned to me again, "Have you seen *Rebirthing Ella?*"

I knew it was a video documenting his process of taking a woman through a Rebirthing session, but I hadn't seen it. "No, not yet."

"You haven't seen it yet?" Leonard almost roared joyfully in a way I had not heard him speak before. "Come here," he said as he led me to the living room, where he opened a large trunk stuffed with VHS tapes, audio, and a few books.

"Here," he said. "Watch this while we're away. You're going to love it. There are some other fantastic videos here that you can help yourself to, but don't loan them out to anyone because I don't have any other copies. This one was sent to me by a neurosurgeon who did scans of the areas of the brain that were activated before, during, and after Rebirthing sessions. He proves that Rebirthing lights up areas of the brain that scientists don't even know what those areas are for." He was chuckling softly now, amused by the scientific community. Leonard showed me how to set up the VCR player with the TV.

"It's going to get very cold here while we are gone. You

will be more comfortable in the house. You are welcome to stay in the house, but it is not a place for giving sessions or having people over." Leonard instructed. That seemed easy enough for me. The log cabin in Afton served as the training center and was where we held all our breathwork exchanges and new trainees had their lodging. I nodded in agreement.

"You're also welcome to use my bath. I'm packing up and will have all this stuff out of here," he said, waving his hand at his snorkel and some items lying around.

It dawned on me that although I had been using my snorkel in the tub for months now, I didn't know Leonard's specific instructions on water rebirthing oneself in the tub.

"Leonard, how long do you breathe with the snorkel in the tub? I know you emphasize mostly breathing through the nose." I asked.

"Well," he started and then paused, taking a gentle breath. "When I do my morning bath, I start with the connected breathing through my nose. Then, when I feel ready, I roll over onto one side and do twenty connected breaths through my mouth with the snorkel in the water. I then roll over to the other side and do twenty connected breaths in that direction. Next, I do twenty connected breaths face-down in the water, then roll back over and finish breathing through my nose. This helps get the energy moving."

"Oh, well, that seems straightforward and simple enough," I replied thankfully. It was helpful to hear the detailed instructions from Leonard himself, as I had asked other Rebirthers, and they all had their own opinions and ideas of how to do it.

Leonard stepped back into the living room and scooted the wooden bed closer to the fireplace. "You should sleep here by the fire while we're away. Fire purification is essential. Fire is as important to the body as food. Bring in your sleeping mat and pillows, and you should be quite comfortable here."

It seemed odd to me to sleep in their house, which was so energetically charged for them. But I welcomed the idea of getting out of the camp trailer and sleeping by a warm fire. Not that I wasn't perfectly cozy and warm in the camper, but I had already learned how wonderful it is energetically to sleep next to a blazing fire through the night.

I took a deep breath. My nerves seemed to settle. I can do this, I thought to myself. I've got this. It would be almost six weeks of them traveling before their return home for a short week and departure again, and tomorrow was our last day together. I noticed a small bowl sitting by the fireplace with a few grains of raw, uncooked rice and raisins.

"I do a simple fire ceremony every day, as many times as I like," Leonard replied, noticing my quizzical face as he picked the bowl up.

"You take just a few grains of rice or your favorite food, anything sweet, and hold it with your thumb, middle finger, and ring finger, just like holding a mala. And very gently offer the food to the fire. Fire is like the mouth of God. You are feeding God, so it should be done with gentleness, like feeding a baby." he showed me as he picked up a few grains of rice.

"Chocolate and ice cream make nice fire offerings, too," he added with a mischievous smile.

"I use simple mantras for each offering. The first is *Om Shri Babaji Jai Shri Babaji. Swaha.*" Leonard softly tossed the grains of rice into the fire. From my previous fire ceremonies with Peter, I recalled that *swaha* means 'I offer.'

"*Om Shri Agni, Jai Shri Agni. Swaha.* Agni is the God of Fire," he explained as he went on making the offerings and continuing mantras.

"*Om Shri Ganga, Jai Shri Ganga. Swaha.* Ganga is the mother and source of all water.

"*Om Shri Lakshmi, Jai Shri Lakshmi, bless me with an abundance of health, wealth, prosperity, and all that is good. Swaha.*

"*Thank you, Divine Mother, for Earth, energy, love, and substance. Swaha.*

"You can also do a mantra for anyone that you want to assist and help heal. Just put their name into the mantra like this, *Om Shri Isabelle, Jai Shri Isabelle. Swaha.*" he finished the last mantra with a sweet smile that made me slightly giggle. What a sweet thing to do for someone.

We sat for a moment, watching the fire as it crackled and now burned more brightly. What a treasure this would be for me to do each day.

We returned to the kitchen, where our toasts waited for us, now cold and a bit soggy. But something in me felt enlivened, like a fire had been lit within me, and I felt something rumbling; I sensed *change* was underway.

∞∞∞

The next morning of their departure, I stood at the dining room table, helping to sort the mail and find their utility bills and other last-minute essentials.

"I like to send back all the junk mail I get," Leonard said with his usual, childlike smile as he stuffed the sales pitch letter and credit card application into the prepaid return envelope. He was always smiling and laughing. I began to notice that I felt rather serious and uninteresting in comparison.

"Oh," I said as I scooped up the junk mail I had just laid on the table and stuffed it into the envelope. It made sense; it did make for less work with recycling.

Isabelle entered the dining room with her soft, doe-eyed gaze now slightly flashing with agitation as she worked to complete last-minute tasks.

"Leonard, where is my flight ticket?" she asked. "I set it on the table here earlier."

"I don't know, let's see," Leonard said as we each began digging through the stacks of mail and papers.

Leonard suddenly laughed. "Look in your envelope there, Sara."

Looking down at my hands, I opened the envelope and, to my shock, there was Isabelle's ticket. I had haphazardly picked it up along with the junk mail to return to the sender.

"You almost mailed my wife's boarding pass to Iowa," Leonard laughed. I handed it to Isabelle, who was now laughing and looking at me, quite amused but relieved to have it in hand.

"You have a self-sabotage pattern to watch out for," Leonard commented as he leaned towards me. He pointed out several other near-catastrophic mistakes I had made earlier that week.

Internally, I squirmed uncomfortably. I couldn't argue Leonard's point. I seemed to be making relatively unconscious mistakes repeatedly, and no matter how hard I tried to remain alert, I couldn't stop it. It was part of my anxiety surfacing all week.

*Self-sabotage*, I contemplated. It sounded so terrible and was a new concept for me. I wasn't sure what to do with it. But there seemed to be no escaping it now. My case was out in the open, plain as day for us all to see.

Leonard loaded the last of their travel items in the van, and we took off for the airport which was just an hour away. We had exactly the time needed to make their flight, maybe a little less.

The next time I would see the house, I would enter alone. I felt both sad that they were leaving and a little relieved that I would have some time to myself and a break from all the emotional processing, or so I thought.

Isabelle and I hugged each other goodbye, and I bade them farewell outside the airport. She had spent several days showing me the ins and outs of caring for the horses and dogs, running the bookstore, calculating shipping costs, etc. She was very industrious. I learned so much from her about running and managing a mail-order bookstore.

Driving their van back home alone, I felt a bit like a fledgling on her first flight. Upon my return to the house, I scanned through my notebook, taking mental notes of the daily tasks already completed and considering where I might pick up on the next. The day flew by, and I found myself feeding the horses outside at night, fumbling around in the dark where there was no electricity. *Mental note taken*, I thought to myself. Feed the horses before nightfall! Ensuring their house was locked up securely, I walked around the side of the house to the basement and took my bath. I would sleep in the camper for one last night.

Tomorrow, I would move into the house and get started with all the work. Leonard had assured me that there would always be more work than could be completed. The trick was not to get overwhelmed by it but to listen to how my body felt and rest when I needed rest. It was not about pushing for productivity every day but managing my energy so that I could accomplish more in a natural, harmonious way. This was a new concept to me, compared to the usual push for productivity and to-do lists to complete at all costs by the end of each day. But I would give it my full hearted attempt.

The next two days were a flurry of animal care, answering the phone, returning calls, and sending out new book orders as they flew in. On my first night in the house, I had built a fire, but it smoked into the house without drafting up the chimney efficiently, and I had to open all the windows and doors for an hour to air it out.

So on this night, I decided to clean out the remaining charred wood from Leonard's fire, as he had advised me to do anyway, and I cracked the window open just a smidge to help the chimney draft better. It was getting late, and I was now covered in smudges of ashes and soot, as I had also cleaned some of the creosote I noticed at the entrance of the chimney just inside the fireplace.

*When was the last time anyone had cleaned this?* I wondered. I put the protective screen up in front of my freshly lit fire, which was small enough to be safely unattended while I took my evening bath. Leonard had instructed me that he was comfortable leaving the fire burning if it was small and putting the screen up if I were to leave the house. He advised never to throw water on the fire unless it was burning dangerously hot and fast.

After my bath, I fell fast asleep in my sleeping bag on the bench by the fire. It had been another full, busy day.

# Babaji

On my third day in the house, I was finally settling into the space. It was different, living in their home. I noticed little dust bunnies on the floor, the way papers could be stacked more neatly together, and, all the while, images of Herakhan Baba gazing over me.

I had no reference to an Indian guru before, as I had been raised Catholic. And the idea that God could be entirely present in one human form almost bothered me. I could not wrap my mind around it. This day was particularly warm and humid, and I had struggled to find the right books from the shelves for several book orders. I had missed walking Hanuman in the morning again, and everything seemed to be difficult. I had not even once yet done the fire ceremony Leonard had shown me before his departure, and I so wanted to make it part of my daily practice.

Finally, at the end of the day, before my evening bath, I stopped, pausing to look deeply at a picture of Herakhan Baba on one of the walls in the bookstore. Nothing, I could feel nothing. In this photo, He looked like some average Indian guy. In other images, He appeared almost supernatural, inhuman, with blazing energy and aliveness. But not this image. It felt ordinary. And in that moment, my agitation and frustration reached its peak.

"What is the big deal? I don't get it." I snarled out loud.

"It's just a man. A man!"

And off I went for my night routine. I lay down in front of the fireplace, still annoyed and wondering what I had gotten myself into. But I was soon fast asleep after another very busy day, I entered into a night of dreaming as I lucidly went from one dream scenario to another in a string of random mental processing.

∞∞∞

In the last dream of my night, I saw Sati, one of Isabelle's dogs, smiling at me, but she was the size of a giant bear. In fact, she looked more like a bear than a dog. She was sort of a bear version of Sati but she greeted me happily. I went to her and hugged her, burying my face in her soft, brown fur.

To my shock, she suddenly transformed into a grizzly bear and gnarled her teeth at my neck. Startled, adrenaline immediately began coursing through my body. I lunged back to get away from her, but she tightened her grip, pulling me in closer, her sharp teeth now scraping the side of my throat.

As a lucid dreamer, this was as real as everyday life to me. I truly felt that I could die in this dream. With my blood pulsing and my heart pounding, all I could think to do was look her in the eye. And so I did.

Immediately, the Sati bear transfigured into a young Indian yogi, sitting cross-legged in front of me, his hand on my cheek and gazing into my eyes. He was the image and energy of perfection, stillness, ecstatic bliss, and spiritual fire, all within an instant of silence. I fell through his eyes into galaxy after galaxy, soft as twinkling stars and spinning planets, hues of distant universes caressing me from the horizon. I awoke.

*Babaji. Was that you? Is this who You are?* I ran to Leonard's office to look again at the photos of Babaji. He looked older in the photos than in my dream. But It had to have been Him.

Stumbling through my morning in a light-filled daze, I still tried to be productive. I had a book order to ship, so I began collecting the books from the bookstore. I pulled a book off the middle shelf, and to my surprise, a book on the shelf above it leaped off and landed on the floor. It was titled, *Herakhan Babaji Speaks*. The book lay face down on the floor at my feet.

Picking it up gently, I read the page it fell open to. It was titled *Fear,* and spoke of the many faces of fear; anger, confusion, inertia, greed, and low self-esteem to name a few. The invitation was to identify your own fear and work hard on casting it out.

It was my first teaching from Babaji. My mind was quiet as I sat with these words, and for the following three days, maybe more, I lived in the hum of the eternal silence.

Everything danced before me in waves of bliss as if caressing me into a marvelous play: the trees, the clouds, the sky. Every blade of grass and falling leaf, the horses prancing with majesty, the dogs in their wagging-tailed greetings, the cat with his wise, quiet, graceful ways. It all felt like an extension of my being, as a living, breathing aliveness that was simply an extension of my body and awareness. I was at peace in a way I could not describe. Babaji, Babaji, Babaji. Everything before me danced in an eternal spiritual fire. I realized I needed to go into town to get food as the kitchen was nearly empty. *Would I be okay? Can I do this?*

To my surprise, driving was simple, with a profound flow of ease. Entering the store, I noticed a young child studying me from the comfort of her caretaker's arms. She smiled at me, and again I was swimming in an ocean of bliss. Joy filled my heart and washed over me like a warm summer breeze as she beamed her joy back into mine.

"Mama! Mama!" she called to me with outstretched arms. "No, that's not your mama," the woman nervously laughed. The little girl didn't care. She smiled and cooed at me, seemingly already in bliss as well. It soon dawned on me that everyone, every single person there, was radiantly beautiful, shining with so much brilliance and light that I felt my heart would burst. But they all looked downcast, overshadowed by thoughts in their minds. I could see both their radiance and their pain. But the radiance was more real, more alive, the true essence of who they were, but they could not see it.

*Babaji, you are everywhere and in everything, in everyone. Om Namaha Shivaiya. I thought to myself. He is the 'you' of 'you' and the 'me' of 'me.' He is the eternal, indwelling Presence, the Isness of all beings, the spark of life that is all things. There is nowhere that He is not. He is the master of the Universe, residing in the space between thoughts, the Ultimate Reality, in the hearts of all.*

# Checkbooks and Runaways

Weeks went by, and my blissful state slowly subsided, but I felt fundamentally changed. A new window had opened for me, and I now had broader horizons within my mind and view. I began reading all of Leonard's books about Herakhan Babaji, trying to understand who He was and is, and why He had come to visit me, a lonely, quiet girl from Oregon, of all people!

It was a time of rich growth and also a dumping of tremendous amounts of mental garbage, insecurities, fears, and genuinely disempowering thoughts and beliefs. It was like a mental purge had begun, and I rode each wave down into the depths of darkness within my consciousness, each time soaring high above the waves in new, expanded states of freedom and bliss.

Menstruation continued to flow easily and comfortably for me. It was marvelous to settle into feeling so at peace with my moontime. As a suggested practice in Lara Owen's book, *Her Blood is Gold; Celebrating the Power of Menstruation,* I began collecting and offering my menstrual blood to a young sapling that had recently been planted in Leonard's backyard. Over time, I began to feel quite the connection with the tree and held a strong affinity for it.

My days flowed in an enjoyable rhythm of work; managing both indoor and outdoor chores, running errands, starting and ending each day with a breathe in my bath, and sleeping next to the fire. It was also a very challenging time. Virginia was having their biggest snowstorm in nearly one hundred years.

Three feet of snow covered the ground, so I had snow to shovel now, in addition to all of the daily tasks. On top of it, Breezy, the matriarch of the four horses, was fearlessly plowing through the electric fence all hours of the day and night. It was not uncommon for me to wake at 1:00 am or so to the sound of galloping hooves racing down the driveway where I had shoveled the snow and hear them pounding over the hill and into the neighbor's yards.

Begrudgingly, I flew out of bed, threw on the warmest clothing I could find over my sleepwear, and shoved my bare feet in boots. It became my worst nightmare each night.

Thankfully, I discovered it was easy enough to find them. I began to keep a halter and lead rope by the front door for easy retrieval in the wee hours of the morning and dark of night. I trudged up the hill through the three feet of snow, apple in hand and calling softly to Breezy. If I could catch her, the rest would follow.

How beautiful they were in the moonlight, though. Their white coats aglow in the full moon's light and breath visibly permeating the air in gentle clouds of warmth on the crisp, frozen night. They pawed most fiercely at the ground, in the neighbor's front lawn to be precise, to get at the fresh, verdant green grass below, ripping it up and chewing happily. I couldn't blame them. What a feast to have in the middle of winter compared to the heavily grazed pasture back home.

Finally, when Breezy had her fill, and I felt I could no longer stand the cold, she let me slip the halter over her nose and buckle it behind her ear.

"Ok, Breezy, let's go home. Enough of that for tonight now, ok?" she hastily chomped on the apple I bribed her with in near defiance. I started to feel a love/hate relationship for her. Leonard often spoke of mastering sleep deprivation, but I was no fan of this.

My days were sleepy, and I watched the horses, ensuring they weren't conglomerating around the fences to escape. They had plenty of fresh hay and food, and huddled together under the shelters on the coldest days. I enjoyed going out to see them, brush them, and love on them as long as I could. It was a mere 14 degrees most days, so much of my time was now spent indoors.

As I opened mail, checks would come in for donations to the nonprofit or to Leonard personally. My job was to collect them, send back thank you notes, deposit them into the corresponding accounts, and pay bills from the money that came in. It was astounding to me that there was a constant trickle of donations via mail coming in, and when the bank accounts seemed like they would bottom out, Leonard would deposit thousands from his most recent training or event. This would cover the travel expenses for the next leg of their travels and the bills to be paid back home in Virginia.

However, several times, I repeatedly overdrafted some of the checking accounts. For the life of me, I could not prevent this from happening. I used a calculator and sat down to balance the books when I was most alert and awake, and still, I made simple, stupid mathematical miscalculations and overdrafted the account. All I could figure was that it was my self-sabotage pattern wreaking havoc.

Several times, I was convinced that Leonard was over-drafting the accounts when he used the ATMs overseas, and I blamed him vehemently. But upon further scrutiny a few days later, each time, I saw that it was I, in fact, who had made the errors. As a person who had always kept clean, accurate records, it was mind-blowing and so frustrating that I could not manage a simple checking account balance. I didn't yet know it, but the pattern would last another year, extending to my own banking, until I could heal it!

Still pushing through my inner, emotional clutter, I cleaned the house as best as possible despite all the piles of mail, books, and papers. I smudged and incensed, I played Aarti and kirtans in the home as often as possible. I opened it to fresh air and, most importantly, kept the fire burning twenty four hours per day, every day of the week.

Leonard claimed that fire could transform the energy of an entire home. I decided that with all the self-sabotage and emotional processing I was doing in his space, it was best to keep the fire going.

It had been over a month since Leonard and Isabelle departed for Europe and India. I noticed that, at times, I would feel Leonard's presence around me as if he were actually in the room with me or observing my task. The phone would inevitably ring a few minutes later, and it would be Leonard, asking how things were going and how I was doing. This became the new norm, so much so that I knew when he was calling. Working with Leonard, indeed, was like stepping into a different and new reality.

It was near the end of November, and Leonard and Isabelle's communications were limited. But when we did connect, I could feel the energy of love and aliveness they were in. They were traveling through South India, giving a training, further adventures, and visiting Sri Aurobindo ashram in Pondicherry. The love I felt from them and for them was profound.

Another short, winter's day gave way to the long dark of night. After finishing my evening bath I sat with the fire for a while before sleeping next to it. I felt the urge to turn off all the lights and just be with the flickering flames.

"Om Sri Ganesha, Jai Sri Ganesha, remove the obstacles in my path. Swaha. Om Sri Agni, Jai Sri Agni, Swaha. Om Sri Ganga, Jai Shri Ganga, Swaha," I made my fire offerings as Leonard had taught me. Upon completion, I stopped and sat in silence,

Within moments, I became aware of a massive shift in the room's energy. It was thick and palpable as if I could wade through the air or even walk on it, it was so heavy with qi (energy). I turned my back to the fire to gaze into the darkness and feel the energy. Excitement and love filled me in a way that words could never begin to describe.

*Babaji! I feel you here! I know you are here!* I wanted to shout, but I knew I needed not to say it out loud. I enjoyed the silence. So great was the energy, the quiet stillness was impeccably serene. I heard the Universal cosmic humm and enjoyed His Presence. Words would have only interrupted the flow of energy that was taking place.

Waves and vibrations moved through the whole house towards me, and in an instant, I could simultaneously see both my view from sitting in front of the fireplace, and above the exterior of the house, the roof, and yard enveloped in the light of the full moon.

All of my senses were heightened in the beauty of it all. After some time, the dual sight and viewpoint of the house from above slowly faded. I was back sitting before the crackling flames, the energy in the house now subsiding. Amazed, I laid down and drifted into an easy, comfortable sleep.

## *Journal*

October 26, 2003
I am awake, alive, and energetic! I had a session with Michael yesterday. I was so tired, it really felt like work to breathe and took so much effort to stay awake. I felt a dull pain in my first and second chakras (base of spine and lower abdomen), then hunger, fear and anxiety, but that didn't last long. Towards the end of the session I had a sensation of falling out of something backwards, head first, with the feeling that there was nothing there to catch me, but something did! (Sounds like birth to me.) I immediately felt very present, here, alive, awake, and breathed in a lot of bliss.

November 9, 2003

Today is the last day of the *Harmonic Concordance,* a lunar eclipse and alignment of six planets forming a Grand Sextile or Star of David. I'm finishing a three day fast. I found that I never really got hungry even though I had a few food fantasies of pizza. The first two days my energy was just fine. The third day I was pretty tired and took a long nap. I was so busy and active the first two days though that this didn't surprise me! I also found that exercising gives me more energy rather than loosing it, as long as I take time to breathe and stay tuned into my body and don't over exert myself. I'm having so much energy that I'm having insomnia, but I don't feel bothered by it!

November 20, 2003,
I've been feeling tired lately, craving junk foods like mad, and giving in to it. My moon time is next week, and these food cravings are a pattern. I feel pretty good, though, aside from a little bloating, probably from all that junk food I'm eating! I feel perfect after my baths. Tomorrow, I will take a day off to fast with the fire. It will just be time for myself and the routine animal care.

Recently, I started reading *Path to Happiness,* a book about Babaji, and I feel stunned with happiness and amazement! I now feel so blessed and honored. I am so grateful for the spiritual insight I received from His Presence. I feel called to Him now; it makes sense. It's beautiful how all the little life adventures build upon one another.

November 23, 2003,
Reading about Babaji makes me think of how I used to say that if I ever went to India, I might not return. It sounds fascinating and harsh like wind and ocean

blasting at rocky cliffs above the shore.

I am still swimming in guilt. I feel guilty for bouncing the check books and costing them so many overdraft fees. I feel guilty for denting Leonard's truck! I feel guilty for spending too much time in Leonard's house, as if I might be changing the vibrations of his house, and he won't like it when they return. I feel guilty for taking so much time alone and not spending more time with the other local Rebirthers at the training center. I feel guilty for having binged on junk food last week. I think, in general, I just feel guilty. I don't even need a reason.

So I've been working extra hard lately like I'm doing penance or something. I am afraid Leonard will be disappointed in me. I'm so scared he will tell me I did things wrong or inadequately. I'm worried about parental disapproval! I know it's ridiculous to ruminate over this, as I'll only feed it more energy and create more of it. I guess I have to trust the process I am in.

Today I have $68 left to my name. I have enough firewood for just a few more days. The dogs will need more food in a week or two, and the horses as well. I didn't want to cash another check from Leonard, but I will need to. With all the overdraft fees I've cost them, I don't feel trustworthy around money right now! I didn't know how much I placed my worth and value on how much money I had. I'm letting that go NOW!

I feel like sitting outside under the stars tonight. It's a new moon, and my moon time will start soon. I wish it weren't so cold here at night. I'm thinking of Hawaii or someplace WARM!

I rode Dancer bareback yesterday. It was a lovely break from all the work to do, and reset myself from all the emotional processing I'm in. I'm so grateful for the love of horses!

November 24, 2003,
Here it is again, 11:30 pm, and I scarcely feel sleepy. So much is happening for me; I sense subtle yet massive energy changes occurring in and about me. All this time alone gives me time to soak in and be with my life experiences and myself in a way I've never done before. It's amazing. I am humbled and amazed, like I'm watching myself unfold. My passion for Babaji is growing. Now, when I see his pictures, it's like he is alive, his eyes always loving, always teaching me something about myself. Babaji is showing me how he has been in my life all along. I almost feel like I have no right to all of this. I feel unworthy. Who am I? A quiet, lonely girl from Oregon. And now I'm openly embracing and loving life!

The more I meditate on His energy, the more I recognize Him in my past. It's as if, I imagine, I have met my creator, who is showing me myself, teaching me about life, myself, the Universe, and Him. It's all the same. It is like he is the thinker and is behind all of my thoughts, witnessing, creating, and the created manifestation itself.

Something shifted in my awareness tonight. I feel a lot of love. I emailed Leonard and Isabelle today, and I have felt them with me, like their presence is beside me. I feel less fearful now because I know Babaji is everywhere and in everyone, every thought and everything. I don't need to control, understand, or manipulate anything anymore. Babaji takes care of it all. I take refuge in Him. Om Namaha Shivaiya.

December 5, 2003,
I had an incredible dream last night. I went to some guy's house; he was a healer and did some energy work for me. I don't remember the details, but he was tall, thin, white-skinned, and had poofy curly hair. I remember lying on my back on the floor on a yoga mat. He was behind my head. At one point, I saw his hands by my throat, one hand pointing up, the other towards my throat, and an intensely beautiful blue and white light beamed out of my throat chakra, filling almost the whole room. Several times, I felt so good that I became completely paralyzed. All I could do was lay there and feel the energy rush through my entire body. He asked if I was okay. I said yes, and then he left. I felt great, and then I woke up. I've been thinking of this dream all day, honestly, I wonder who he was!

As of late, I'm noticing that I feel terrified of intimacy, not physical intimacy, but emotional intimacy, letting people see myself, my authentic self without any hiding, as if I could hide! I'm stuck in my Personal Law or something. I know all this is coming up to be let go. I know I am in purifying mode!

December 10, 2003,
I feel like I am in another dimension and never want to return. Leonard said, "once your consciousness expands, it can never return to its former, diminished state." I feel that right now.
I am in love. In the Light of Love!

# Fire and Snow

It was a few days before Leonard and Isabelle would return home, which filled me with excitement. However, I also felt a little out of sorts. I had horrible neck pain, and a rash had appeared in perfect hand-like stripes around my ankles. Nothing I did for it could make it go away, and I had a strange, inexplicable sense of urgency that Leonard and Isabelle should not see me like this with this rash.

Amazingly, it completely disappeared on the day they returned, aside from one small stripe on my right ankle, which was easy to hide. I was sure this was more of my birth trauma, as I could not explain the irrational fear of being seen nor quite fathom a rash that appeared simultaneously around both my ankles, looking like I had been gripped by my feet. Indeed, I had been, and held upside down, upon my birth! Leonard taught that every symptom was a healing in progress. I was quickly catching onto how this worked.

Upon his return from India and Europe, Leonard looked worn and aged. He had gained weight around his belly. Even though there was a foot of snow outside, he spent three days by the fire doing a liquid fast. I continued to help with the care of the animals and enjoyed having Isabelle's company. It was a nice rest for me too.

"Doing fire purification in the snow is one of my favorite things to do," Leonard smiled as he approached me. I had hardly seen him since his return home three days prior, aside from a few glimpses of him standing outside in the snow with the fire. He looked ten years younger. The lines, fatigue, and weight were gone, and he was back to his radiant, smiling self.

He led me around the house to the north side where he had been spending his days with the fire. Isabelle had asked me to prepare for spending time with Leonard by taking some hours with the fire first. I was bundled up in all the layers I had, and as I walked around the corner of the house with Leonard, it was so beautiful to see the fire flickering in the white of the snow all around. He left me to stay with it for several hours before going inside to meet for the day's work.

∞∞∞

*Rap tap tap...* I knocked gently on the front door, feeling absolutely sparkling after just a few hours outside by the fire. Leonard opened it, beaming with energy and seeming taller. He smiled like a kid on Christmas morning, which was just a few days away!

"Come with me!" he grinned and nearly bounced through the living room and down the hallway to his office. I entered and was stunned.

Leonard stood in the middle of the room, glowing with a smile from ear to ear. His desk was completely cleared of clutter. The boxes of mail were mostly gone, aside from a few tucked neatly in the corner. Everything was polished and shiny clean. It felt good to be there.

"I cleaned my office all night last night," he proudly said.

"I was up until 3 am. Do you approve of me?" he jokingly laughed with a childish twinkle in his eyes.

"Leonard, this is amazing! You did all of this last night?" I was impressed, and I did approve! It would be so much easier to work in his office now.

He showed me some letters he was responding to and the stack of donations he had found. He invited me to write to the people who had sent them while he was away. Leonard had such an amazing relationship with so many people. He was so very attentive and thoughtful with each one.

"And you know who this is, don't you?" he asked, pointing to a small, 3 x 5 photo at the top of his file cabinet. It was an image of a tall, pale complexioned man with poofy, curly hair.

"Oh!" I exclaimed. "I saw him in a dream that I had recently, but I don't know who he is."

"That's Babaji in His Italian body."

"Really?" I gapped as I took a closer look. "He worked on my throat chakra in my dream. It felt so good and intense that I was completely paralyzed during parts of it."

"Yes," he said, as if he already knew somehow. "That is called Shaktipat. It is a special energy transmission you received from Babaji that awakens kundalini and heals the mind and body from the root cause of disease." He studied me intently.

Unable to speak, I stared at the photo with astoundment. Shaktipat. I had already received two from Babaji then. First, in my dream, with His hand on my cheek gazing into my eyes, and the second, His Italian body healing my throat chakra. I pondered how He appears in multiple forms, or in any form. There are no limits to this divine leela (play)!

"Isabelle tells me you had a dream of Babaji, one of your first nights here in the house?" Leonard inquired.

"Yes. I'm certain it was Babaji, but he was younger than how he looks in most of these photos." I motioned to the walls of Leonard's office, where he had framed images of Babaji from the 80's. Leonard went to his file cabinet and pulled out some pictures.

"He looked like this?" Leonard asked with a puzzled look on his face, almost troubled.

"Yes," I replied. "Exactly. Babaji sat before me with his hand on my cheek, gazing into my eyes. And I saw the whole universe in Him like I was falling into the stars and galaxies. I was in an altered state for at least three days. Maybe more."

Leonard was silent as if he was integrating something in his internal process. I felt a bit shy about sharing my experience, but knowing Leonard, everything was perfectly okay and just as it should be. He put the photos away without saying another word, and we returned to the tasks for the day.

Enjoying having them both back at home, I watched as they unpacked treasures from India and shared stories and adventures. Leonard was all work, finding articles and books for his next trip, going through mail, and returning phone calls.

"Argentina is a fantastic place." he smiled at me. "My organizer lives in a small town where kids can ride their horses into town and pick up a pizza. It's a beautiful. Would you like to come with us?"

Leonard had planned a spontaneous training there with an organizer he knew well. They would be leaving on Christmas day, an easier time to travel as most people would have already arrived at their destination for the holiday.

"Oh, I couldn't," I replied. "I don't have my passport. And who would take care of the animals? And I don't have money for an airplane ticket."

"We could work that out," Leonard replied with calm intentness.

"No, I don't think I should. I'm happy to stay here. But thank you!" I pondered how I had read that one should have a passport in hand if hanging out with Leonard Orr.

I also remembered hearing rumors that he liked to purchase one-way tickets for Rebirthers that traveled with him and leave them in other countries to work out their prosperity consciousness until they developed a high enough self-esteem, eventually earning enough money through their connection to infinite intelligence, infinite being, and infinite manifestation to get the money for the flight back home. I did not feel up to the task! I did, however, decide to get my passport application turned in. One never knows what the future may hold.

∞∞∞

In the wee hours of Christmas morning, Leonard and Isabelle were rushing to prepare for their next adventure in Argentina, no doubt happy to leave the cold for warmer skies.

"Let's all take a quick shower before we leave for the airport. It's an early flight, but we have time." Leonard commented when I knocked on their door at 3 am, ready to drive them to the airport.

It was an awkward feat, but I managed to shower while crouching with all of my six foot body in the basement tub, using the hose I would normally fill it with. It was fun and invigorating. I rushed to get dry, hovering near the propane space heater to stay warm. I returned to the house, where Isabelle and I sat at the table as Leonard had ended up taking a bath.

"He often does this," Isabelle smiled with a twinge of annoyance. We waited half an hour until he drained the tub and turned on the cold shower.

"Uhhhhh ughh!" he shrieked, sounding like a woman. Isabelle rolled her eyes and quietly laughed. Leonard had no reserves of self-expression, and no doubt, the water was very, very cold this morning.

He came bounding out of the hallway, happy and fresh as a 6-year-old child, ready to depart. It was still dark outside, and we chatted quietly on our drive to Dulles International Airport, discussing details of what work was due for the next month.

The horses would need another large, round bale of hay. There were some bills and personal finances that would need tending to; temperatures were below freezing, so there were some things to know about starting his truck in the cold weather and tending to the house, dogs, and cat through the winter.

And, of course, there were the bookstore orders, phone calls, and the usual routine of opening mail and responding to people who sent donations. I had plenty to manage while they were gone.

We arrived at the airport, still in the darkness of a typical early winter morning. We bid our farewells, and off I drove back to Staunton. As I arrived in town, the sun was just beginning to shine over the horizon.

Another month on my own here. I wondered what further adventures awaited me. It was just a few days before the new year. I stopped at the local grocery store to get a few items and use up some coupons Leonard gave me for soy ice cream. It was an indulgence he got me started on that felt sinfully delicious after fasting on liquids one day per week. Leonard was a strange mix, or balance perhaps, of discipline and luxury.

*Staunton, Virginia, 2004,* read a stand of New Year's t-shirts in the store.

*Why not get a souvenir?* I thought to myself as I picked up a gray shirt with the US flag and big white lettering. *I may as well celebrate that I am here!*

Upon returning home, I tended to the gently glowing

fire in Leonard's fireplace. I scooped the ashes into a metal bucket but kept the burning embers and added more wood. This was a sacred fire, our sacred fire. I kept it burning constantly when they were gone, and Leonard tended to it when they were home. I was happy to be picking up the practice again after my short break from it and resume the simple fire ceremony Leonard taught me twice per day.

And the fire was getting plenty of soy ice cream. It was nice to have something to indulge in, in what otherwise seemed to be a pretty ascetic life.

## *Journal*

December 18, 2003,
Leonard said I have a self-sabotaging pattern that shows up every day, and it's unconscious. He said to stop beating myself up! So, I am using these affirmations and new thoughts now:

I am no longer harsh with myself.
I am gentle with myself.
I love myself.
I am kind to myself.
I am compassionate with myself.
I treat myself with all the tender, loving care of a gardener handling soft blooming buds.
I nurture myself with peace.
I love God, and God loves me!

Leonard had also mentioned something many people

have in their psyche called a 'learning barrier.' People, myself included, have a barrier to learning and genuinely receiving new information because they listen to what their mind has to say rather than truly listening to the new information. He said repetition is necessary to overcome the learning barrier. He recommended that I listen to the Money Seminar audio every day for 30 days. One more thing to add to my daily routine that I haven't done yet!

December 19, 2003,
Today was a hectic, long day for me. I woke up at 4 am, so I did over an hour of mantras and got blissed out!

December 20, 2003,
It is so freezing here. My eyes were watering by the time I got back to the house after taking Sati for a walk. Leonard and Isabelle returned today. It's lovely to have them back. Leonard was so impressed with the energy in the house and said I had cleared it for them. He loved that I kept the fire going all this time, and he will keep it going while they are here. They leave for Argentina right around Christmas. I'm glad they are here.

I've been feeling timid around Leonard. I wanted to tell him how thankful I am and how blissful it has been for me to be here at their home, but each time I tried to speak, my mind went blank. Somehow, Leonard is gently processing me through a ton of fear around disapproval, unacceptance, and rejection. He keeps supporting and encouraging me through every mistake I make, even all the overdraft fees on their checking account. There is no vibe of disapproval or punishment at all!

December 22, 2003

I am overwhelmed with love, at times I almost fear I cannot contain it and might burst into a thousand cosmic pieces, but here I am.

December 24, 2003

Leonard is gently processing me through a TON of childhood stuff... and a lot of fear and mistrust of being emotionally close to anyone. I am grateful.

December 29, 2003,

I feel more grounded and rooted in knowing who I am than ever. After all this emotional clearing, I haven't had any symptoms at all again for two months now. I feel even ten times healthier than I did before! I've been watching my interactions with people and observed a significant change in myself. I no longer look to define myself by what other people think or have to say about me. I know myself. I know myself more intimately than any other human being knows me. And while I still listen to advice and others' opinions, I know that my life and my own self are the greatest teachers and guides I could ever need.

I had a great talk with a longtime friend today. We connected in ways I have not experienced with her for a long time. I shared so much about my healing process and things I had never told her before. I didn't know that by healing my body and health, I'd be healing my relationships, too!

# Walking Hanuman

It was December 31st, 2003. With Leonard and Isabelle in Argentina now, I was back to my daily work rhythm with the house, animals, and office work all flowing along nicely. Each morning, I managed to do the fire ceremony, get a light breakfast, and take Hanuman, for a walk up the hill to the mailbox and around the neighborhood while doing the breathwork routines as he had shown me before.

Feeling exceptionally light and free, I enjoyed the pristine, crisp winter air with the sunshine blazing across the landscape. It was a wild change from the blanket of Oregon's cloudy skies that seemed to hang low in the Willamette Valley. Hanuman and I were getting along fabulously, and I felt good being with him. There was not an ounce of tension between us as Leonard had cautioned of.

We made our way up the hill and turned to go back home. I had finished my rounds of twenty connected breaths and began the alternate nostril breathing. Feeling the smoothness of the energy flowing through my inner, central column along the core of my torso, I relaxed and bathed in the sunshine. I heard a gentle wind that soon became like a soft whispering roar. Funny, I thought. A few more steps later, it was as if the sun was right before me, or perhaps I had stepped into the sun.

I could see nothing but an illuminated golden light and

gentle wind that seemed to permeate the entirety of 'me.' Did I even have a body? I no longer felt my feet on the ground; it was as if I was floating. I had a vague sense of holding Hanuman's leash but could not sense him there.

A radiant, rapturous tickle spread through me. Yes, I was nothing but light, energy, warmth, and pure ecstasy that only comes with a completely silent mind. There were no thoughts, just being. It was beyond words, beyond description, and all I could do was feel the bliss.

Sometime later, moments perhaps, a car slowly came into view as if it were driving directly into the light and my path. And along with it, it brought back the world: the trees, the houses, rolling hills, and the banked roadside.

Once again, thought took over. At first, it was an irritation. *Why did that car have to interrupt my experience?* And then the usual cascade of mental activity: *What would have happened if that car had not driven by? What did the driver see, if anything? Where is Hanuman?*

Looking down, I saw him walking alongside me calmly as if nothing out of the norm had happened. He glanced up at me, wagging his tail and enjoying himself. I breathed in deeply and gave thanks for whatever had just occurred. Gazing at the sun on my way home, I will admit I tried to repeat the experience, but it did not return. However, I felt light and relaxed in my body in a way I hadn't felt in a long time.

# *Journal*

January 1, 2004,
Happy, Joyful, victorious New Year! I really did feel like I was lifted into the wind, sun, and light yesterday when I was walking Hanuman. My body felt like it was made of pure light.

I love doing the fire ceremony twice a day, every day! I love to share my food with God/Goddess. I love offering and sending my prayers on the smoke. My relationship with fire is changing a lot. I love this fire. It burns brightly and beautifully, and it is easy to keep it burning. I am writing in my journal by its light now.

Today, I saw something different that I'd not seen before. It was like tiny particles of light (substance?) were being released into the air with the smoke. It was stunning. It looked like golden dust falling upward into the air.

# A Bale of Hay

It was another sunny winter day in Virginia, but the wind blew stronger than usual. Vayu, God of the wind, teased at my hair and sent little blasts of hay and dust in my face as I fed the horses that morning. They needed another bale of hay, a large, circular bale that the farmer would load into Leonard's truck for me. I had been with Leonard before they left to meet the farmer and his wife, so I knew the routine of hauling it back home. The bale was so large that I would need to park his diesel truck on the hillside in the pasture and push it off to roll it out the back. Today was the day to do it before the next snowstorm blew in.

The wind occasionally pushed against the truck as I drove down the highway, forcing me to turn the wheel into it to keep straight on the road. At last, I arrived on the farm. The husband and wife came outside, bundled up in the wind to greet me. I opened the truck door just slightly, preparing to step out, and the wind ripped it from my hands, slamming it forward full force. Surprised, I hopped out and quickly shut the door. To my horror, I noticed a huge dent at the door's hinge, leaving a gap between the door and the truck's body. Had I seriously just dented Leonard's diesel truck in the wind? What kind of misfortune was this? How long were these mishaps to go on like this?

"Gosh, it sure is windy today!" The farmer called out to me as his wife stood by his side. He had a thick, southern accent that had nearly shocked me the first time I met him. I had never spoken with anyone with such an accent before. They were a sweet couple, perhaps close to my age, and had recently taken over his father's farm. They insisted they find me a man to help with all this work! I laughed and assured them I was ok.

Hopping in his tractor, he loaded the hay bale onto Leonard's now-dented truck, and we bid farewell. I drove home with a heavy cloud of dread hanging over my head. How would I face Leonard when he returned with this considerable dent in his beloved truck? Would he demand I pay for it? I had no money!

I parked the truck on the hillside, lowering the electric fence as Isabelle and I had done before. However, I did not have her help pushing it off this time. I parked on a steeper slope in the pasture and climbed into the back of the truck. Leveraging my leg and buttocks against the cab, I began pushing and rocking the bale back and forth until, finally, it tipped over the edge and down the hill. The horses were soon happily munching away.

# Chandra

The next day, I mainly spent indoors, working on bookstore orders, responding to phone calls and letters, and paying bills. Throughout the day, one word repeated over and over in my head. It would not go away, and I had no idea why. Chandra. I didn't know what it meant.

*Chandra. Chandra. Chandra.* It rang in my ears like a mantra, louder than all other thoughts. Had Babaji placed it there? *Yes!* I nearly heard audibly out loud. *Chandra!*

Babaji regularly gave spiritual names. Was this mine? A warm, soothing sensation eased through my body, and I softened. I picked up the phone and dialed Yasoda Susan Deschenes' number. She was a longtime Rebirther living in California, and Leonard had said she would welcome my call anytime and be of tremendous support. He felt we would have a remarkable connection, and he was right. We did.

I found Yasoda so easy to talk with and to laugh with, and she had the most unique, outrageous stories as a former Rajneesh. She had traveled the world as a Rebirther and had a witty, sharp mind, deep, loving heart, and, at times, a nearly naughty sense of humor. She told me that Chandra meant the moon.

I thought about my love and near worship for the moon, as well as how I had named my periods my moontime, and was quite amazed. It made sense that it would be my spiritual name, but in my analytical mind I still doubted it. She assured me that if I sensed it was given to me by Babaji, then indeed it was.

Chandra. It was simple, only one word, compared to the longer string of Indian names I had heard of others receiving. But I was fine with that and felt happy. So I accepted it. Sara Chandra Dawn, it was then. Om Namaha Shivaiya!

Looking intently at the snow falling now furiously outside, I took a quick mental inventory of what might need to be done. It was mid-February, and the snow was piling up again. I decided to shovel the front door area and pathways, as it looked like much more snow would fall that night. I was so grateful that I had picked up the hay bale before the February weather arrived, just as Leonard had recommended. At least now, the horses would be less likely to jailbreak out of the pasture to dig up the grass in the surrounding neighbor's front lawns!

## *Journal*

January 11, 2004
Chandra. God of the Moon. I love my spiritual name.
Thank you, Babaji. I am so happy, everywhere I go! I am in Bliss! Everywhere I go!
Om Namaha Shivaiya!
Bhole Baba ki Jai! (Victory to Divine Father.)

# A Surprise Rebirth

T he snowstorm had finally passed, and the roads were clearing up as all that remained were the soft, powdery snow drifts playing in the wind at the roadsides. The sky was stark naked blue again, and the air was positively dry and crisp with sunlight.

However, I felt tired, moody, and tearful for no identifiable reason. Regardless, I had decided to take a trip to Charlottesville for food and supplies that I couldn't get in town. I was fighting back tears, insistent on being productive. I was confident that I would feel better once I got on the road.

Loading up my day's items, I sat in the truck, bundled up warm, and watched the swirls of snow blowing in the wind. I went to turn the ignition key and burst into tears. What in the world was wrong with me? Why couldn't I just go? The sobbing became more vigorous, and it finally dawned on me: I was having a spontaneous Rebirth. I realized I was not going anywhere at this time, no matter how determined I was. Through sobs and tears, I trudged back into the house and lay on the bed in front of the fire, the sacred fire I had maintained for nearly three months. The breath took over, finally, now that I gave it my full attention.

Still crying, I became aware of a presence in the room. It was a kind, powerful, protective presence, but I could not sit up and look around. Suddenly, it was as though

I was paralyzed, and I felt this presence pressing down on me, on my whole body from head to toe. Fear surged through me, and then it surfaced; my body, the cells of *my* body, wanted to die. It was like my body had a mind of its own, and without my mental consent, it was going to get up and kill itself. Terror could not describe the emotions I felt as I experienced what seemed like a total loss of control. My breath powerfully surged on.

Overdose, a knife in the kitchen, drowning in the bath, freezing to death outside. Each option was like a massive urge activated in my body. I was convinced the urges were so strong that had I not been physically held in place by this Presence, my body surely would have gotten up and committed suicide without my mental consent or emotional desire.

It was clear to me this was the suicide urge I had felt as a teenager. But now, alone in Leonard's house in front of his fire, my body was having the experience all on its own.

I breathed and sobbed and breathed and sobbed. I remained paralyzed by the pressing weight but could no longer feel the loving presence as the sensations seemed to rip through me with ferocity. Through my tears, one of Leonard's most popular affirmations came to mind;

*"I am alive now; therefore, my life urges are stronger than my death urges. As long as I continue strengthening my life urges and weakening my death urges, I shall go on living in increasing health and youthfulness forever."*

The bodily death urges kept surfacing as my breath

raced on, and now, in my mind, I repeated the affirmation as a self-soothing, self-affirming action. It went on for what seemed an eternity, but at least now I had a coping mechanism.

Slowly, the urges subsided and gave way to tingles and warmth. The fire still burned next to me. Still unable to move, I watched the flames flicker and lick at my aura. The sun shone through the windows, and the air began to feel light again. Breathing in the affirmation over and over, it took on a new life for me. These were no longer just inspiring words; they lived in me like a vibration of their own.

*"I am alive now; therefore, my life urges are stronger than my death urges. As long as I continue strengthening my life urges and weakening my death urges, I shall go on living in increasing health and youthfulness forever."*

Cautiously, I began to move my body. I was a bit bewildered, but now complete with the most wild, spontaneous rebirth of my life up to that time. The house and immediate space around me felt charged with a loving, light energy. It was nearly palpable, and I felt safe and supported. I thanked my angels, guides, and the very presence of life and love for helping me through this rebirth.

Finally, I decided to stay home that day and care for only the necessities and my body. I tended to all the animals and finished my outdoor work before dark. I enjoyed a long bath and more time by the fire. I called Kim at the training center in Afton and chatted for a while. I set out to do my evening yoga routine and was amazed at how easy it was to stretch and hold the positions. I could reach my toes easily. I was so much more flexible and light.

Contemplating what had happened that day, I remembered Leonard's words, *"Each one of the Physical Immortality affirmations that we master becomes like an angel that can save us, over and over, every time we need it."*

*Yes, indeed, Leonard. Yes indeed!*

# Unconscious Death Urge and Physical Immortality

The unconscious death urge is any anti-life thought. When you start looking for anti-life thoughts and identifying them, you can see it is a vast topic. Humanity is in a hypnotic state, a sea of anti-life thinking and feeling. The idea of Physical Immortality is that you have the potential and the right to maintain a physical body peacefully and blissfully as long as the physical universe exists.

I have been pondering and questioning the idea that we are given only a certain amount of life force energy at birth, and then it runs out. Is this just a reflection of scarcity and deathist belief systems? I believe we are energetically made of an eternal life substance. There is only eternal life, changing in its many forms.

If we have only a limited reserve of life energy that we quickly consume at an unforgivable pace, wouldn't we just be mere victims of a stingy and limited universe? What gives us the energy or sustains us in the afterlife? What gives us the energy to be reborn? Or if you don't believe in either of those, what gives our body the energy to disintegrate? Are we entirely separate from the life-sustaining pulse throughout the entire universe?

Science has known for a long time that almost your entire body, every cell, organ, and tissue is completely replaced within ten to fifteen years. Studies conducted by nuclear physicist Dr. Paul C. Aebersold, in his article titled *Radioisotopes - New Keyes to Knowledge,* revealed that 98 percent of all the atoms in a human body are replaced yearly. Your skin is replaced approximately every month. Most of an adult's skeleton is replaced every 10 years.

Perhaps, like the legendary phoenix, we, too, can purify ourselves and rise above our deaths. Change, or transformation, is like death and rebirth. Personally, I have not been afraid of death in the number of times I faced it. This does not mean I want to die. This means I don't see death as an end. I don't see it as being permanent and irreversible. I see it as a transformation. The cells of our bodies die every day and are replaced with new ones. Therefore, ultimately, death as a complete and final end to life, does not exist. Only life, changing and transforming, exists. Perhaps, there is no logical reason why anybody should die.

It is challenging, if not impossible, to be fully alive and, at the same time, be fearful of death. Having an Immortal philosophy is not about avoiding death. It is about mastering it as a process that supports the ever changing flow of life.

At a cellular level, we die and are reborn every day. Why is it that we take on signs of aging? Why is illness still manifesting in our bodies if 98% of all the atoms are replaced yearly? Science is beginning to find answers in mitochondria and telomeres. But I like to consider that our consciousness recreates or sustains the disease in the cells of our body. The cells and atoms of our bodies listen in on all we think and do and say, in all we believe and hold to be true.

Life is eternal. Within this context of the body's atoms replacing themselves every year, we are already masters of death and life, day after day, every moment. Wherever you are, whatever your circumstances, admire yourself! You are Alive! You are miraculous!

I am no longer willing to live as though death is the only option. It seems that is what most of our society is doing. Most people are living, or more accurately, dying, as if Earth were the worst possible place to be, the lowest realm of the universe, the lowest form of existence. I've heard many spiritual people refer to Earth as the universal garbage dump. This is just one idea, a tiny, teeny-weeny thought. Take the time to ponder this; for centuries perhaps countless lives have been spent living with the mere idea that there is some better place to be than right here, right now. What would happen if we began to question this? If we all felt that EARTH was the absolute best place to be and we showed up for it every day, 100% in on the game of making life work for everyone together?

Early on in my mission to be completely disease-free, I experienced a deep, dark depression that lasted three days. I had experienced depression many times before, but those were a walk through the park compared to this. I recalled walking outside my house and looking around at the countryside. The birds were singing, the big, blue sky was filled with white, puffy clouds romancing the sun, and tons of roses were bursting in full bloom with marvelous color and scent; it was a gorgeous Oregon summer day, and I hated it. I was furious at all the life around me in its untamed splendor and joy. I felt disgust at the brightness and beauty that surrounded me. I went back into my house, where I lay down, and just wanted to die.

In that moment, I was wholly convinced that all of life and the Earth's beauty would perish at the greedy hands of humanity, and I, too, was a part of that. Where was the glory in Life? What joy is there to behold when it will all end? What kind of God would allow this to occur? I just wanted to quit. Never, never in my life did I remember having felt this so strongly. I was always the optimist, with just a few rainy days. I was always passionate about the beauty of life and nature. I was an artist, for heaven's sake; it was like my natural tendency to see the beauty in all things!

I didn't understand what was going on with me, but at the same time, I didn't care. I felt like a prisoner, sentenced to confinement in my body, stuck on this dying, diseased planet as punishment. I wanted to be free. I prayed for my death, "Dear God, just let me go, just let me go."

Believing there was so much more I could accomplish if only I were in Spirit, unbounded by the limitations of physicality, I wanted to quit and just go 'home.' A dark cloud had fallen around my head, blocking my vision of anything but this.

Angry and in tears, I called several good friends and asked for support. They gently reminded me that being here is a great gift and much can be accomplished. They reminded me of the great saints, yogis, and teachers who have changed the course of our future, and without their physical incarnation, this would not have been possible.

After three days of this impenetrable gloom, one of my friends adamantly said, "Sara, there are people here who need you, people you haven't even met yet!" And for some reason, this shook me out of the death urge.

No, I had not been thinking of other people. I had only been thinking of my unhappiness. Sometimes, I think it's egotistical to think other people might need me. But I also think it is egotistical to believe that I have nothing to offer to anyone else on the planet or that I don't need them just as much. We all need each other and are equally important and necessary in each other's lives.

I once passed a huge church while driving down a freeway in Virginia. The building was enormous, spanning at least three city blocks with a massive billboard facing the traffic. Its giant letters loomed over my vehicle; "You matter to us! And to God."

Noticing at first some irritation I had about organized religions and dogmas, I then let the message sink in. *You matter to us! And to God.* I had often heard the *I matter* concept, but seeing it in giant, unmistakable letters in broad daylight was fantastic as a complimentary road sign!

It is a fundamental truth that we do matter, our presence matters, our contributions, or withholding of contributions, matters. Like it or not, we are impacting other people's lives. Life is working through us all of the time. Higher energies, thoughts, and frequencies are always available to us. We are expressions of Divine love. We are the manifestations of Divine love. We are precious. To deny this kills off a piece of ourselves every time.

You don't know what life would be like for others without you here. There is a greater purpose and reason for your existence. So intricate, so delicately unfathomable, is the weave of life that I do not doubt that we are all exactly where we need to be all the time.

## Invitation - Death Urges and Life Urges

What if, whenever you experienced an anti-life thought or painful emotion, you simply understood it was an opportunity to let it go? That's it. That's all.

I realized that it was futile to attempt to heal my body when I had a deeply rooted belief that it was going to die someday anyway. To first believe that your body must perish someday and then set out to heal it when disease arises is an act of insanity. An immortal philosophy is the basis of all healing. You don't have to die. Your physical body is not the source of your life. It is a manifestation, an effect of your life, and life is unlimited, eternal, ageless, and indefinable. YOU are life. How could you not be?

Try saying the following statements out loud, and notice how your body, emotions, and mind respond. Write down your reactions in your journal:

Someday, we all must die.
I am going to die.
Death is inevitable.
I can not escape death.
Each year I get older, I am closer to death.

My body is aging and deteriorating.
I have no choice.

Now, try saying these out loud, and notice how your body, emotions, and mind respond. Record your reactions to these as well:

I am an Eternal Being.
I have an abundant supply of energy.
I choose life.
I can live forever.
My body is brand new every day.
I am made of exponential energies.
There is nothing that can destroy my Infinite Being.
My body is the physical manifestation of my Eternal Spirit.
I Am the power of Eternal Life.
I Am alive right here, right now.

Listen closely to your internal and external dialogue. Do you have thoughts and emotions such as, "I'm not needed here, no one would miss me or even notice if I were gone, I'd die before I'd do that, that just kills me, the Earth is better off without us if only I weren't stuck in this body," and so on. What are some of your favorite anti-life thoughts? Write them down in your journal.

Here are some prompts to get you writing and exploring your unconscious death urge:

If you believe death is inevitable, what would be the purpose of going for optimum health?
What is optimum health?
How long would good health last?
What would be the deciding factor?

Do you believe you are in a dying body?
Where did you get these ideas about death?
When did you decide this is so?
Are you more afraid of life than you are of death?
What would happen to you if you embodied life to the
fullest, a life without death?
Would it kill you? Would it be too much for you to take
or more than you could handle?
Would being fully alive be too good to be true?
Do you think you could handle feeling ecstatic, joyful,
and serene all of the time right now?
What are your ideas and beliefs about Heaven?
Are you separated from Heaven?
Did Heaven abandon you here?
Are you here as punishment, to learn lessons, or to get it
right?
Why on Earth would we want to be immortal?
Why wouldn't you want to be immortal?

By purifying ourselves of negative thinking and pain,
we are mastering our consciousness and are one step
closer to perceiving Heaven on Earth.

# I Am Love

In the following weeks, I was feeling pretty victorious within myself and fully competent in caring for Leonard's home and business. The animals and I had survived the previous snowstorm and the weather was calmer. The horses were more settled and no longer running through the fence at night. I had stopped bouncing checks, at least for the time being, and although I was still a bit unnerved by my last rebirth, I felt fantastic in my body, and my self-guided breathwork sessions were feeling great. I was vividly alive among the sunshine and sparkling clear night skies, and I looked forward to my day's planned adventure.

George, an older gentleman and Rebirther who lived a day's drive away, was in town visiting Kim and Michael at the training center. He had offered to pick me up for a drive to Charlottesville. Given that there were several larger health food stores carrying items I couldn't find in Staunton, and since George was also very calm and pleasant company to be with, I jumped on the occasion. Early that morning, he pulled into Leonard's driveway in his immaculate, four-door, gold-colored car.

George had a reputation for driving well below the speed limit and pushing the limits of his passenger's patience levels. I was about to see how I would pass the test.

"You can always find where the Rebirthers are in town, just follow the chimney smoke," he laughed as he greeted me. The fire was gently smoldering, and the smoke billowed out the chimney rather pronouncedly. I had placed the safety screen over the fireplace and was ready to go.

We enjoyed the day leisurely, and I was happy to get some much-needed items I was looking for. On the drive home, I confessed to George about denting Leonard's truck and my emotional agony of how I would face him when they returned. I shared that I wasn't sure why I felt this way so intensely.

"Am I overreacting?" I pleaded with him in the car.

He drove quietly and slowly around the winding road through the Blue Ridge Mountains. Time seemed to pause as we rolled along the highway in slow motion. As if in a movie scene, George looked intently at me and calmly said, "Well, Leonard is Love."

"What?" I asked, surprised by his response.

"Leonard is love," he smiled gently and began to hum a soft melody. We swayed slowly around the next corner with the naked winter trees slowly dancing by in the sunbeams streaming along our path.

*Leonard is Love,* I pondered. *Okay then. George has known him long enough. I'll adopt this mindset.*

Back home that night, I took my evening bath in Leonard's bathroom, as he had welcomed me to. I brushed my teeth in front of the mirror.

*I Am Love,* a teal blue sticker on the mirror said. Every day since I moved into the house I had seen it there, but this night, I pondered it more. What does it mean to *be* love? I knew that we couldn't be anything but love at our deepest level of being. But I felt so many tumultuous emotions and agitation in life and with life. How could I *be love* here on Earth? I decided to let this new thought percolate.

∞∞∞

Leonard and Isabelle returned from Argentina with suntans all aglow. They laughed in disbelief as I described how much snow there was to shovel while they were gone. I didn't mention the wild, unconscious rebirth I experienced in their living room. I figured some things were just fine left unspoken.

To my amazement and relief, Leonard was not at all concerned about the dent in his truck.

"Well, these things happen," he said as he exhaled loudly, putting his hands in his pockets and smiling. "It's alright, and there's no need to pay me for anything. The truck is getting old, I probably won't bother fixing it."

And that was that. All of my anxiety seemed ridiculous now. But I was genuinely amazed that Leonard was not upset about it whatsoever.

The following day, we met outside and hopped into his lovely, freshly dented truck. We were running some errands together in town. Before starting the engine, Leonard paused, and this time, with a more serious tone, he looked at me intently.

"Babaji says you will be my publicity manager," he said.

"What?" I gaped in surprise and confusion.

"I have a personal relationship with Babaji, and He says you are going to be my publicity manager," he repeated matter-of-factly.

"Publicity manager? But I don't know anything about that. How could I possibly do that?" I asked in disbelief.

"Well, maybe we will see as time unfolds," Leonard smiled as he started the truck. It seemed there was never a lack of surprises around Leonard.

A week after their return home, I departed for Oregon, certain I would return again soon or see them during their travels.

# Back to Oregon

A return home revealed my housemate in a bleak situation. The heating oil for the home had run out, and he was almost out of firewood. I wondered why he had not called me. The house was in disarray, and my cats were brilliantly excited that I was home. I went straight to the bathtub and then to bed, where I fell fast asleep. It was a bit of a culture shock to be back.

I spent the following few days getting the house in order and catching up with my housemate. We had more heating oil delivered and were settling into our new routine. I began doing agnihotra and the fire ceremonies I had learned from Peter in my backyard fire pit, weather permitting. Now that I was house-sharing, I no longer slept in front of my woodstove in the living room at night. Instead, I laid out a sleeping mat on my bedroom floor surrounded by at least four candles in front of the large, sliding closet doors made of mirrors.

One of my first nights back home, I had an interesting experience. The unexpected was becoming my new norm. I went to bed early as I felt quite tired. I finished my evening bath, lit my usual candles around me and fell fast asleep. I had just one, simple dream. I was in a desert with iron-red mountains and plateaus, illumined by a larger than life full moon rising over the horizon. It emanated a silvery blue hue, and the red desert seemed to permeate me with an energy of its own.

"So this is what Chandra is about," I was surprised to hear myself say. And then everything went black as I passed out in my lucid dream. Seemingly only a moment later, I awoke feeling a soft, glowing peace about me. I opened my eyes and gazed into the closet mirror doors in front of me as I lay on the floor. A beautiful, gently shining woman with auburn hair dressed in teal and white robes stood behind me. She held her arms outstretched at her sides, her palms facing me. Light was emanating from her hands and entire body to me. She was filling me with such peace and soft joy. I turned to look over my shoulder at her, but in an instant she was gone.

A little confused, I sat up and looked at the time. It was nearly noon! How was that even possible? I was accustomed to waking at 6 a.m. for my morning bath at the latest! Stumbling to my feet, I quickly dressed and stepped out of my room, feeling hungry and disoriented by the full daylight.

"Are you ok?" asked my housemate.

"Yes, I'm fine, thanks," I mumbled, still looking around, a bit disoriented.

"What were you doing with a Coleman lantern in your room last night?" he asked.

"Coleman lantern?" I asked with total confusion as I now realized how concerned he was.

"Yes! I woke up around midnight and heard a strange hissing sound that sounded like a Coleman gas lantern for camping, and there was blue light coming out from under your door. Those really shouldn't be lit indoors, you know. And then you slept in until noon, which is not like you. I started to worry if you were ok. I wanted to knock but felt I shouldn't disturb your space." I saw the furrows of worry on his brow and forehead.

"Oh my gosh," I stuttered. "No, I didn't have a Coleman lantern in there. I don't know what that was. I was exhausted last night. I had a fantastic dream, though."

He looked at me wearily but with more calmness. "Well, as long as you are ok!" he laughed, shaking it off.

I didn't know what to make of it either, and the shock of it all hadn't settled in yet. I could not even speak about the woman I had seen and the peace I had felt emanating from her. I thought of Leonard saying many times that he had met several immortals. Eight in total, to be exact. And of how people always questioned him, asking him how he knew what their age was. And he would laugh and reply that if you meet one, you will just know.

Years later, when I shared this experience of seeing the woman with auburn hair upon my waking, Leonard was very pleased. He felt strongly that she was Mary Magdalene. And he encouraged me to learn about her. The idea felt so foreign and far-fetched to me, but it seemed reasonable to start at least learning about her.

∞ ∞ ∞

The following month I was back in Portland, for Matt's advanced course, *Awakened Potential, again.* It had been a remarkable day that blew my mind open, but the day wasn't done with me yet.

It was well past dark as I was leaving town, and I had become lost, not knowing my way around the city yet. This was in the days before smartphones and driving apps. It was late at night, and I found myself on a one-way street going through downtown. I had driven on it twice but could not find my way to the freeway entrance. Homeless people and party goers dotted the streets. I was growing tired, and I still had an hour's drive ahead of me, if I could get out of the city!

In the left lane of a one-way street, I drove slowly as the lights turned yellow, red, and green again as the traffic lulled forward, bumper to bumper. I found my eyes drawn to my left, where there was a large, covered entryway to a closed business. It was glowing with golden light.

Confused, I looked closer at the steps leading up to the doors where a homeless person sat, wrapped in blankets. It was Babaji. He radiated such masterful gold light and energy that my senses immediately heightened, and I desperately wanted to leap out of my car and sit at his feet. However I found myself unable to move. It was as if my hands were glued to the steering wheel.

*Don't place your trust in the world,* a thought entered my head, louder and more precise than any other thought I had ever experienced. *Place your trust in Me.*

In a breathless state of spiritual ecstasy, I searched for a place to pull over but found none. Traffic was urging me on, and I drove away. Suddenly, the missing on ramp I had been searching for and must have passed several times already, revealed itself before me, and I merged into the speeding traffic. Within moments, I was flying down the dark freeway on a cold winter's night.

*Don't place your trust in the world; place your trust in Me,* I repeated over and over in my mind. What exactly did that mean? How was I to do this when I lived here in this mess of a world, and Babaji seemed so far off? Regardless, I had received my next assignment from Babaji. It would take me years to integrate.

∞∞∞

While it felt good to be back home in Oregon catching up with clients and taking day trips up to Portland to visit with friends, things felt different. I had outgrown my home sanctuary of solitude, and the housemate situation was temporary. I also had very little money, as I had spent the last several months without earning any money but doing a work exchange for room and board at Leonard's.

Fortunately, my dad offered to have me stay in a little white cottage at his property. It was a one-room tiny house split into halves; one half consisting of a greenhouse with ceramic tile flooring, the other half carpeted and lined with cedar plank walls and a mini wood stove. It was perfect.

Having grown accustomed to the biting cold winter of Virginia, I found Oregon's springtime bursting with fragrance much more blissful than I had ever remembered. I spent so much time outside in Virginia the past fall and winter that I preferred to be outdoors almost all of the time if it wasn't raining or snowing. So, I slept outside the small white cottage on my dad's property, next to a fire under the stars.

Inside the greenhouse half of the tiny house, I had a mini fridge and blender, a place to chop veggies and fruit, and a small rug and space to do yoga. I was enjoying eating mainly raw foods, as I had been inspired by Isabelle. The other half of the tiny house was carpeted and had a small wood stove I could sleep in front of on colder, rainy nights. I hung a large poster of Haidakhan Babaji on the wall by the front door, blessing the rest of the house.

I kept in touch with Leonard and Isabelle weekly via phone and email and learned that they would soon be traveling across the USA by car on a tour of events. I planned to meet them in Chico, where Leonard had lived after selling the infamous Campbell Hot Springs, and to have some fun with them in California before they went on to San Francisco, New Mexico, and then back across the USA to the East Coast.

So that spring, I drove to Chico in my little red Volkswagen Jetta. It had many miles on it but still had plenty of life left in it. I was off on another adventure with Leonard and Isabelle.

# My Coldest
# Cold Water Rebirthing

I pulled into Chico and met with Leonard and Isabelle at the hotel they had stayed at the previous night, as they had just arrived the day before. I went upstairs to their room and visited for a while as they packed their things. Leonard's sleeping pad was on top of the dresser. He disliked the energy pollution from hotel room floors and mattresses so much that he often slept on the dresser top as a bed.

We soon departed for Mt. Shasta, as they had some items of interest to explore there. We headed to the local health food store and deli for lunch. From there, we meandered through town and visited some shops. In the late afternoon, we made sure to stop at the local spring and fill as many water bottles and jugs as possible. At that time, it was still permissible to enter the springs, so we enjoyed a light splash in place of an evening bath. It was the best spring water I had ever tasted, and was believed to have special healing properties. This was Mt.Shasta, after all, the famed mountain where St.Germain appeared to Godfré Ray King and birthed the I Am Discourses series.

We ventured up the mountain and walked along some of the trails, intending to sleep the night in our cars.

However, when we returned to where we had parked, a large group gathered around partying. To my surprise, Leonard said we couldn't stay the night there as it wouldn't be safe.

"Can't we just intend it to be safe? What about manifestation?" I asked, somewhat disappointed not to be sleeping and dreaming on the side of the mountain.

"It's good to read the energy of your surroundings and act accordingly," Leonard responded. "I know a campground we can go to where we can bathe in the lake in the morning."

We finished our breathing exercises and returned to our cars. I followed them in my car, through winding mountain roads and towering trees as the sun set, giving way to a dark, starlit night. Finally, we arrived at a small campground with no amenities. It was quiet and secluded.

We found spaces near each other to park for the night and waved goodnight. I sat outside, taking in the fantastic aroma of the trees and pines as I finished my leftovers from lunch.

Leonard had purchased me a small wooden spoon to eat with. Over the years, it became apparent to me that he would always have one with him when traveling in the USA or overseas, especially to enjoy some soy yogurt or ice cream. It was easy enough to rinse in a little water, wipe dry, and store away in a pocket.

Curling up in the backseat of my car with my sleeping bag and small travel pillow, it quickly became apparent just how small the backseat was. I had never slept in this car before, and I spent half the night pushing against the cramped confines of the backseat and the other half of the night in the passenger seat reclined.

It was late spring but still reached freezing temperatures each night at this elevation, and I could feel the cool breeze coming off the lake. I dozed between shifting around in my car and waking to a mild nip of cold night air. I put on another layer and slept again, mildly stirring until, at last, sunrise broke in her radiant beams over the tops of the surrounding evergreen trees.

*Ooof. A morning bath in the lake,* I thought. Since I had spent my childhood playing in the cold Pacific Ocean and mountain streams, this seemed doable, although not as appealing as a warm bath.

Leonard and Isabelle were already awake, and we soon gathered at the lakeside. I could not see it in the dark of the night before, but the view at dawn was stunning. It was a vast lake of crystal clear water surrounded by snow and ice at its edges, embraced by a beautiful snow capped peak directly opposite of us.

This lake would be a challenge for a morning dip. I could still see my breath in the air and remembered that Leonard generally advised against doing cold water rebirthing if the air temperature was below 60 degrees, which it certainly was this morning.

"You two can enter the water here, and I'll go over this way," Leonard motioned around some trees to another entrance point on the lake.

The air was still, and hardly a bird was singing. It was certainly a fresh spring morning. Isabelle smiled at me whimsically and said, "Just remember, gentle connected breaths, and there is no hurry. One toe at a time. And when you are comfortable with that, go a little more."

We undressed to our underclothes and began the gentle, connected breathing through the nose. I felt the ice crunching at my feet as I stepped in, but I was surprised that I easily had both my feet submerged in the water so soon. Isabelle was slightly ahead of me.

By the time the water and ice were nudging up against my calves, I heard a loud splash in the lake to my far right. Leonard had plunged into the water immediately, a distance away, and was now exhaling loudly. We laughed with incredulity. So much for the gentle, slower cold water rebirthing technique he taught!

Isabelle and I continued and eventually fully submerged into the lake. I could not bring myself to dunk my head under more than a few times. Tingles spanned through my entire nervous system. My heart beat vigorously in the cavern of my ribs, and I could see it sending ripples out into the still, icy water. Everything took on a crisp clarity; the trees, the sky, the water, the mountainside, and the ice were all vividly alive.

Just as Isabelle turned to exit the water, I reached my maximum point of tolerance and happily followed her back to shore. We breathed deeply and wrapped up in our towels. I quickly began drying off, my body buzzing with prickles and tingles as I changed into dry clothes.

Leonard had built a lovely, large fire in a nearby fire pit for us to warm up afterward.

"But Leonard, only one fire? You do not share fires with

people," I questioned, as I knew his sensitivity to energy and had not shared a fire with him before, aside from a few moments at a time.

"This is fine," he smiled.

Gratefully, I huddled close to the fire but felt strangely, intensely warm at my core. After a few moments by the fire, Isabelle stepped over to the nearby picnic table and got out a large, white, husked fruit of some kind and a cutting board.

"What is that?" I asked as she took out a large chef's knife.

"A young coconut," she replied. "Have you ever had one?" I nodded my head no, still feeling my heart and blood coursing through my body as I stood by the fire.

"This is what they look like when the outer green shell has been removed before it reaches maturity. You have to cut the pointed top like this," she said as she wielded the knife sharply against the husk, removing it from the light brown shell and striking it with a loud 'whack. Whack!'

The coconut cracked open at the top, and a little water spilled. She sliced the top off and handed it to me. "Here, you can have this one. You can drink the water straight from it and then scoop the coconut pulp out with a spoon. It's very soft and delicious."

Isabelle was beaming at me. She seemed delighted to introduce me to young coconuts. I took it with both hands and held it to my lips. The water was very sweet and pleasant to taste. It was like nothing I had ever tasted before. I strangely felt as though I was drinking milk straight from Divine Mother's breast!

"Oh wow, that is good! Thank you!" I smiled.

"It's very healthy too," she replied.

Later on, I learned that coconut milk is excellent for building blood, especially when combined with chlorella or spirulina, something that could come in handy for recovering from heavy periods and anemia.

After some time with the fire and sharing a delicious but simple breakfast, we bid farewell. I had a bit of a drive ahead of me, and they were heading to San Francisco. I had no desire to go to a big city, but was grateful to visit with them for a while.

For my entire eight-hour drive home from Mt Shasta, I still had that tingling, invigorating energy of the lake. Thinking I must be cold, I took a warm bath upon returning home. But the water felt strangely annoying like it was just too hot.

*Sometimes healing requires hot water, and sometimes it requires cold,* I remembered Leonard's words. *Warm water teaches us about life and birth. Cold water teaches us about overcoming fear and death.*

Overcoming fear became a passion of mine. I pondered how cold water could assist me with this. And given my recent spontaneous rebirth of purging death urge, it seemed like appropriate timing to focus on cold water rebirthing.

# Virginia Again

In the summer of 2004, Leonard invited me once again to come housesit for them in the fall and winter while they traveled to India and Spain. Although I still didn't have much money, I had enough to purchase plane tickets and a few necessities. I would be doing a work exchange for food and lodging again, and I wanted to be back in the community of Rebirthers to deepen my understanding.

So, I began to wrap up my breathwork practice and prepare my clients for my departure. I would be gone for at least another three months this time. Continuing with the long, arduous work of inner inquiry and healing, I found myself in the throws of purging out so many unconscious beliefs, identities, suppressed emotions, and grief. It was a real rollercoaster, and the floodgates were wide open. What a perfect time for me to return to Virginia and be around Leonard and Isabelle again.

## Yogananda

I was to leave for Virginia again in a few days, and I was flirting with the idea of moving there, but I felt unsure. The autumn rain and cooler nights had picked up again, so this night, I slept inside, across the room from my Babaji poster.

The following morning, I lay with my back to the front door. I awoke feeling someone in the room, and I opened my eyes suddenly. I felt a tap on my shoulder. I rolled over to see Yogananda sitting in a lotus position on a cloud, smiling, just a foot away from my shoulder. He beamed with golden and earthly brown hues. I stared at him in astonishment, and then he floated away from me, still smiling and gazing at me, as he dissolved directly into Babaji's image hanging on my wall.

What on Earth was happening? It was like an information highway had opened up while I was at Leonard's. And it seemed the more I raised my vibrations through the practices Leonard adopted and taught, the more experiences and interactions I had with high spiritual beings. Yet, in my mind, I still doubted my experiences.

Had I really just seen Yogananda? I had heard that he appeared to students and devotees, but I felt no ties to him. In fact, I felt an aversion, as my ex-husband had introduced me to his autobiography and often pushed me to read it.

*Okay then. Time to read Yogananda's Autobiography of a Yogi,* I thought. I still had the copy my ex had given to me, so I pulled it off my bookshelf and stuffed it in my carry-on bag. I could easily start reading it on the airplane and finish it while at Leonard's. I had no doubt now that the Babaji Yogananda referred to in his book was the same Babaji embodied as Herakhan Babaji, and it was time for me to read it.

∞∞∞

My stay at Leonard's home this time was routine. I settled right in and picked up where I had left off. But this time, it felt different. It was clear that I wanted to put roots down in Oregon. I was softly pulling my energy back and away from Virginia. I spent a little more time with the horses and by my favorite tree with which I had shared my moontime blood. I snuggled Hanuman a little more and took him for longer walks. I left a small white teapot my sister had given me in their kitchen cabinet as a small token, hoping I would return soon for a visit.

I would also be bouncing back and forth from the East Coast to West, as Matt had multiple trainings happening in California that I did not want to miss.

Yasoda's daughter, Becky, was stepping in for me at Leonard's home for a few days so that I could attend Matt's events. She had the most striking blue eyes and blonde hair, accompanied by an exuberant joy and warm heart. She already knew the animals and property well enough to be there alone. The timing and synchronicity seemed divinely orchestrated for both of us. I was at Leonard's home for one week before Becky arrived, and then off I flew to California to volunteer at Matt's Liberty Experience.

# *Oneness*

Sitting in a state of alert, quiet attention, I watched the group of Matt's trainees break out into smaller groups for the next activity. My venture out into the world again was a striking contrast to the quiet solitude and sadhana of daily life at Leonard's home. Now, I was in the vibrant, stimulating city with a roomful of people for nearly sixteen hours each day. I was working as a mic runner. My sole job the entire weekend was to sit in a chair at the side of the room and bring a microphone to a participant when they raised their hand and were called on to share.

There were very few breaks, so it was like I had been doing a working meditation for two days. I could not space out, lest I miss seeing someone raise their hand, which could happen randomly and frequently throughout the expanse of the entire crowded room. I was as invisible as possible to avoid disturbing or distracting from the conversation or activities. I often crouched on the ground beside the person speaking and watched Matt respond to their questions, fears, emotions, breakdowns, and transcendent breakthroughs. It was totally fantastic!

At this moment, Matt finished speaking and the attendees were busily chatting with each other. I remained vigilant, lest someone need tissues, which I had a hefty stash of next to my chair. Within a single breath, a stunning moment of otherwise ordinariness,

I found myself floating, entirely within my body and view, but also merging with everyone in the room. I heard what each of them were individually saying. I felt their energy, but instead of feeling their nervousness, joy, or fear, I felt the flow of life force as if it were all my body and mind. I was merged energetically with the entire room in a state beyond words or description.

It was a spontaneous, transcendent state of pure *being*. My mind was tranquil in this state of oneness. It was as though every movement in the room was a part of my being, a simple and exquisite flow of energy within me but also beyond my local body. I was everything, and everything was me. It was blissfully, calmly, ecstatic.

One thought entered my mind as I saw Matt stand up and walk to the back of the room, leaving for a short break. "Don't go," I asked. *"Don't go!"*

To my amazement, he stopped immediately and turned back into the room. I felt him in the same way as I felt everyone else in the room in this expanded state. He watched the room, studying the energy, perhaps in a similar fashion to how I had seen Leonard 'read' a space. Matt sat down in an empty chair directly across the room from me.

Still blissfully poised and immersed in this newfound energetic oneness, I became increasingly aware that Matt was directing his attention on me. I grew more deeply aware of my body as a separate thing. Yes, he was watching me and smiling. Self-consciousness crept in, and my energy concentrated into my own body again. Blushing, I scooted around in my chair a bit and nervously smiled.

The oneness subsided, but I felt permanently changed. How could anyone shrink back to a previous, more limited perception of life after such an experience? I was entering new states of expansion, awareness, and ways of living I never even dreamed of.

The training completed in a few days and I headed back to the East Coast. The gifts I returned home with from these trainings were always unique and varied. No matter how many times I attended Matt's events, each experience was brand new and always a gem of self discovery.

Back home in Virginia, I was happy to return to the quiet countryside. I welcomed the time of solitude and nature to integrate. But it was only a short time before the next challenge arrived.

# Hanuman's Healing

The following week, my heart sank when I went out to feed the dogs one evening and found Hanuman lying by the gate, unable to stand up on all four legs. It was evident that his hips were nonfunctional and he was in pain. The cold winter nights had settled in that week. Isabelle had mentioned that his hips often bothered him in the winter months, but from what she described, it had likely never been this bad. I realized that I needed to get information on which veterinarian to take him to, and of course, it was a weekend and after-hours.

Speaking to him gently, I rubbed his back. He looked at me uncertain and slightly alarmed, but I kept gently massaging along his spine and talking slowly. He began to relax as it felt good to him. He could not walk, so I carefully scooped him up in both arms. He was not a small dog, probably closer to fifty pounds. But it was similar to carrying a sack of grain, so I was able to waddle over to the basement and lay him on some old blankets. I brought him some food and water, but he was uninterested in eating. I pondered what to do.

Recalling two other occasions of finding cold or near-freezing animals having a hard time, I searched for memories of what had worked in the past. One instance was with a tiny kitten that had wandered out of the mother's nest or perhaps had been kicked out. I found her on the floor, stiff and appearing lifeless. But to my shock, when I went to scoop her up, ready to bury her, she let out a small, tiny 'meow.' I placed her in a warm water bath, and she fully revived.

The other instance was a limp and lethargic lamb, born just a few hours prior, that had fallen into an old post hole in the field which had filled with water during winter rains. The farmer called the vet who recommended placing it in a warm bath immediately. Seeing the little lamb revive within minutes to its spunky, bright new life was beautiful!

So, it seemed the obvious thing to do; Hanuman was going to have a warm bath in my bathtub. I lit the gas water heater and began filling the tub. Hanuman looked rather displeased with me as I lifted him into the tub, but tolerated the water for some time. *May as well shampoo you too while we're here,* I thought.

He loved the attention and massaging as I scrubbed and lathered his long white hair. I rinsed him and lifted him out, wrapping towels around him and rubbing him dry. The basement was now toasty warm from the water heater running. He still could not stand, so I began giving him some Reiki. I chanted Om Namaha Shivaiya for a while and started singing my favorite kirtans to him. I soon visualized and felt him in a column of white light and laying on a bed of violet, healing flames, as described in *The I AM Discourses.* He finally ate a little food from my hand and soon drifted off to sleep.

I went upstairs, locked up the house, and slept on the bench in the basement with Hanuman asleep on the pile of blankets on the floor beside me. I prayed this would work but had doubts about what this night would bring. I fell fast asleep.

What felt like only moments later, I awoke the following day to a cold nose and a wet lick on my face. I opened my eyes, and Hanuman was just centimeters away with his nose. His eyes lit up brightly upon my waking, and he revealed a cute, sort of young puppy grin on his face that I had not seen him express before.

"Hey, Hanuman!" I sat up and stroked his head. To my astonishment, he barked a joyful, playful 'yip!' and began running around the basement like a young pup! He was jumping, wagging his tail, running over to me, and licking my feet. I had never seen Hanuman so happy and playful! I was utterly relieved. Praise be, Hanuman was in excellent shape! I would learn years later that the seasonal aches and pains in his hips would never return. The healing was permanent.

## Journal

October 11, 2004

Today I mowed the lawn, it was twelve inches tall in some places! I also finished raking the grass, cleaned off the back porch, swept the garage, spread mulch in the garden, returned phone calls, assembled a bunch of mail to send out, plus my regular duties with the animals. I also had an interesting phone conversation with a friend.

Angels Divine, be with me!

October 21, 2004

There is always something extremely good and potent in the air, the excitement of God/dess!

November 4, 2004
The past few days my breathing has felt very light and easy. My body feels smooth with soft energy flows.

I felt Leonard's presence again today, about five minutes before he called. This is getting kind of fun!

November 12, 2004
I felt nauseous with my period today and almost vomited. I spent some time by the fire and then breathed in my bath. My spine felt tight and I had some pain from my mid back to my tailbone for a few moments, then the worst of my symptoms were gone. I felt totally fine after breathing through an energy cycle in my bath! A few moments after I felt complete, the phone rang and I answered it. It was Leonard. I asked him what he thought of my symptoms returning.

He said this is how it is released. Each time the symptoms return and come to the surface, they become less and less intense until it becomes nothing but a ghost of a memory.

December 2004
I, Sara, am now safe, loved, and wanted. I am safe to be me. The past is now forgotten. I am free at this moment. I release, I relax, and I let go. I am safe in life.

# *Leaving Virginia*

**M**issing the verdant green of Oregon springtime that would soon be arriving and missing my family and friends, I was eager to return to my breathwork practice at home and start building my profession again. I felt like a fledgling leaving the nest, but I knew I could return anytime. Leonard had said their home was my home, and I was welcome anytime, as were other longtime, dedicated Rebirthers in the community.

With stories of yogis and Babaji teleporting and achieving magical feats swirling in my head, I pondered how wonderful it would be to teleport myself back and forth from locations as I pleased.

"Leonard, what do you think of teleportation? Can people really do that?" I asked him in all sincerity.

"Well, yes, it's possible," he replied matter of factly.

"Have you done it?" I asked, sensing that he knew much more about the topic than I had imagined.

"No, but I am learning. Would you like to learn it also?" Leonard asked with a twinkle in his eye.

"Yes, absolutely," I answered without a doubt in my mind. Teleportation seemed like an entirely practical thing to master in this world. He leaned in closely as if to let me in on a big secret.

"Ok. So, when you lie down to sleep at night, imagine

yourself standing next to your bed and looking down at your empty bed. Keep doing this until you can do it and see your bed empty where you were laying," he explained.

"That's it? Isn't that the same practice for astral projection?" I inquired.

"Yes, but it's different. Instead of looking at the bed and seeing yourself asleep there, you will look at your bed and see that your body is not there; it is standing beside the bed, and you will realize that you have teleported your body to stand beside your bed. When you master that, you can practice going a little further, perhaps to the living room or outside. But be certain you don't envision yourself too far away and get into trouble, like in some snowy mountains," Leonard laughed.

"Wow, that is not something I had even thought of," I laughed.

"Exactly," he said with a smile. "It's good to start very slowly and take your time."

Isabelle drove me to the airport that afternoon, and we bid farewell. In my heart, I resolved to see them again soon. There were signs of trouble between Leonard and Isabelle. Their relationship was strained, and it was too much for me to bear. I loved them like family but I could not stand to see them go through a divorce, as it was triggering so many emotions from my childhood and my parent's separation. I left Virginia in hopes that they would work things out. I didn't know it yet, but it would be the last time I saw Isabelle and Leonard together. The following year they separated.

∞ ∞ ∞

My flight home was filled with people coughing and runny noses. I realized how completely immune I had become to that. In past years, I had colds and sinus infections, one right after the other, all through the winters, but I had not had a single cold or flu since I started Breathwork and the purification practices!

The airplane drifted through brilliant, sunny skies that looked like Heaven herself. We sailed over the blanketed ocean of dense clouds that so often settled over the Willamette Valley, in truth, the entire western half of Oregon. Lower and lower, we descended, and the brilliant beams of light gave way to the heavy, dense fog that would shame even the mists of Avalon. As I entered the dark, rainy day, the city and airport lights flickered below. I could almost feel winter's cold humidity seeping through the airplane windows.

Upon returning home, I found myself without a space to give breathwork sessions. Every job inquiry and rental space I sought were dead ends. Life was, again, pushing me in a new direction. I moved to Portland with my last $400 to rent a small room at a Nila's house, and I resumed my work and clientele building.

Living in Portland offered me many exciting new opportunities to learn and to grow. It also offered an abundance of Breathwork clients. I enjoyed giving one day workshops and initiating many people into the power of their breath. On occasion, I gave sessions in groups, although I knew it was not Leonard's way of doing things. I had breathed in groups before I met Leonard, but I always felt fortunate that my first session was within the serenity of an individual session. The last group rebirth I facilitated was for about twenty friends who were deep into personal growth and healing.

We all had done group breathwork before. We were aware of clearing and grounding energy. I called in my guides and Divine protection and grounded the room energetically so that anything being released would not be left floating around.

The group's breathe went beautifully. Everyone felt great. But as often was the case in a group session, I could see that many people got into emoting more than breathing, no matter what guidance I offered them.

After this last group rebirth I gave, I left feeling a little off. It wasn't anything I could locate or identify as 'my stuff.' By the time I arrived home, my head was spinning. I felt depressed, anxious, completely ungrounded, and like something was seriously wrong, but I didn't know what. I went into a spontaneous rebirth. I happened to have my phone with me, and of course, Leonard called me right in the middle of it.

"Leonard, I'm in a rebirth right now," I answered the call, weak and panting between breaths.

'What's going on?' he inquired.

"I just finished giving a group rebirth. I feel terrible,'" I managed to stammer. It felt like a confession.

"Oh. Well, you're processing the group's energy. And group rebirthing causes an imbalance in kundalini. Call me when you get complete," he answered calmly.

"Ok." I set the phone down and continued breathing.

I never went back to groups or needed any more evidence of EEP (emotional energy pollution) or the value of one-to-one breathing guides. Individual sessions were my path.

# Animal Totem

We sat in a dimly lit room, a circle of ten or so people journeying together on a shamanic drumming vision quest. I was at a friend's house for a one day workshop. She was guiding us to meet our totem animal. Although we had just begun, I was surprised by the rapid visions flooding through my mind's eye.

"Find a hole in the Earth, your very own entrance to the center of the Earth," our guide said.

Almost immediately, mine appeared in my mind's eye. It was like a wormhole or snake's hole, and I dove into it head first, slithering around the bends and curves. I thought perhaps I had become my animal totem!

Within moments, I popped out in the center of the Earth into its sky. I was floating above an island adorned with a fairytale-like castle. Under the castle was a mass of heat and energy. I landed on a wall overlooking the countryside. Out of the sky, a phoenix came swooping down. A phoenix!

He was magical. Luminous flames of vivid colors emanated from him, striking me with an aliveness I had only dreamt of. We had been told beforehand that our animal totem had to be a real animal, not a fantasy creature.

"If you are my animal guide, you're going to have to take a different form," I called to him.

Immediately, he turned into a golden eagle, brilliant like the sun, and landed near me. A wave of energy washed over me as I saw flashes of his eye, talons, and beak as if magnified a hundred times larger.

He soon took off flying, and I ran after him. He flew past a wolf. I stopped to ask the wolf if he was my guide, but he just looked over his shoulder at the eagle and walked away. So I ran after the golden eagle again. We were both going so fast, but I finally caught up to him.

"Fly! FLY!" He commanded with his immense, powerful light energy. It was so intense that I thought I would burst. Incredibly, I took to the air, and we flew faster now through vast open blue skies until we landed in a large, verdant green meadow.

"Where have you gone? Why don't you fly?" He asked while cocking his head and looking at me intensely.

Instinctively I knew he was referring to my life, to how I had shut down internally. I had no answer for him, just silence and a mild pang of heaviness in my heart. Our attention turned to the sun, which was now setting.

"As you are spending time getting to know your animal totem, ask if they have a gift or talisman to share with you," our guide said in a soft, gentle tone.

A necklace appeared in the eagle's talons, and he dropped it over my head. It landed around my neck, a long silver chain with a crystal that shone like the sun, setting right over my heart center.

"Anytime you need to find me, look to the sun," he said.

With gentle tears filling my eyes, my body radiated with warmth and vibrated with energy.

"Thank you," I managed to reply, gasping for breaths as though I really had taken flight.

Over the following days, I learned more about the phoenix. According to Egyptian mythology, it is a legendary bird that was said to live no less than five hundred years. When its life was near the end, it built a nest made of boughs and spices and set it on fire to be consumed in the flames. The phoenix was reborn from the ashes, springing forth in a new, rejuvenated life. The phoenix is the bird of Immortality.

## *Journal*

February 12, 2004
Pardon me, I couldn't help but notice your beauty,
You, with the twinkling eye
Your old and wrinkled you, with the furrowed brow,
You, with the laughing glee
You, the child flying free.
You, sitting alone in contemplation, isolation.
You, preoccupied with worries and fears.
You, scared and alone.
You, with the glamor and plastic faces.
You, in the street and desolate places.
Pardon me, but I just couldn't resist to notice,
You, in all your unseen, unknown beauty.

# Growing into the Role of Rebirther

As Leonard had predicted, I developed quite a friendship with Yasoda. She had greatly supported me while I was alone at Leonard's home managing the circus of events and tasks there, and our continued mutual support and love grew over the years.

I first attended Yasoda's Return to the Sacred training and West Coast convention in 2005, not as a participant or trainer, but as a personal retreat after working hard at one of Matt's events in San Francisco. The Return to the Sacred retreat was held annually at Sierra Hot Springs, formerly known as Campbell Hot Springs, which Leonard had previously owned. It was a marvelous opportunity to spend time with Leonard and the spiritual community that gathered each year to do the purification practices.

It was easy to fall in love with the hot springs and Yasoda's raw honesty and authenticity. Her sharp wittiness and often hilarious personality seemed to perfectly compliment the rugged mountains and seven winds gusting through the valley. Yasoda's love, honesty, joy, and gentle tender care, at times seemed bigger than life. I went on to volunteer at her breathwork trainings as a seminar leader, lead Rebirther, and all-around breathwork mama to anyone who needed support during the training.

It was not uncommon for Leonard to occasionally

disappear on some day's venture, and Yasoda, Aaron Overstreet (another longtime Rebirther), and I would take over the entire day's tasks. I regularly gave two to three sessions every day for the nine days, aside from the one day of fire. It was hard work, and the sessions could be pretty wild. Many people came straight into the nine days without prior experience and were holding years of deep trauma. It was sacred work that was humbling, inspiring, and awe-provoking to witness the healing power of breath and elements in the ever-changing community of people that came together year after year.

In those days, people were allowed to have their own individual fires on the property, so it was a deep immersion in the complete healing system with all the elements. I grew into my own as a Rebirther there, and it became my spiritual home and family for many years to come.

Thanks to Yasoda, I truly fell in love with Aarti, devotional songs and offerings of light to Babaji the Divine, and havan, a sacred fire ceremony of offerings and mantras that purifies each participant and the atmosphere about them as well.

I loved to sit next to Yasoda every morning I could, to sing Aarti with her and feel her vibrations lift higher as she sang and played the harmonium. Often stopping in silence, our eyes would fill with tears and we simply had to pause, breathe, and take in the outpouring of Divine Grace and Love we received. I sat next to her during the havan as well, to help with the sacred fire offerings of food and ghee and to hand out the Prasad, a special food for the participants that had been prepared and consecrated by the fire ceremony, at the finale of the mantras and offerings. It transformed me. It transformed all of us. I volunteered at *Return to the Sacred* at least nine times over eleven years. In years that I couldn't attend in person, I still diligently worked to promote the event through newsletters and websites.

Over these years I also put my roots down in Portland, Oregon, working as a Rebirther and Organizer, creating client support groups and events. During these years, I wanted to diversify my income, as it was stated as one of the principles of prosperity in Leonard's infamous *Money Seminar*, so I started my own house cleaning business, jewelry-making business, and launched LeonardOrrBooks.com to make his works available in a digital format.

Since Aaron Overstreet and I both lived in Portland, we supported each other for a total of nine years doing breathwork trades with each other. We organized One-Year Seminars that met one day every month for a year, for Rebirthers who had completed their ten sessions. Each month at our One-Year Seminar, the group paired off and did breathwork trades with each other. We also chose a topic to discuss on Leonard's teachings and supported each other's growth as Breathworkers.

During my time in Portland, I completed three years of professional training, exams, and oral panels to become a licensed Prayer Practitioner with the United Centers for Spiritual Living, founded by Ernest Holmes, author of *The Science of Mind*. We studied the works of Mary Baker Eddy, Ernest Holmes, Thomas Troward, and many other new thought pioneers who launched the Christian Science movement that inspired the basis of Leonard's ideas on spiritual psychology. I was well received by the community and invited to continue to become a Minister within the organization, however I opted not to pursue that path. I frequently did affirmative Prayer for Leonard, which he enjoyed and received often from his local Christian Science community in Virginia. He loved Affirmative Mind Treatment and said I could pray for him anytime. (Affirmative Mind Treatment, also called Affirmative Prayer, is a five step approach to prayer based on the faith that the desired outcome is already fulfilled, and aids to overcome blockages and fear.)

Continuing my work with Leonard, I edited, formatted, and managed the publishing of his *Conscious Connection* newsletter, as well as creating Spanish editions and coordinating teams of translators. Leonard and I continued a close connection, as I was in constant communication with him, editing his latest articles and fresh ideas.

His ongoing emotional and spiritual support was a total life-enriching gift that would continue to grow within me as though a beautiful, immortal garden of life had been planted, present to me through any of life's ups and downs.

# My First Dance with Modern Medicine

It had been many years since I maintained my healthy lifestyle changes, so it was quite crushing that the disease reappeared in 2007. When I first moved to Portland, I failed to find an acupuncturist that could help me manage the symptoms successfully, so I decided to give birth control a try. It was six months before I found the right pill for me that would not cause massive mood swings, uncontrollable sobbing, and miserable side effects. I stayed on the pill for several years, with the symptoms of endometriosis always lurking just beneath the surface as my abdomen ached and swelled. I suffered from migraines so severe at times that they impacted my sight. I knew that using birth control pills was just a temporary fix to band-aid these symptoms until I could find another avenue to shift things again.

A year later, I had debilitating pain on my right side almost daily. A visit to my gynecologist revealed normal results, and they told me everything was fine. However, I insisted that I receive an ultrasound as I knew something was just not right. The imaging revealed a cyst on my right ovary, large enough that my doctor recommended surgery. At his advice, I decided to have a laparoscopy to remove the cyst and also look for endometriosis. If any endometriosis was found, it would be ablated (burned away with a laser). I hoped this would finally give me some answers and permanent relief.

At that time, a laparoscopy was considered the go-to treatment for endometriosis, but years later, it would be understood that excision surgery offers far better outcomes. Excision surgery is the complete surgical removal of visible endometrial lesions and the underlying tissues. There are risks and unwanted side effects associated with any surgery. Excision surgery, in my opinion, would only be an absolute last resort since it scoops into the tissues of any organ in the abdominal cavity that has endometriosis lesions. I have personally known women who had the procedure and were dealing with horrifying side effects and/or saw the symptoms reappear with time. While it has given some women relief, it is still not a cure.

The laparoscopy revealed that I had endometriosis adhesions wrapped around my ovary, fallopian tube, and ascending colon, pulling everything up out of place and adhering to my abdominal wall. The laparoscopy also proved to be extremely hard on my body and did not help with my symptoms at all. I could not urinate for two days and had seemingly permanent symptoms of a damaged bowel. My life was never the same after that surgery. There is perhaps no such thing as minor, noninvasive surgery, especially one that involves multiple organs in the abdomen. Surgery is traumatic to the body.

Soon thereafter, I chose to return to Traditional Chinese Medicine and began weekly acupuncture sessions with Peter. I made the hour-plus drive to his office and spent the night at my father's home each week. It was like a revival of my earlier years of treatments with Peter. Within a year, my symptoms disappeared again.

In 2010, I met Jesús Meca, a new Rebirther finishing his one-year professional training with Leonard. He had been traveling the world with Leonard and working at all of the trainings on Leonard's schedule when he attended a two day event I organized for Leonard in Portland, Oregon. It was in early June, and the annual Return to the Sacred retreat was coming up a few weeks later in California. Jesús and I fell quickly in love with each other. He invited me to travel with him in Spain for three months. Leonard was also in Spain leading trainings, and encouraged me to go. I realized I would regret it if I did not follow my heart and take this leap of faith, so I closed my three businesses, and ended the leases on both my apartment and office as quickly and ethically as possible. I took off for Spain after completing my promises and commitments to my clients. It would be my first adventure overseas. I was also excited to have time with Leonard and his new wife, whom I had already met several times and hosted in my home as his organizer for the Portland events.

# Adventures Overseas

The train sped past a blur of olive trees that stretched for miles. I had been traveling for twenty-five hours via car, multiple airplanes, and metro. Now, for the final length of my journey, I experienced my first high-speed train ride. My travels had not been without a few tears. The only Spanish words I knew were hola and gracias, which made it a bit challenging to navigate my way through the airport and Madrid's mass of confusing metro lines. With all the work it took to wrap up my life in Oregon, learning Spanish was something I needed to do on the fly.

It had been an intense time. There were many goodbyes, and the pull for me to stay in Oregon was strong. I felt like I was breaking up with someone every day, and I was leaving the country to potentially marry a man whom no one in my family had met, and only a few of my closest friends knew!

Butterflies flipped like acrobats performing wild feats in the pit of my stomach. I already missed the evergreen trees and soft humidity of Oregon. I was going to Seville to meet up with Jesús at Leonard's latest training in Seville, which was wrapping up shortly as I joined them near the end of it. Thereafter, Jesús and I made our first road trip to the East Coast of Spain. Arriving in a day, we entered the city under a full moon and dark, moody, cloud-filled skies. The towering rooftops of the city emitted an eerie Gothic feeling. We were in Valencia.

In the following weeks, we stayed at the Bam Bam

Bhole Center, a Rebirthing Breathwork and yoga center founded by famed Rebirther Mavi Carreres, a longtime Breathworker who had brought the movement to Spain. She had organized a three-week professional training with Leonard, and we were enjoying a day on a mountain, where we had been practicing water rebirthing in beautiful, calm, aqua-colored pools and gentle waterfalls.

A group of ten or so of us trekked along the mountainside with Leonard, making a long loop back to our cars in the parking lot. It was a hot, dry, dusty trail that dropped off on one side and had a steep slope up the other. The return to civilization felt very welcoming. I could feel the group's fatigue as we all plodded along, nearly three-quarters of the way there. The dust billowed in small clouds around our group, mingling with our sweat and leaving little streams of mud on our brows. The hot midday sun shone down on us relentlessly. It was a stark contrast to our water rebirthing sessions the day before.

Suddenly, without saying a word, Leonard turned and went back down the trail by himself in the opposite direction, leaving the group out of sight.

"He probably has to pee," Jesús joked with me and we laughed.

Moments passed by, then more, and more. No one had any sight of Leonard. People in the group began to worry.

"Where is Leonard? Did he get lost? Should we go back for him?" Whispers broke out in the group.

The fear and concern grew to near panic for some, and a mild drama unfolded before our eyes. Some wanted to keep walking; others wanted to turn back and search for him. A few insisted that we stop and wait awhile.

Jesús assured us that Leonard made these kinds of disappearances all the time during their year of travel together, and he was sure he was just fine. The group finally conceded to finish the walk back to the parking lot and wait for him, as we were already almost there.

To everyone's amazement, when we finally arrived back at the parking lot, Leonard stood calmly in the shade, sipping some water with no hint of exertion or exercise. People were freaking out.

How had he done that? There was no other trail back but the way we had come. And there was no logistical possible way he had returned so quickly. Yet there he was, having returned to the cars before any of us!

Leonard offered no explanation but whimsically smiled and said, "Let's return to the center. We have a lot more ground to cover."

I quietly pondered the situation and thought back to the conversation he and I had had years ago about teleportation. *Has Leonard been practicing all these years?* I pondered. I intended to ask him, but the training schedule was busy and demanding, and the time never seemed right.

Although we seemed to be in constant communications regarding newsletters, articles, and events, I never followed up or asked the question about teleportation.

The next time I saw Leonard again was at the Meeting of Immortals in March, 2011, in Junagadh, India.

# Meeting of the Immortals

The airplane circled the runway below as my heart sank to the pit of my stomach. Gentle clouds of smog sat snuggled around what appeared to be miles of little shacks nestled at the base of towering, modern-day skyscrapers, crammed directly up against the airport fencing. The afternoon sun beamed across the horizon, striking the sharp lines of the monolithic buildings and penetrating through the air pollution in glowing hues of pinks, oranges, and reds.

People were living right next to the airport runway with countless thundering take-offs and landings day in and day out. It was the most drastic contrast I had ever seen of poverty and wealth. I had never encountered anything like it. I felt like I was stepping onto another planet. What had I gotten myself into? I choked down a hard knot forming in my throat and took some deep breaths. The reality of what I had heard it would be like to visit India for the first time was hitting me hard, and there was no escaping it now. We landed in Mumbai, India.

Jesús and I were there to meet with Leonard and a group of other Rebirthers for the 2011 Maha Shivaratri, literally meaning, 'the night of Shiva.' It is the celebration of the divine union of Shiva and Shakti, of consciousness and pure energy, the masculine and the feminine, the formless, ultimate reality, and the primordial force of creation in the ultimate, sacred union of creation.

Leonard had caught word of a meeting of immortals that takes place on Mount Girnar every year in the state of Gujarat, Northern India. It is said to be older than the Himalayas and is a sacred place of pilgrimage for both Jains and Hindus. It is home to various Shiva sects and is also believed to be the place of enlightenment for one of the last Jain Tirthankars, a human who attained liberation and can now lead others to their personal moksha (enlightenment). In this sense, Mount Girnar could be described as a sort of mystical, spiritual hub for enlightened masters.

And so in Leonard's typical fashion, it was a chance to seek out immortals, people living in a physical body beyond 300 years. He claimed to have met nine of them in person so far and often shared fantastic, mind-blowing recounts of interacting with them.

Inside the airport, I was able to relax and breathe a bit. I gathered myself while watching my surroundings as women in beautiful saris and men in kurtas bustled through the airport, speaking in accents and languages I couldn't quite place in my mind. We located our gate to catch a connecting flight to Rajkot, the closest airport to our final destination, Junagadh, at the base of Mount Girnar.

Our flight was delayed by several hours, and after a long wait, we readily boarded the plane. Although the airplane was small, I was grateful it was not as tiny as my flight from D.C. to Charlottesville years ago on my way to Leonard's home.

Shortly after take-off, we were offered cucumber

sandwiches and raita. We both fell into a light sleep as the airplane bounced randomly through small pockets of turbulence. After a mildly rough landing, Jesús and I gratefully descended the steps from the small airplane and walked the tarmac to the entrance of the Rajkot airport. To my surprise, it consisted of one cafeteria-sized room.

Jesús went into the building first, and I followed directly behind him. As soon as we set foot indoors, everyone stopped what they were doing and stared. We stood there in total silence.

Hesitating to even make a move, I, a caucasian woman of six feet in height and still dressed in Westerner clothes standing next to Jesús in his jeans and travel cap, stood out in stark contrast. We were possibly in as much shock as the locals were to see us. The silence was astounding.

Within moments, several men approached us, offering taxis and rides, wanting to know where we were going as they crowded around us. Jesús took the lead in trying to find someone reputable who he felt confident would drive us to Junagadh.

After some negotiation and sorting things out, he chose a driver. We loaded up in the back of a small car and were taxied off into the night.

"Does he know where to take us? Do you think he's going in the right direction?" I nervously asked Jesús as we drove into the Indian countryside. The sun was already setting.

"I think so," Jesús responded. "I'm not one hundred

percent sure he understands exactly where we want to go, but I think we're going in the right direction."

I studied the strained look on his brow and tried to convince myself we were okay. Jesús had been to India before, so I gathered that he knew what he was doing. And if not, what else was there to do now but remain calm, alert, and let go? It seemed India had already swept me away into the vast mysteries and enchantments of a play I could only hope had a Divine director and amicable script.

Each time it seemed we were far off in the remote countryside with not a soul in sight, we would suddenly come upon bustling streets lit up with shops and open-air food courts filled with Indian people in their bright colors, motorcycles, bikes, pedestrians, dogs, and the occasional free-roaming cows, which are held as sacred in India.

Whole families rode together on one motorcycle, straddling the seat with their children sandwiched between them. Lacking helmets of any kind, they seemed to comfortably nestle in and cling snuggly to each other as the motorcycles veered through the crowds and traffic. Aromas of food, exhaust, incense, and the occasional drift of fresh mountain air filled my lungs in an intoxicating, bewildering dance of the senses. The star-lit night was upon us as the dark, towering treetops silhouetted against the heavens.

Exhausted after a day of travel, I struggled to stay awake, still unsure that this driver was taking us where we wanted to go. I slept just moments at a time, my head bobbing on the rough road below us and leaning on Jesus's shoulder, who was also struggling to stay awake.

At last, we entered a small town and were greeted by two arches adorned with bright orange Sanskrit writing. To my relief, we arrived at the gates of our resort, the meeting point for Leonard's group and our lodging.

After some mixup about our reservations, a room was procured, and we settled in for the night. It was a large room with two beds and a walk-in shower toilet combo. It was the only room they had remaining, as it was also the tail end of Northern India's wedding season. They were now full to capacity. We purchased some bottled water to quench our thirst, and after a quick shower, we fell fast asleep. The next day would be busy, as Leonard was wrapping up his week of staying there giving lectures and a training. We had joined the group just in time for the celebration of Shivaratri.

The next morning, I gazed out the window over the courtyard. Palm trees danced gently in the wind. My eyes rested on the towering mountain range beyond the resort's perimeter fence. The air was humid and warm as the pinks and blues of sunrise bloomed in the air about us, and drifts of fragrant sweet incense sang on the wind.

We grabbed a few snacks and headed outside to the courtyard, where Leonard was finishing up one of his lectures. He smiled and greeted us warmly before disappearing off into his accommodations. We met with other Rebirthers and began making fast friends as we meandered into the resort restaurant for a very spicy, somewhat heavy Indian cuisine meal.

After lunch, we left the highly manicured resort grounds and ventured into the city's streets, finding our way to nearby temples. Towards the base of the mountain range, the unpaved roads were dusty and peppered with litter, dogs, and sacred cows, exuding an extraordinary sense of calm as they chewed on the trash. Leonard and our group enjoyed strolling along as we meandered and played like the tourists we were. Leonard, smiling mischievously, approached Jesús with a paper bag in hand.

"Happy birthday," he grinned as he handed the package to Jesús.

"Oh, Leonard, you shouldn't have!" Jesús laughed as he accepted the gift. Leonard knew we had arrived just in time to celebrate Shivaratri and his birthday. Jesús opened the gift to find a small, shiny metal wind-up toy boat for the bath. We all shared a good laugh and continued on our way.

We spent the morning exploring the local temples dedicated to Shiva. We left our shoes at each entrance and walked barefoot through the small, concrete rooms and corridors, each imbued with an almost electric, sparking energy amidst drifts of incense. Mantras of Om Namah Shivai played on repeat from little mantra chanting boxes placed throughout each temple. I peered in at a large Shiva linga, considered to contain the energy of Shiva Himself, sitting on a rock in a small cave at the center of the temple. Offerings of water, ghee, milk, and flowers had already been poured over the linga that morning.

"What is the significance of a Shiva Linga?" I asked Leonard as we stood outside some temple doors. I knew that in ancient sacred texts, Shiva originally appeared as an infinite, fiery pillar of light with no visible end or beginning, and from there, manifested in His first physical form as the Shiva lingam.

"Well," Leonard paused and took a thoughtful breath as he often did before speaking.

"A shiva lingam is a phallus sitting in a yoni. It is a physical representation of Shiva and Shakti, the creative principle of the masculine and feminine in all creation. It is a physical representation of Shakti, the feminine principle of eternal, unchanging, and unconditional life force energy impregnated with Shiva, the masculine principle of conscious awareness. Thought is creative. Thought and feeling impress upon pure life energy and are the source of everything in the physical world and all creation."

My Catholic-conditioned mind was spinning out in a daze with the thought of a penis and a yoni representing God and life itself. I intellectually understood what he was saying and tried to take it all in. I certainly could feel its representation of energy, creation, and the source of all that exists.

We returned to the resort in the afternoon, which soon became a welcomed retreat from the dusty roads and sea of people descending upon the small town for the night of Shivaratri. The following morning, we were to hike to the Jain temple and Shiva temple at the summit of Mount Girnar, via a path of 10,000 steps carved into the mountainside.

Well before sunrise, a small group of Breathworkers convened with Leonard to begin the ascent up the mountain. Jesús and I were a few hours late, as we were still recovering from the travel, time changes, and adjusting to the spicy, dense foods of Northern India. We were joined by a few others from the group who were also starting their trek up the mountain a bit late, and we walked together just as the sun rose over the horizon.

Usually, I would not have had a worry in my mind about a hike like this, but just two months prior, I had been bitten by a dog. I was breaking up a fight between a friend's two dogs and got caught in the middle of them, and the larger one had sunk his teeth into my calf muscles. I had barely had time to recover, but here in the energy of India, I felt ready to take on the journey one step at a time.

Many locals and pilgrims were making their way up the mountain, happy and eager to say hello and have a picture taken with us. It seemed they were quite surprised to see Westerners making the pilgrimage, too.

Every so often, we crossed paths with a Saddhu, who approached each person and offered a blessing of kumkum in exchange for a monetary gift. As soon as they caught sight of me, each would approach, speaking in Hindi and raising the kumkum paste to my third eye, the inner eye of spiritual sight located just above the brow at the center of the forehead.

The Saddhus were a mix of fantastical, uplifting,

calming, and sometimes intense and frightening energy. Dressed in red and saffron robes, weighted with rudraksha seed malas, covered in ashes and brilliant markings, they were a sight to behold.

At halfway to noon, we arrived at the largest of several Jain temples on the mountain. The temple was enormous, with beautiful white marble peaks hand-carved in intricate designs. We were nearly halfway up the mountain. Rather than enter the temple, we decided to continue our ascent, aiming to reach the summit before the afternoon heat became too much to bear. We continued up the carved steps, enjoying the vistas of forests and foothills below us, with Junagadh visibly nestled at the base of the mountain range.

Wild monkeys romped freely along the trees lining the pathway and occasionally came down to beg for food. Many were sitting on the edges of rocks overlooking the valley below in a sort of meditative state. Vultures and various birds soared high alongside the mountain. The silence was stunning and alive with energy. Occasionally, a group of pilgrims passed us with smiles and jubilant proclamations of "Jai Girnari!"

"Jai Girnari!" we called in response, meaning victory to Mount Girnar and all Her blessings.

Feeling the effects of the altitude, we stopped in shaded areas to sip on water and catch our breath. Amazingly, older women and men carrying large loads of supplies on their heads easily passed us and continued singing out Jai Girnari all through the day. I was amazed by their vibrancy and stamina.

The carved steps of the mountainside continued, as it soon became steeper and more demanding. I fell into a sort of walking meditation, as each step synchronized with each of my breaths. The steps were painted in the center with a white rectangle outlined in red, marked with the number of steps since the beginning. 6,000. 6,001. 6,002. 6,003... I marched onward, allowing the numbers to blur as I moved on in a trance of simple movement, breath, repeat. Occasionally, we would pause to look out over the horizon, the town of Junagadh now a mere mirage in the distance. Birds were soaring by at great heights, now at our eye level. Monkeys still scampered along the rocks and pathway.

Fewer and fewer people passed us by as we reached what appeared to be the mountain's summit. A steep stairway of carved steps, now no longer numbered, traversed up and down the final crest of the mountainside, dropping off dramatically into the depths below. The steps were lined with a stone wall on each side, and we made our way reverently and silently in the wind, sun, earth, and sky.

Pausing at the top of a steep incline, I turned to gaze behind me at the height I had so quickly climbed. To my surprise, there was a Hindu woman whom I had passed earlier on the steps far below. Whisps of her silvery hair danced in the teasing wind, pulling at her white and pink rose-printed sari, the loose end of it draped over her head as a ghoonghat veil. Her gaze met mine, and she beamed at me joyfully, proclaiming, "Jai Girnari!" and other words I did not understand, but they were clearly a celebration and a blessing. She looked fresh and radiant, and again, I was surprised at the level of vibrancy and aliveness present here. I smiled at her, holding my hands together in namaste, the traditional Indian way of greeting and honoring of each other. She continued on her way.

Quietly, I took in my surroundings. A Saddhu sat in meditation near the entrance of a small structure, and a woman leaning over a container of water, washing dishes, smiled at me. I felt surreal, as if in a dream.

A colorful, square mini temple sat at the peak, with a pointed roof and a bright orange dome resting on top. Shiva tridents and a large brass bell sat at the entrance. It is said that the impressions of Goraknath's footprints are here. Goraknath is a Hindu yogi and saint revered as one of the founders of the Nath tradition. The religious Nath sect seeks physical immortality by transforming the body into a divine, imperishable body made of the Eternal Spirit. Leonard, through his studies and research on immortals, claimed that Goraknath was thousands of years old.

We rested and stood in quiet reverence at the summit. To my astonishment, I saw the path of steps continuing beyond the summit, down a distance, and up another peak where a less elaborate, plain, square temple stood. After some time of taking in the energy and view, we decided to turn back and trek down the mountain. It was well past noon and would be very hot on our return.

My legs wobbled a bit at the new movement of stepping down instead of up; however, I soon found my stride. We left the rocky summit and entered the forests again. With each step, the crowds of pilgrims grew. Soon, it was a sea of never-ending people and Saddhus, marking us with kumkum after kumkum on our descent down the mountain. The sun was unforgivingly hot, and I needed to rest in the shade every so often. The crowds of people wanting to say hi and catch my gaze, wanting photos and staring, overcame me quickly. I stopped again and closed my eyes, finding rest and quiet within myself.

"You need to get her out of the sun," a stranger said. "Yes, yes, I know," Jesús replied in agitation. We were nearly out of water, but thankfully, we were approaching the lower steps where we could purchase some. I pulled my sunhat down over my face to block the views of the constant stream of pilgrims pressing around me, and I stared at the steps below my feet as I marched onward.

By the time we returned to the town, it was clear that within another day, seemingly all of India would descend upon the hills of Junagadh. We rushed back to the resort and found some respite with a shower, rest, and a good meal.

Returning to the resort's restaurant, we found one of our new Rebirther friends, Jesse, excitedly sharing about a yogi he had found off the main trail of the mountain.

"He's living in a cave there and meditates all the time. He says he goes into samadhi each night, and his Master appears to him at a location near the cave." Jesse's eyes flashed with enthusiasm.

There were so many Babas (Saddhus) from various sects gathering in town now. It was easy to spot them gathering in their orange robes, some embracing each other in clear friendship and camaraderie. Others remained aloof and silent, their eyes flashing with a wildness I had only seen in books before. Some were dressed in black robes, others dressed only in a loin cloth and covered in ashes from their sacred fires.

We agreed to go with Jesse the following day up the mountainside and off the main path to visit with the yogi. I had no idea what to expect. My mind was swimming with the day's activities. As I closed my eyes, all I could see was Saddhu after Saddhu, reaching for my forehead in blessing as I fell into a light, restless sleep.

The next morning, our alarms went off well before dawn. Feeling incredibly sore and drained from the previous day's hike, I could not believe I was going anywhere near the steps of the mountain again, but I could not resist. We left at dawn with a small group of Rebirthers, our new friend Jesse, and a translator.

To my surprise, the trek was easy enough, and we arrived at the spot where, almost invisibly, a narrow path veered off the main steps and led into the forest. We followed Jesse and his guide down the path in single file, as in some places, it dropped off sharply into the ravines below.

It amazed me how anyone could live out here. I recalled that Leonard said there were many sects of Saddhus living in these forests doing practices such as panch agni, purification with five fires, and surviving in the wild, even amongst the jaguars and lions.

We soon arrived at an opening in the side of the

mountain, and entered a small cave we had to duck our heads under to squeeze into. We were invited into a room at the back of the cave. There were benches carved out into the side of the cave walls, and we were motioned to take a seat.

Light filtered in from the entrance, making it comfortable on the eyes. Two men were present in the cave, one dressed in white and lying down, seemingly asleep. We quietly gathered as the translator was speaking with our host, who informed us the yogi would soon wake to talk with us.

We awkwardly squeezed ourselves onto the stone benches, and I looked around the room, taking it all in. What a sight we were! Curious Westerners dressed in non-traditional clothes crammed into a yogi's cave to inquire about enlightenment, spiritual gurus, and immortality.

My eyes landed with curiosity on the yogi who called this his home. I couldn't help but notice his breathing. How smooth and connected it was! I watched as both his ribs and belly simultaneously expanded gently with each inhale and effortlessly receded with each exhale. There was no pause in between. I could not sense or feel any restriction or tension in his breathing mechanism. His breaths became more rapid and stronger. The previous whispers and anxious giggles in the room fell silent. Our new yogi friend, our gracious host, was waking. He blinked his eyes and slowly sat up. He seemed totally unbothered by our presence and not at all surprised we were there. Jesse and the interpreter began speaking, and the yogi shared with us his experience.

He had been meditating in the cave for many years. A friend had been watching over him and bringing him necessary supplies. Each night, he said his guru appeared to him, and he went into samadhi, a supreme meditative state where one merges with everything, entering into the ultimate reality of consciousness, existence, and bliss. He slept only a few hours per day. He was calm and his presence felt very clear. There was a soft lightness to his eyes and I did not detect an ounce of superiority or egotism in him. He felt as a pure, natural being and his heart was sincere.

The conversation continued, and a few members of our small group asked questions. I couldn't help but feel entirely surreal. In speaking with the yogi, it felt like the most natural thing in the world that he lived there and had these peak experiences daily which could easily be described as spiritual enlightenment. Yet mentally, I marveled that this could be happening at all.

We thanked him graciously before taking leave, and his friend handed each of us a small sticker with an image of his guru. All of the writing was in Sanskrit, and as if in a dream, I could not manage to hold onto the memory of his guru's name once we returned to the daylight and crowds of people on the mountain. The following day was the much anticipated Shivaratri Festival.

# Shivaratri

We gathered again with the group of Rebirthers. However, Leonard was nowhere in sight, as he had planned to spend the day elsewhere. We climbed aboard multiple buses that the resort had arranged for us. We would attend the festival close to the Bhavnath Mahadev Temple, near the sacred bathing pool.

The day felt unusually hot, and the air had an indescribable sort of unusual charm to it. Our buses caravaned slowly through crowds of people before stopping abruptly behind a crowd control fence. We all piled out and followed the guides assigned to us from the resort, with the manager himself joining us for the day's festival. We began a long walk through streets partitioned off with crowds piled on each side. It soon became clear we were parading through the town to arrive at our destination, and people were happy to wave and catch a smile from our group of Westerners.

As we turned through the streets and rounded each corner, I became increasingly aware of how many people were in the tiny town of Junagadh. What were just days ago, relatively quiet, quaint streets were now amassed with people crowding in every available space, step, door front, or perch. People sat enmeshed together, their legs dangling from walls and rooftops. I had never seen or imagined anything like it. It was a massive sea of humanity as far as my eyes could see

We passed a gathering area of Naga Babas, ascetic worshippers of Shiva, literally meaning 'naked yogis.' Naga Babas wear only a loincloth, as even clothes are considered an attachment to the physical world of material possessions. Instead, they adorn their bodies with ash from their sacred fires, tilak (a sandalwood paste on the forehead to bring inner peace and mental stability), and garlands of bright marigold flowers. We stopped for some time, watching them perform their superhuman feats and displays of swordsmanship. One such feat was to lift the total weight of a man on a walking stick wrapped around the male genitalia, holding the stick horizontally to the ground and the other Saddhu standing with one foot on each side of the stick. The spiritual and mental powers of these Saddhus were incredible to behold.

Reluctantly, we passed the gathering at the urging of our guides and arrived at our final destination: a stage of chairs under a tarp covering with a loudspeaker and a stage of performers adjacent to our left. The heat, dust, and massive crowd of onlookers parading by were nearly suffocating. However, the procession of Saddhus would pass directly in front of us on their way to take a dip in the large Mrugi Kund (sacred bathing tank) in a ritual of purification. It is believed that Shiva Himself comes to bathe in the water on this sacred night.

The day stretched into night, and we were offered supplies of bottled water, chips, and snacks in plastic bags and boxes as processions of Saddhus of various sects paraded by. Babas blowing victoriously on conch shells, resounding music, and mantras made it an overwhelming sight and sensation to behold. At times, I needed to close my eyes and breathe deeply to take it all in.

Approaching midnight, a gloriously decorated palanquin bearing a Lord Dattatreya Murti, an object or figure said to be an embodiment of the divine, in this case, the Divine Trinity of Brahma, Vishnu, and Shiva, was carried to the water. In completion, a massive crowd of Naga Babas came celebrating in procession to take their bath in the holy waters. They leaped in rhythm to their repeated chanting, "Hara Hara, Maha Deva, Hara Hara, Maha Deva," the name for Shiva as the destroyer of illusion and ego. The throng of Naga Babas continued on in a crescendo of energy and sublime ecstatic union with the Divine, dancing and chanting just inches away from us.

Glancing at my friends by my side I could see I was not the only one overcome with the energy and joy as our eyes were open wide with wonder and complete awe. Occasionally, the Naga Babas paused in their procession, pressing together in a crowd of naked ash, flowers, ganja, and praise of Shiva. We chanted with them, and one held out a hand to me in request of a financial offering. I nearly reached into my pocket for some coins but realized I had none, and my friend called out to me, "Sara, be careful!" At that moment, I noticed a flower lying on the folds of my skirt, and I lifted it and offered it to the Saddhu's hand. They roared with laughter, and he placed the flower on my head before continuing their procession.

I stared in awe at the mass of human bodies rounding the corner to enter the holy bathing tank. In one surreal moment, I saw a single man in white robes calmly and directly stride towards the water. He stood out with a golden hue about him, the Saddhus seemingly unknowingly parted as he stepped into the crowd towards the water. It seemed as natural a thing as breathing to him despite the ongoing velocity of the festival's peak celebrations. *Babaji?* I pondered.

In a daze, the energy receded, and we left with our group back to the sanctuary of the resort. My entire being buzzed with electric energy. I fell fast asleep and again had dream after dream of Saddhus and Naga Babas blessing me.

With the festival coming to its close, we had one more destination before parting ways with Leonard and our new friends: Somnath Temple.

# Somnath

The dust blew in small billows of clouds at our feet and occasionally into our faces as our small group of Rebirthers traversed the dirt roads. Our driver had dropped us off near the Somnath Temple. The sun in India felt notably hotter to me, but perhaps it was due to my long skirts and clothing covering most of my body, as was culturally appropriate in India.

We stopped near the shade of some trees and a small, covered, open-air structure nearby. Some of our group gathered under the structure away from the sun's rays. Not many people were around yet, and we seemed to be the only ones on this road. However, a short distance away, I noticed a Saddhu in bright orange robes looking our way and laughing with hilarity. I couldn't help but giggle at the sight of him laughing so hard, bending over and slapping his knees, pointing at us, waving, and clasping his hands together as he openly and loudly howled in laughter.

A few in our group chuckled and waved at him. We couldn't help but wonder, what was he laughing about? Maybe it was the sight of a bunch of Westerners huddled together in the structure out of the sun. Perhaps the structure was a bus stop or a former bathroom facility. We had no idea. But seeing this Saddhu roaring with laughter and joy felt like a beautiful way to start our day. We continued, eventually reaching the grounds of Somnath and more crowds of people. It was breathtaking.

Towering at the edge of the Arabian Sea, Somnath stood in its amber-colored grandeur of carved stone. A few in our group mentioned it is known as the Shrine Eternal, as its original form is mentioned in the ancient sacred texts the Rig Vedas, Shiva Purana, Bhagavad Gita, and Skanda Purana. Within dwelled a sacred jyotirlinga, the symbol of Shiva. I studied its many intricate columns, carvings, and levels, as we began the long procession down the paved pathway through manicured gardens to the entrance. Something about the majesty of the temple and the fresh ocean air felt so freeing to me, liberating.

As we approached closer and entered the temple doors, I began to feel another layer of wind around me. It was energizing, uplifting, and brightening. Gazing at the now visible jyotirlinga in the temple's main chamber, I became aware that the wind was emanating from it. It blew through me energetically in a cyclone-like fashion, as if an indescribably powerful yet gentle storm was swirling around it, washing away the heaviness of human conditioning. I breathed connectedly and tuned into what was happening energetically. I felt as though the jyotirlinga, within moments and beyond any rational or reasonable explanation, had washed away several diseases lying dormant within my body. In a stunned, reverent silence, I exited the temple along with the procession of people. Our small group meandered outside its walls and came upon a stone pillar.

"It points directly to the south pole; there's no land between this point and the shore of Antarctica," one of the Rebirthers mentioned. Gentle tears were now filling my eyes. The peace, the freedom, the Divinely romantic atmosphere of Somnath filled me with exquisite lightness and splendor. I had just learned of the temple that morning and knew almost nothing about it, except that everyone assured me that visiting it should not be missed. We visited the Krishna temple as well, as Somnath is the recorded place of ascension.

"Somnath," I pondered. Further inquiry into the temple revealed that it was said to have originally been built in gold by the god of the moon, Chandra, also known as Soma. Jyotirlinga means linga of light. There are twelve jyotirlingas in India, each said to be a self-made, spontaneous manifestation of Shiva as a column of white light. The jyotirlinga of Somnath was the first of the twelve to manifest.

After my blissful experience at Somnath, I began to ponder what it might be like to visit each of India's twelve sacred jyotirlingas. However, our stay in India was coming to an end. I felt both sad and relieved to be returning home.

Walking the streets of Spain once again, I marveled at how empty of life it seemed. There was scarcely anyone to be seen in our neighborhood, though it was lined with a multitude of flats and high-density housing all around. There were no beeping horns or motorcycles veering through traffic and crowds of people. No cows serenely chewing and meandering wherever they pleased. It felt entirely void of any aliveness, just bricks, cement, and sky. It was shocking, but my heart was full with the blessings of India. *Mother India,* I silently marveled as if in a trance. Knowing that there were still such wild, untamed, and unstructured places as India in the world was deeply comforting to me within the confines of a highly structured, inanimate place.

∞∞∞

The year 2012 was soon upon us as time rushed on. Still living in Spain, Jesús organized an event for Leonard in Galicia and we enjoyed a reunion there for nine days. I later conducted a series of teleseminars titled *Ask Leonard Orr,* taking callers and participants from around the world to join us for my live interviews with Leonard, including time for interactive questions and answers on different topics. These were recorded and are still available today at LeonardOrrBooks.com.

During my time living in Spain with Jesús, my endometriosis symptoms yet again returned after two years of being symptom-free. In 2013, we moved to the United States, and I suddenly found myself back in my hometown, attempting to recover and overcome the next round of debilitating symptoms. This time, it led me to the profound work of women's mystery menstrual teachings.

# Into the Woods

*Aren't we all*
*little red riding hoods*
*heading into the woods*
*to face the wolves*
*who plagued our Grandmother's days,*
*Generation after generation*
*Forgetting our Goddess ways.*
*The wolves of shame*
*the wolves of pain*
*suppression, rejection*
*neglect, and abuse,*
*centuries of power misused.*
*So I shall don my red cape*
*to reclaim my feminine space*
*and turn with the tides.*
*These many, many lost years*
*shall not go to waste.*
*Into the deep dark woods, I ride.*
*Dropping to the center of my core*
*I am lost no more.*
*Fearlessly, I stand in this dark moon*
*and I wait*
*for her to come to me.*
*Now is the time,*
*it is not yet too late.*
*I shall kiss all the wounds*
*and hug all the hurts*
*knowing that as I do this*
*I am giving birth.*

SARADAWN

*Wise Woman shall rise*
*above all the lies*
*and reveal her majestic power;*
*her power to love*
*her power to heal*
*to connect and ignite all that is real.*
*To protect and replenish*
*this great garden Earth,*
*to revel in her beauty,*
*her sacred wild jungle hearth.*
*I have not forgotten her.*
*I will not leave her with this deep wound.*
*It is time my sisters*
*to do all of this*
*For we are reclaiming our sacred blood*
*Our sacred time of the moon.*

# The Magical
## Qualities of Blood

**B**lood is a perfect combination of the elements: earth, air, water, and fire. The elements are the building blocks of all of life.

Every month following the natural lunar cycle, each menstruating woman rebuilds and renews, physically emulating the process of life, release, and rebirth within her own body. It is a physical initiation and process of creation, manifestation, release, destruction, and rebirth. It is an eternal, ongoing, energetic renewal in the body of humanity, full of all the freshness of beginning life anew again.

Since this physical process is also energetic, the energetic pattern of the cycle stays with a woman for her entire lifetime. She is a microcosm of the macrocosm, a system of the cycles and seasons of life changing in her own body, as they do externally with our mother Earth. This is the magic of menstruation. This is the creative power and process within our bodies.

The follicular phase is the building up of the uterine lining, where all of the elements are present in the building, creating and growing potential new life. The ovulation phase is the tipping point for new life to be seeded. What dreams are you sowing and manifesting from this perfect creative medium? What is gestating that will emerge as new life?

The luteal phase of menstruation is a time of cycling down and letting go of what is no longer needed. It is the time of release, shedding off and returning to the Earth what no longer serves our purpose. It is the little death before the rebirth into renewal as the cycle begins again.

Had I understood this cycle of life, of blood as the alchemical magic that it is, since my menarche, perhaps my menstruations would have been different. It is a blessing that we have leaders, authors, and guides in the great women's mystery teachings.

∞∞∞

## Menstrual Cycle Awareness (MCA) -

## RED SCHOOL

There's a super positive side to periods. It's a path to enlightenment on its own. While menstruating, the veil is lifted between a woman's consciousness and Source. It is a physiological, biologically designed rhythm of entering into deep meditation and close connection with Spirit/Soul/God/dess.

In a natural, Divine world, this would be revered, and women would be allowed time to drop everything of the external world, and go within to access messages and insight from Source. The days following menstruation are for integrating the experience and downloads of information and adjusting to returning to the external world.

There also needs to be that transition time beforehand for a woman to prepare to leave and have the space to leave and go within herself. It may be for many women that a result of not doing this every month is PMS and other physical afflictions.

Menstrual cycle awareness can be a life-changing education. I learned it from Alexandra Pope and Sjanie Hugo Wurlitzer, co-founders of Red School and authors of *Wild Power: Discover the Magic of Your Menstrual Cycle* and *Awaken the Feminine Path to Power*.

# A Journey to the Womb

A fine mist enveloped the air. I sat on the damp, mossy forest floor under a canopy of cedars, firs, maples, and lichen, dancing like a tribe of protective grandmothers above me. I inhaled their scent, soothed by the collective aura of the forest, and sank deeper into the Earth. I wrapped up in my blankets with a canvas of treetops and blue sky holding me from above. I had driven to one of my favorite river parks on the eastern side of the Willamette Valley, McDowell Creek.

The sound of the rushing river became my guide for the sacred inner journey I was about to embark on. I was journeying into my womb to meet her for the first time, my inner womb Goddess, the gatekeeper of life. My recent experiences with the Red School sparked the inspiration to do this.

I had no herbs, no medicines, not even shamanic drumming. Instead, I followed the rush of the river and the sound of my pulsing blood. I breathed it all in. The edges between myself and the river blurred as I felt my heartbeat and the rhythm of my pulse become one with the river. I began my journey in consciousness.

Approaching my vulva in my mind's eye, I entered into my womb space. I quickly noticed a gold door over my cervix. It was in the shape of an intricate cross inlaid with jewels, an ancient cross representing the four elements, four directions, the meeting point of Heaven and Earth, above and below.

Feeling a tremendous urgency, I ran to the gold cross door and opened it. Surprisingly, a vast gushing river of black oil came pouring out. It poured and poured and poured until finally, the water ran clear. It then became a light flow of bright red blood and then stopped. Was this the hemorrhaging I often had with my periods? I stepped through the doorway and walked into my uterus.

The walls were a purply black color, and it was dark and empty. I waded through a pool a few inches deep in my womb blood. I stroked the walls a bit and wondered where my womb goddess was. I lit a small flame, tiny enough not to burn my body but bright enough to light the place.

In response, my womb pulsed three times as the walls contracted and released softly. They transformed from the purply black color to a bright, vibrant red.

I noticed a small table and two chairs to my left. I decided my womb goddess must be here somewhere, so I waited for her and made a pot of tea. I set the lit candle on the table and poured two cups. I quietly asked if she was there. A figure came swimming over from the pool of blood on the floor, and she rose from the blood to greet me. She was a mermaid!

She swam directly to me at the table, and her tail transformed into two legs. She stood across the table from me, and we gazed at each other face to face. She had fair skin, hazel eyes, and soft black hair. She wore a crown of green vines adorned with pearls all around.

She smiled at me.

"Well, we have to adapt, you know?" she said as she waved her hand about being a mermaid.

Smiling, I sighed in awe and relief. I had no idea what I would find here, and to my delight, she had such a charm and sense of humor; so beautiful, cheerful, and nonchalant about the whole thing.

A mermaid! It was quite funny to me. Given the amount of blood loss I had last month, she probably did need to adapt to the torrents of blood flow. She sipped her tea contently, her eyes shining over the rim of the cup and smiling at me.

'Why are you alone? Where is everyone else?" I calmly asked.

"I am sufficient enough for now," she replied. She was, is, so beautiful, confident, and secure. She seemed to be studying me, and waiting for me to direct the show.

"So, where are my ancestors?" I asked as I held her gaze steadily.

She said, "They are trapped in there," and she motioned at my right ovary. "They are stuck, they can't get out."

Logically, I couldn't understand why this would be or what she meant by this. But I immediately sensed I was here to liberate them. So, I climbed up into my right fallopian tube.

It was a bit of a tight squeeze. I cleaned out some dried, crusty blood and made my way to the ovary. It glowed a beautiful, luminous, soft blue. I could see a dark spot in the center of my ovary. I held out my hands, and as if of its own accord, it came to me and landed in my opened palms. It was a soft, translucent, dark gray cell sort of thing. I turned around and pushed it through my fallopian tube, following it back into my womb.

When I emerged, I saw my womb goddess holding it in her hands. She nodded to my left ovary, indicating another gray cell was stuck in there. So, I did the same thing for my left ovary. This time, when I emerged from my left fallopian tube, I saw her standing there laughing, holding both of the gray cells against her chest like they were seashells covering her breasts! She laughed and caressed the gray eggs fondly.

I asked her, "What do we do with them?"

Still laughing, she said, "This..." and she rolled them like two bowling balls down the length of my womb and out the cervical door. They rolled out my vagina and dissolved into the air, returning to the Source of all life. A bit bewildered, I gazed at her in awe.

"What is your name?" I asked.

"You can call me Leela," she responded with a confident warmth and joy.

We hugged and I thanked her. She sat happily in my now brightly lit womb, warmed by the tiny flame, and sipped our tea. I would be back again, this we both knew.

Feeling victorious, I opened my cervical gold cross door and closed it behind me. I buffed it with my sleeve until the gold shined brightly and the gems glittered. I exited my vagina and raised my hands, giving it a protective seal of gold light.

Light, warm, and relaxed, I felt very happy with this. What an interesting journey!

After integrating and relaxing where I lay in the forest, I sat up, snacked on some nuts and dried fruits I had brought, looked around at my surroundings, and soaked it all in. Soon after, it started getting dark, so I collected my things and returned to my car. In meditating on my experience, I decided to do more yoga and spend more time in nature.

Later in the evening, my mind kicked in, and I wondered if what I did was ok. I don't know much about journeying, ancestors, and ovaries, and I started to wonder if I'd done something I shouldn't have, like kick my ancestors out of my womb! I shared this with Jesús, and we laughed as he helped me realize that whatever it was, it wasn't serving me or them, and they returned to the Source! So all is well.

∞∞∞

## Invitation - Journey to Your Womb or Sperm palace

Our sexual organs and pelvis contain the seat of our life force energy. There can be so much information and healing there: ancestral energy, shame, fear, pain, pleasure, expression, aggression, repression, grief, joy. Taking the time to consciously go there and symbolically meet our inner guardian can be insightful to what is going on in our subconscious awareness and body.

For women who have had a hysterectomy or those who identify as female but have no physical womb, you can still journey to your energetic womb space. Men are welcome to journey to their sperm palace.

Find a relaxing, calm place where you can remain undisturbed. Perhaps listen to a sound or music that can carry you through the experience. Drop into your body by being relaxed, warm, well-supported, and taking deep breaths.

Simply using your imagination, visualize yourself at the entrance of your root chakra, the entrance of your sex organ. Begin by seeing or feeling the door to the entrance. What does it look like? What material is it made of? What colors or designs are apparent there?

When you feel ready, in your mind's eye, open the door and enter, slowly making your way to your womb space or sperm palace, with the intention to meet its inner guardian. Follow the flow of information that comes to you without judgment. Trust that what you see or imagine is coming from your subconscious and will give you insights into yourself, your feelings, beliefs, etc.

When your visit feels complete, return through the door you entered and close it with love, making a final blessing on the closed door to complete the journey.

Write your experience and any insights upon completion. Some may find it helpful to journal as you go with this inner journey.

# The Second Dance with Modern Medicine

In 2014, with all of my symptoms still persisting, even Peter, my Doctor of Oriental Medicine, began to advise me to have a hysterectomy. He had tried everything and was at a loss for what else to do. It was difficult for him to see me suffering and struggling in this way.

Simultaneously, my ob-gyn recommended that I go on birth control full time again and stop having periods. In desperation, I agreed to try this under the guidance of my gynecologist and as a result, nearly hemorrhaged to death. The bleeding had been ongoing for several weeks, and at the last attempt to stop it with continuous birth control, I passed tennis ball-sized blood clots all through the night. I could not stand or get out of bed. I only got up to crawl into the bathroom. I was so accustomed to being intensely sick and exhausted that it didn't occur to me I could have died.

Finally, the bleeding stopped in the morning, but I still went to the emergency room as I also had intense pain in my head and neck and found it difficult to move. There was an outbreak of Meningitis from a Listeria contamination in the food I had just eaten the day before. I was as pale as a ghost and could barely walk.

The doctor seemed unconcerned about my description of bleeding but ordered some bloodwork to confirm that I did not have Meningitis. A few days later, my doctor informed me that my iron levels were so low that I was at risk for a heart attack. My ferritin levels were almost non-existent at five nanograms per milliliter, the lowest my doctor had ever seen in his twenty year career. He urged me to go to the hospital for a blood transfusion, immediately.

After receiving this news, I lay in my bed, looked in the mirror, and realized how puffy and white I looked. I realized how much of my life energy had drained from me. I became very present in my situation. What was I going to do? What would help me heal from this? To my surprise, a jolt of energy sang through my body with one word, "Write. Write!"

It was as if my soul had heard my plea and responded. I suddenly sat up in my bed with this newfound energy. I remembered the book I had begun scribbling out years ago after my first healing of symptoms. I had to return to writing my book. It seemed a matter of life or death for me.

I began writing that day. I also started researching more ways to heal from anemia with vegetarian-friendly methods. Fortunately, I could restore my iron levels with two iron supplements, Floradix and Ferrasorb, a diet high in leafy green vegetables, vitamin C, black strap molasses, young coconut water, chlorella, and other excellent iron-containing foods, and blood builders. The worst of my symptoms were over within days and I could now walk about the apartment with ease. I decided not to go for the blood transfusion, but continued my iron building foods and supplements instead.

Quickly, I found a new gynecologist who gave me an ultrasound to see if we could discover what was going on. The results were obvious. In the mere two years of using birth control, I had developed four fibroids; one of them was submucosal and, in her opinion, was unable to be operated on because of its location. She informed me that all I could do to stop the hemorrhaging was to have a hysterectomy.

Once again, I faced a modern medicine doctor and replied, "I'd like to try some herbs first." She gracefully accepted and supported this idea and asked me to keep in touch and let her know how things were going.

∞∞∞

## A Midwife Saves My Uterus

Immediately, I went off birth control and was able to get the bleeding under control with herbs recommended to me by my friend Danielle Kitt, a Rebirther who had just completed her license in midwifery. I wasn't pregnant, but she sure did help me with menstruation!

Following all of her recommendations, I used a tincture of Cinnamon Erigeron on days that I had heavy bleeding. A week before menstruation and during my bleeding, I took tinctures of Partridge Berry and Chastetree (Vitex) three times daily. While I menstruated, I also took a tincture of Cramp Bark to help my uterine contractions relax and soften.

Each month that progressed, my periods became

lighter. It worked beautifully! Danielle's advice saved my uterus. It was another marvelous success and demonstration for me of the healing power of herbs. It took me more than six months to recover from the severe anemia. I could not have done it without slowing the hemorrhaging that was happening every month. However, the debilitating pain, vomiting, etc., all continued without any change. I found that a good, non-psychoactive CBD oil could help with the pain, which is saying a lot because no over-the-counter pharmaceuticals I had ever taken could come close to relieving the pain. However, the CBD did not stop the vomiting. I tried medical marijuana for a short time, and while it helped with the nausea, it did not stop the pain.

Committed to my cause, I remained focused on natural approaches as it was where I found most of my success, and knowing that I wanted to have children, I began to get as healthy as possible and tried to conceive. In 2016, at age thirty eight, I enjoyed a very healthy pregnancy. It was a miracle in the minds of many who believed I would never conceive.

## *Journal*

May 2015
Last night, I had a dream where a priestess healer visited me. She told me, "When the heart is open and expanded, if it is connected to the womb, the whole body will benefit."
I'm meditating on this daily.

# A Door Between Worlds

U rgently seeking some privacy, I stood in the stall of the women's bathrooms where I had been shopping for maternity clothes. I felt a weird rush of energy while strolling around the store. The air about me became thick with Babaji's presence. I felt myself rising from my body in a sort of bilocation. I was in my body but also several meters above my head, similar to when I had been at Leonard's house offering mantras to the fire.

In a moment of irrational fear, I took deep breaths and pulled my energy into my body. I did not want this 'bi-location' experience in a public place. It subsided, but I felt a soft energy flowing within me. I wondered if I were pregnant.

*Not likely,* I thought and brushed it off, as we had only just begun trying. Ignorantly, I continued about my day and headed for my acupuncture session that afternoon. I had been nauseous and had breast tenderness for three days. Both were typical symptoms of my usual PMS with endometriosis. I was sure my period was on its way, and it was going to be a doozy. I chatted with Peter as he tapped the needles in, and I lay under the heat lamp over my abdomen.

"Relief at last," I hoped. I took a few deep breaths and drifted off into relaxation. Five to ten minutes into my session, I suddenly felt my friend Binah enter the room. She had died just over a year prior, a tragic and unexpected loss in my close circle of friends. Binah's love and art exuded from her like a magical courtress of mysticism. And now she was standing next to me in her energy body, her hands on my abdomen protectively and lovingly. She was holding me steady. At that moment, I wondered if I could actually be pregnant. I felt so very much like my period was coming, and I had had some light spotting the last two days. Again, my mind discounted it. I focused on Binah's energy and sent her love as I received hers. It was magical, and I shed tears of gratitude.

Later that evening, at a friend's suggestion, I took a pregnancy test. If I were pregnant, it would be very early. I couldn't imagine it would have happened so fast. Then it appeared: two pink lines. It was positive. I was pregnant! Jesús and I locked arms and were jumping up and down in wild excitement! We were having a baby!

In the following weeks, I could barely eat. It seemed the nausea increased with each passing day. Exhausted and worried about not getting enough nutrition, I fell into a deep sleep early one night and had many vivid dreams. In the final dream before waking, a tribal woman carrying a baby on her hip told me to eat a raw cacao bean every day to dispel the morning sickness.

Waking up thinking what a ridiculous excuse it would be to eat chocolate, I decided to look up the cause of morning sickness. Many sources said it was due to a lack of magnesium. I also remembered learn about raw cacao beans having a high amount of minerals, including magnesium.

Quickly, I dug out a bag of raw cacao beans I had

purchased and frozen months ago. I popped one in my smoothie, and my nausea disappeared within the day. I tested it several times, and each day I omitted the cacao bean from my smoothie, I became nauseous again.

*Alright then, cacao beans for my baby and me!* I rejoiced! That was an easy fix. I wondered if this would work for other women as well.

After discovering the raw chocolate cure for the morning sickness, I continued working on newsletters and events with Leonard throughout my pregnancy. In addition, from my years of experience in leading seminars on Physical Immortality at the annual Return to the Sacred Retreat, I wrote the Physical Immortality Consultation, a workbook designed to introduce people to the concept of physical immortality and begin to uncover their unconscious death urge. Leonard gave me permission to include several of his best articles on the topic and he enjoyed utilizing it in his training center with his students.

When we met up again in person at Return to the Sacred that summer, I filmed an interview with him and created the *Leonard Orr Rebirthing Breathwork Video Course*, complete with his demonstrations of various breathing techniques. As I was pregnant and preparing to give birth in a few month's time, it was a marvelous time to be with him and Yasoda at the hot springs.

# Breathing with the Braxtons

eeling the same as most mornings, I woke up to another early autumn day. I was four days away from my estimated due date. Throughout the night, I experienced mild cramping that felt like menstrual cramps. They were not as bad as my period pain but were strong enough for me to be aware of them and wake up slightly through the night. I was having Braxton-Hicks contractions. These are the normal, healthy uterine muscles toning and contracting lightly in preparation for birthing, like strength training of the uterus! I'd had them mildly since my second trimester of pregnancy, so this was a regular occurrence for me.

However, on this day, they were stronger and sometimes required me to sit down and breathe as if my body were exercising and needing more oxygen. I was excited but knew this could go on for days or weeks before actual birthing would begin.

So, I spent my morning cooking, cleaning the house, and vacuuming the car. Jesús had taken our pickup to a nearby town to run errands. I spoke with one of my midwives, Danielle, and we both felt that possibly my baby would be born today, but more likely tomorrow at the earliest.

My day went on, and by late afternoon the Braxton Hicks were a little stronger, sometimes requiring me to lay down and rest. I called Danielle again and asked her to come to my house, a two-hour drive from where she worked. She agreed it was a good idea. Jesús had already returned from his errands with groceries in hand.

By the time she arrived, I was lying down and breathing with the gentle, sporadic Braxton Hicks. It was easy going but exciting! My Braxton Hicks were spaced out irregularly and did not follow any of the usual patterns of early-stage labor, so I was hanging out and resting. Danielle arrived and took my vitals. All was good, and there were still no signs that actual labor had begun.

Early evening arrived, and my Braxton Hicks still followed no regular pattern; some were long in duration, and some were short. Some came four minutes apart, some were twenty minutes apart. However, their intensity grew, and I soon reached a point where I could not talk during the Braxton Hicks. I had to breathe and focus on the sensations.

We all agreed it was a good time for Lisa, my second midwife, to join the party. She had over 35 years of experience and did home births with all five of her children. I loved that she would be with me for this, as I would have another woman present who had given birth many times before. She carried within her body the cellular knowing, experience, initiation, and memory of what birth is.

Shortly after calling her, I suddenly wanted to get up and be in our bathroom, a tiny, closet-sized half-bath attached to our bedroom. I began to feel intense pressure moving down into my pelvis. I stood in the small bathroom, unsure if I should stay standing or sit on the toilet. I felt no pain, only the tremendous pressure and heaviness in my pelvic bowl. Each Braxton was now more like a surge of energy, stretching, widening, and weight moving downwards.

Ahhh-ohhh! A moan came out of my body, and just like that, the energy of birth descended upon me and awakened within me. It came like lightning! It was powerful, magnificent, overwhelmingly strong, wild, and primal. There was no controlling it. No taming it. No managing it, just surrender. How thrilling and, at the same time, terrifying.

I let it take me like a wave and did not struggle against it. Although I could see how tempting resisting it could be, I was sure it would unforgivingly be a brutal experience. I rode the wild, crashing waves with all the relaxation and openness I could muster. I said YES. I offered my entire self up to the experience: my body, my mind, my heart, my Spirit, my emotions, my deep inner self, my feminine goddess, my spine, my hips, my yoni. Each wave carried me further and further out to sea, farther and farther from the shores of the Earth beneath me, deeper into the oceans of just *being.*

It was a space where neither time nor thought could reach me. It was as empty and void as the darkness of the universe, yet filled with the untamable energy of all creation. 'I' had to let go. 'I' had to let it annihilate everything I ever thought myself to be. I instinctively knew I was to give way to it with every surge and let it carry me entirely into the world between physicality and spirit, form and formlessness.

As each surge passed, I found myself back in the room, as if I were laying on the shores of a sandy beach with the giant waves receding behind me. Only my connected breathing remained, enabling me to regain my energy in time before the next wave picked me up and carried me to the otherworld again.

# Birth Demands Presence.

J esús joined me in the bathroom as soon as he heard me moan. He was well prepared from all his years of supporting me through the symptoms of endometriosis plus our childbirth classes and years of Rebirthing. I alternated between standing and sitting, all the time leaning into him, moaning into his body, lifting my arms, and sinking into my pelvis. I vomited six times. Still, there was no pain, just energy and intensity. The vomiting was effortless compared to the contortions my stomach went through with endometriosis.

Jesús held me like a rock as the storm thundered through me. "Fill the birthing tub! I want to be in the water," I managed to say between surges. Birth is well-designed. The space between surges was, for me, incredibly calm and peaceful.

Danielle rushed into action, connecting hoses and filling the tub. Jesús started to leave to help her.

"No!" I nearly shouted. "Stay with me!" I needed him there right where he was. "Is Lisa here yet? Where is Lisa?" I struggled to both catch my breath and get the words out before the next surge came.

"She's on her way. Any minute now." A voice informed me from afar. I was drifting in and out of a magnificent sea that swelled with energy on each crashing wave.

Still in my tiny bathroom for what felt like an eternity, I finally heard Lisa quietly come in through the front door, greeted by Danielle, who was still filling the birthing tub in our living room. Could they feel the energy of the vortex opening up in my body? Could they sense the magnitude of the vast, wild, beyond-the-senses world of Spirit crashing into the physical through my very own body?

"Ahhhhhhuh..." I moaned as another wave forced down through me into my pelvic bowl and then left moments later.

"Well, that sounds like birth!" Lisa greeted me.

I was between surges, and we smiled at each other. Lisa went to the living room to set up and get ready. A few surges later, another deep, guttural, grunting moan came out of my body as I felt a push. It wasn't me pushing, but rather my baby moving through me and my body responding.

"Guuuhhhhghhh," I vocalized uncontrollably. This was not at all like the gentle, quiet births I had watched in Elena Tonetti-Vladimirova's film *Birth Into Being*, nor in my birthing classes.

"Push! That felt pushy!" I called out to her at the end of the surge.

"I heard that!" Lisa responded as she moved quickly towards me and called to her assistant. Everyone was hustling to set up in time and be prepared for this baby.

"Water," I pleaded. "I need to be in the water!"

As I wanted to be held by the soft warmth of the tub in the gentle caresses of warm water, this couldn't arrive a moment too soon. The tub was not full yet, but we began the procession out of the tiny bathroom. Our goal was to walk to the tub set up in our living room. In between surges, Jesús and I walked from the half bath, out of our bedroom, and down the hall. I arrived, feeling precarious on my feet. The lighting was gentle. The air was warm and filled with qi (energy), but I also felt very high, as if the room were a vortex I was stumbling into. Nothing felt solid or certain. My eyes focused solely on the birthing tub. I was ready to get in no matter what.

The water was not yet deep enough for a baby to be born in, but Lisa suggested that Jesús get in to displace some of the water. It worked. He sat behind me and massaged my back while I squatted in the tub. It was the only position that worked for me.

"Ghhhaaahhhh ohhhhhh!" Moans continued to ricochet through my body as each surge grew stronger. My body was responding by pushing with all its might.

"Would you like me to check and see how much you are dilated?" Lisa offered.

"Yes!" I wanted to know. I heard my baby's heartbeat as she finished listening with the Doppler, a non-invasive device that allows the monitoring of the baby's heart. It sounded strong and beautiful. All was going well.

With gentle yet steady hands, she checked my cervix. "You're close to 8 centimeters." she smiled. This baby is ready to go!

Danielle appeared at the tub's edge before me, holding a glass of water and a straw to my lips.

"Drink," she said calmly with a smile.

"But I might vomit!" I said.

"It's alright," she said, "just try."

She was right. I was aware that if I became dehydrated, it could be dangerous for both me and the baby, and we would be required to transfer to a hospital, so I carefully took a sip. To my amazement, the water stayed down. The vomiting had ceased.

With each surge, the pressure grew more vigorous. My energy body broke open, expanding to fill the entire room and, at the same time, condensing down into the core of my body and pelvic bowl.

"Look at the water; it is slightly red. I think the water broke." I heard Lisa say. I looked into the water and saw a soft beam of light shining into the tub. It looked rosy and warm as it was tinted red.

The surges came faster and harder. With each one, I groaned wildly, primally, and then managed to go into rapid, connected breathing. I marveled again at how perfectly birth was designed. The minutes between surges gave me time to go deeply into serenity and to cope mentally with what was occurring so quickly. Just hours ago, I wasn't even sure this would happen today! This dance of surges and resting points continued throughout the birth, right up to the moment my baby emerged.

"Are you breathing to escape the sensations or to cope?" Lisa inquired.

I could hear concern in her voice and the strength of a wise leader who knew where I was physically. She was inexperienced with Rebirthing, and although I had previously forewarned her that I could sound like I was hyperventilating at times, I had assured her everything would be fine. In the reality of the moment, it seemed she had forgotten.

"Cope," I replied as I went into the next surge, groaned, and then breathed my way through it.

Rebirthing Breathwork and Birth are made for each other. I could not imagine going through this without breathwork. It was as if the energy and power of every successful, victorious Rebirthing session I had ever done in the past was in preparation for this moment. Of all the intense, insane sensations and experiences I'd ever breathed through, this was the most demanding. It took everything I had as a Breathworker to breathe through the surges as my baby's head began to crown.

In moments of doubt, I felt Jesús supporting me calmly from behind, massaging my back and telling me how great I was doing. I saw Danielle kneeling before me, telling me how awesome I was doing and that I was *rocking it*, and I believed her. I listened to Lisa and Emily communicating, handling technical logistics, and holding me in a loving, powerful place.

There were a few moments where I began to resist the sensation of weight bearing down through my body. My moans turned to a higher pitch, and I felt myself nearly crawling out of the tub and wanting to climb higher to escape the weight pressing within my pelvic bowl. There was one moment of fear where I did not believe this baby would be able to pass through. My open, moaning mouth landed on Danielle's arm, and I nearly bit her!

She gently laughed and said, "It's ok; you can bite me if you need to. You are not biting as hard as you think you are."

But I had held back the urge to bite as I saw myself going for her arm. She offered to place a cotton rug on the side of the tub for me to bite, and I did. It felt good to physically release the tension in my face and jaw. I was able to breathe through the rest.

My baby's head was crowning fully now. I placed my hand in the water and moved through it in a state of timelessness. I felt my tissues stretched and taught, gently cocooning the top of my baby's head and hair. What hair this baby had! And how large its head felt to me! I could not believe it was so large!

I continued to surge and moan, breathe, and bear down as the energy moved through me. It began to feel like an eternity. I could not feel the baby's head progressing or coming out. I patiently continued and started to spiral my hips gently and rotate my right leg out.

"Good, that's it. Make room, find the space," Lisa encouraged me.

She was checking for the baby's heartbeat again with the doppler. But this time, it did not sound. We waited. I could feel the tension rising in the room. I breathed and continued. Again, Lisa was checking and listening. Still no heartbeat.

In between surges, I looked at Jesús as I realized what was happening. I had no doubt my baby was fine; I just knew it, but I could feel the concern building in the room, and I did not want to try to argue with three concerned midwives who wanted me out of the tub, while I was in mid-birth and fully crowned.

At that moment, I felt fear creeping in as I began to doubt my intuition. What if I was wrong? These ladies are experts and have been at hundreds of births. Jesús saw my thoughts and knew; he responded with a steady gaze and deep breath. I breathed deeply and surrendered to the experience again, trusting everything was ok, and agreed to leave the tub and lay on the nearby futon where Lisa could better listen for the heartbeat. I knew this was a possibility and was willing to let it unfold if necessary. It was the right choice for me to do.

Jesús and Danielle took my arms, and miraculously, I could stand and lift my legs and body over the edges and out of the tub. I laid down on my back, and for the first time, I felt pain. It was the exact pain I had with my periods and the endometriosis.

It surprised me as the entire time I had not yet felt any pain and I cried, "It hurts!"

I began breathing faster and harder to cope with the pain. It was a familiar pain, so I knew I could do this. I wanted to know if my baby was ok. With full-blown, breath-stopping anticipation, everyone paused in silence, listening for the heartbeat. It was there, fleeting momentarily, and all breathed a sigh of relief. But it was barely distinguishable from the rushing sounds of my blood pulsing and fluids moving.

Lisa set the Doppler down, looked me in the eyes, and said, "I want this baby to be born now."

With no hesitation I replied, "I agree!" To the best of my ability, I would not let this drag out and crescendo to a state of emergency.

"One push and the head will be out," she told me. I nodded.

I took a few deep breaths, felt the next surge arriving, and pushed with all my might. A loud groan rose from my depths, and the surge passed.

"That all went out your mouth," Lisa said as I breathed and relaxed into the resting space before the next surge.

I nodded. Lisa was right. The baby had not gone anywhere, and I was all too familiar with my body's energy leaving through my mouth instead of going downwards into my root chakra. I was escaping. The subsequent surge came on. I covered my mouth, and though I still groaned, I directed the energy down and felt the head pop out.

"The baby's in the sac! The water didn't break," I heard someone say.

Then Lisa's voice came through a now seeming cloud of fog, "Okay, the cord is around the neck. Pause, Sara. I'm going to move it."

I held back between surges and relaxed my pelvic floor, meanwhile breathing softly yet connectedly as I felt Lisa's hands at work. Fast, gentle, confident, and without hesitation, I heard her break the water and felt her maneuvering as she removed the cord from around my baby's neck. It was a soft tugging yet slightly uncomfortable as I sat with the sensation of my baby's weight and shoulders right there, ready to emerge. I waited, and again, time stood still as this fresh new life was held there, mid-exit.

"Ok, it wasn't wrapped around the neck, just draped around from behind. One more push, and this baby is out."

"Really?" I questioned. I could not intellectually believe this was one more push. It all happened so fast!

"Really," she reassured me.

The next surge came on. The pain was still there, but I breathed deep and felt the surge move through me, more gently now, as I pushed. These last two pushes were the only time I felt I was doing the pushing alone. I felt the energy of the surges retreating, like a storm passing in the distance.

Feeling a pop and a moment of intense pain, I realized the shoulders came through, followed by an intense flood of pleasure as the rest of my baby's body flowed out of my body in one fluid motion. I tilted my head up to see what was happening.

I will never forget the moment I first saw my baby's face. It was purely thrilling. Baby's whole body turned from blue to a rosy pink and red right before my eyes as the first breath was taken. Thick black curls of wet hair framed a soft, round, angelic face, the eyes gently opened.

"It's a boy," Lisa smiled at us, but her smile quickly turned to a furrowed brow. "He's floppy. Why is he floppy?" she said with unmistakable concern.

"What do you mean, floppy?" I asked with alarm. He was the picture of perfection to me.

"He is not holding in the fetal position. His arms and legs are straight and relaxed. Newborns are always curled up in the fetal position," she said as she looked him over closely.

"I am going to use the aspirator just to make sure he's fully oxygenated. It's very gentle, don't worry," Lisa assured me, as she knew how vital gentle birthing practices were for all of us present.

She placed a small, clear mask over his nose and mouth, gently pumped it with her hand, then released it. He let out a small cry. Assured he had adequate oxygen and was breathing well independently, she handed him to us. I felt as though time itself stopped and everything in the Universe became perfectly still as I held my baby in my hands for the first time.

"We have Ademar; it's Ademar!" I cried gently.

I was in such an altered state. One beyond words. One beyond thought, time, or space.

Lisa placed him on my stomach, and we let him look for the breast. He attempted latching on several times, and we both fumbled around, new to all of this. Lisa offered to assist, and I happily accepted. She helped him latch on perfectly. I held my hand on his back, feeling the thick layer of vernix and softly massaging it into his skin.

*Ademar, Ademar, Ademar!* The joy overwhelmed me.

Once Ademar finished his first nursing session and took a few swallows of the liquid gold colostrum (the first milk that flows), he fell asleep and lay swaddled beside me.

The placenta came out quickly with a few cramps and a slight push. The cord had stopped pulsing, and all of the blood had transferred to Ademar, so the cord was cut with my consent.

Again, Ademar let out a cry, and I had a deep sense of sadness. If I ever did this again, I would surely attempt a lotus birth, allowing the cord and placenta to remain attached until it fell off naturally.

Some of the water sac remained in my uterus, and Lisa had to slowly and carefully traction it out. It was a bit nerve-wracking, knowing that it could perhaps break off and cause infection. However, it was painless for me, and I waited patiently, conversing with her and whoever was around.

I had torn deep into the muscle and was bleeding quite a bit, so soon after Lisa removed the remaining sac, she began the tedious work of stitching me up. This also was reasonably painless, although uncomfortable and time-consuming.

All was done, so the next task was to sit up and pee. Yes, pee! The uterus begins shrinking to the size of a grapefruit immediately after birth, and if the bladder is too full, it can block or displace the uterus from returning to its normal size. I slowly sat up with Lisa's help. I was clearly on a cocktail of natural endorphins and new mama hormones. I leaned towards the portable toilette station my midwives had set up for me and told Lisa I felt dizzy. "Do you feel like you're going to pass out?"

"Yes, I think I might..." These were the last words I remembered before succumbing to a complete euphoria in a trance of deep peace and perfection. I became aware of three feminine energies (my midwives) before me.

"Sweetie... sweetie... sweetie!" I heard Jesús calling from a far distant place with increasing concern.

"She's alright, this is normal." I heard Lisa's voice assuring him.

I came to and laughed. I had passed out, and it was so delightful! I was slightly irritated that my husband's urgency had rushed me out of it.

"This was fun. I would do this again!" I beamed and exclaimed.

Lisa laughed with amusement. "This was fun for you?" She smiled. "Okay then," She glowed back at me as she helped me sit up slowly again.

After I had successfully peed and taken care of a few more items, my husband and I lay beside our son, swaddled in the middle of the bed and sleeping so serenely. We oohed, and ahhh'd over his features.

"Look at his lips, how perfect they are! And it's so cute how they are turned up like this! I love his eyes, and his nose is so cute! He looks like a sleeping Buddha," we cooed over him.

With each passing breath, I fell deeper and deeper into love.

I reveled in the glory of this day. It changed me forever. In giving birth, I was once again reborn.

With us all tucked in for a rather sleepless first night, Lisa departed as one of her other families had already started labor. "I'll come back first thing in the morning," she assured us.

The morning quickly dawned upon us, and we were adjusting to the cries of a newborn. He was nursing like a champion. I loved his full head of hair. It was curly, soft, and brown, like mine was as a newborn. I looked down at his chubby cheeks and scrunched-up nose while he nursed. "You're like a little bear," I thought. "Mama's bear."

# A Little Extra Surprise

"**L**ook at you!" Lisa exclaimed as she walked into the living room. I was kneeling on my knees with my feet tucked under me, holding Ademar to my breast, and nursing him cradled in my arms. It was too painful to sit yet, as the tearing and stitches were quite fresh, but sitting on my knees worked well for me.

"This looks beautiful; he has a nice latch," she commented. Jesus joined us and greeted her.

"I'd like to take a closer look at the baby again," she shared. "Just to make sure everything is alright," she mentioned.

"Of course!" we exclaimed, handing him over to her gentle, loving hands. She spoke sweetly to him as he gazed at her, letting out little squeals of delight. She gently played with his limbs and then looked over his hands closely. Very closely, I thought.

I started feeling concerned as I could sense her energy becoming more serious. When she was done examining him, she handed him back to us sweetly but with a visible furrow on her brow. My heart began to pound. I knew something was about to be said, and it was solemn.

Calmly and quietly, with a face of utter compassion and neutrality, she gently placed her hands on my knees as she sat across from me and looked straight into my eyes.

"I think your baby has Down Syndrome," she said calmly and matter-of-factly.

I felt as though the weight of a thousand tons of bricks had suddenly slammed into my lap.

"What?" I asked in disbelief.

"I think your baby has Down Syndrome," she repeated, eyes full of concern and compassion.

She pointed out a few features: his almond-shaped eyes, relaxed and loose limbs with low muscle tone, and a palmer's crease in one hand. "I'd like to come with you to see a pediatrician this morning."

My heart raced like thunder. I could see nothing of Down Syndrome in my baby. He looked and acted perfectly normal to me. I trusted Lisa, but I could not believe her. However, if this was her assessment, I wanted to investigate it thoroughly.

I could not imagine how I would walk or ride in a car in my post-birthing condition and with my freshly newborn baby, but we managed. Danielle and Jesús held me on both sides as I wobbled down the hall of the pediatrician's office. She was a sweet, optimistic, and very loving person who confirmed, yes, he had markers of Down Syndrome.

That night, after returning home and sneaking away after Ademar had fallen asleep, I crept away to the guest room and sobbed every last bit of my heart out. My child, *my child,* had Down Syndrome?

I wasn't so concerned about Ademar himself; I already

knew since my pregnancy that he was the highest being of love I could ever imagine. I recalled the first dream I had of him, when I was a mere two weeks pregnant. He appeared to me as a small bird with long, curling feathers that continuously changed colors, shining like a rainbow. Actually, he appeared to be a fledgling phoenix!

My mind raced back through time, gathering just two memories of interactions I had with a person who had Down Syndrome. My first memory was in high school. One of the boys in the special needs class had Down Syndrome, and he passed by me almost daily between our classes. He had dark brown hair and large brown eyes that always gazed into mine when we passed. His gaze always had something soft and open, like that of a gentle deer. I towered over him in height by at least a foot and a half. I never said a word to him that I could remember. Did I even smile?

The second memory that came to me was in Madrid. It was just a week before Jesús and I were to meet with Leonard in India. Back in Madrid, it was a dry, sunny, cold day. We had to travel to the embassy to pick up our visas, which were finally approved just weeks before our trip.

It took us over two hours to arrive at the embassy via walking, metro, and bus. After waiting to retrieve our visas, we left the embassy, wiped out and tired. As we barely caught the correct bus to take us to the metro, a young, blond-haired man with Down Syndrome dressed in a suit and carrying a briefcase boarded the bus and sat across from us, beaming with joy. Just smiling and gazing at us, he said hello. What transpired blew my mind. Although my Spanish was still lacking, I understood most of what he said.

And the more we talked, the more joyful and light I became. I felt revitalized in a matter of minutes. I was so confused as we got off at our stop. What had just happened? Who was this man? Jesús commented that there was a center nearby for people with Down Syndrome, and it was very esteemed and successful. But that didn't account for how I felt in my body after our brief interaction. I felt lighter; all of my fatigue and weariness was gone. It was like the weight of the world had been lifted from my shoulders, and all I could feel was joy.

Remembering this the first night after Ademar's diagnosis, I knew we would be just fine with him. Magical, even perhaps. But my heart ached to think of how the world would treat him. I feared how the world might see him, judge him, and discriminate against him. And in those achingly piercing moments, I felt for the first time the indescribable depths of what it means to become a mother, giving freely a piece of one's own heart, body, and soul to this world.

∞∞∞

"You can do it. Remember, his natural divinity is enough, and he is manifesting perfection. You can do a good job as parents, presence to presence," Leonard encouraged me in his most recent email.

Leonard was totally unfazed by my son's diagnosis and

knew he was already perfect. He told me that his first teacher, Joelle Teutsch, loved to work with children with Down Syndrome. I fondly remembered his stories of Joelle, as he had described some of her miracles and mystical life in detail during an interview I conducted with him during the *Ask Leonard Orr* series. She was a medical mystery and a phenomenal presence.

Her way of working with children with Down Syndrome was to keep them relatively isolated with herself and a select team of people explicitly chosen by her. Leonard believed she did that because children may absorb and become what the adults around them perceive them to be. In her times, the typical attitude towards people with Down Syndrome was not so welcoming. People with intellectual disabilities were left in institutions and very rarely raised with their families.

There were minimal opportunities for education, work, or social inclusion. However, Leonard knew Joelle loved to work with them, and many thrived in her care. He said she naturally treated them as perfect, healthy, divine beings and kept them surrounded by people who supported their natural perfection at all times.

Nowadays, the common standard for educating children with Down Syndrome is to presume competence. If they need help, adjustments can be made accordingly. However, the energy and expectations directed toward any child will very likely impact their self-perception and growth.

It felt good to have Leonard's understanding and support. I literally could not see anything but perfection in Ademar. He was absolutely beautiful to me! I sang to him, spoke to him, and held him constantly. He was already the biggest gift and Divine surprise of my life, and we had just begun our journey together!

∞∞∞

What followed over the next weeks after Ademar's birth were a flurry of blood tests, echocardiograms to check for heart defects common with Down Syndrome, and a very intense few nights stay at our local hospital due to jaundice. After far too many tests, pokes, and prods, the hospital granted us release to be free at home with our baby, where we could get back to life as usual and spend every moment with him.

There was a delay in the karyotype blood test for the medical confirmation and diagnosis of Down Syndrome, Trisomy 21. I still could not see anything 'wrong' with his eyes or limbs. He looked like a lovely baby to me. Free from all of the monitoring devices and tubes, I rolled onto my back and laid him on my stomach. He looked up at me and gazed directly into my eyes.

"You are perfect. I don't see anything wrong with you. You are total perfection." I told him, beaming with love.

He let out a little laugh, and we began our long journey of his first year of life. It was the longest, slowest flurry of sleepless nights, messy kitchens, piles of laundry, constant middle of the night wakings, far too early sunrises, laughter, fear, worry, and a huge learning curve as I took in and digested all I could about Down Syndrome, motherhood, and Ademar.

After a grueling first five months of struggling with 'failure to thrive,' meaning he was growing in length but was far underweight, we finally discovered he had gluten and dairy intolerance. I had heard that it is common for people with Down Syndrome to have Celiac disease and be lactose intolerant, so I stopped eating all gluten. He gained a pound that week on my breastmilk alone.

The following week, I also stopped all dairy, and he gained an additional two pounds. All of our doctors, including us, were astounded. Ademar was healthy, strong, and thriving.

## *Journal*

October, 2016,
Dearest Ademar,
You are the most prized
Gem of the sea,
Twinkle of the stars,
Flower of Heaven
Center of my heart.
I love you forever and always,
Your Mama

August 2017,
In a guided meditation, I saw my menstruation as ocean waves moving in and out on the shore. I saw it as a

heartbeat, expanding and contracting in sync with my heart but at a slower pace, stretched out over time as my menstrual blood built and released. I saw it as breath, inhaling and exhaling as the leaves and foliage of the Earth inhaled and exhaled with the seasons. My blood was a wave, the pulse of all life, my ovaries released a shining pearl of light, and it washed out with the flow of the tides.

My pregnancy was a huge, long, drawn-out inhale and exhale. In my womb, I still feel my newborn son's peace, perfection, and tranquility. My womb breathes and pulses with all of life. And I love it deeply in a way I never imagined I could have before birthing my son.

I felt so cozy in my first few days of menstruating. I took naps (my husband and baby survived). I ate well. I claimed it as my time, knowing how well I rested or didn't would impact me for the rest of the month.

In meditation, I see my menstruation as a ball of energy, hollow on the inside, where I sit and watch the energy move across the sphere's surface. In my most recent meditation this summer, it was aqua blue, radiating energy as a white light. For the first time, it looked wholly balanced and synchronized.

The message of this meditation was clear; this work is a spiritual path to enlightenment for women and perhaps the men who love them: a brilliant light, Enlightenment, Shakti of love embodied through the energy of menstruation. I am in Awe of where cycle awareness is taking me.

Moontime Day 5 - Love. Centered. Calm. I am trusting

life. All this after several days of tumultuous stress and pain in my marriage, pulling at the ground beneath my feet. Change is here without knowing what it will look like. Fear creeps in, too. Anger. Grief. I am softening into surrender. I am tenderly holding myself in this springtime and contemplating more ways to bring myself back to my deepest nature. Trust. Breathe. Let go. Repeat. Autumn is here externally, and it is becoming so clear to me how much the external seasons pull on me and influence my energy.

December 2017,
I feel like I stumbled too quickly through my whole period, as my menstruation may be ending today and I haven't felt prepared for it or present to it—a quick summary: Day 1- reverent. Day 2- derailed. Day 3- renewed. Day 4- depleted. Day 5- depressed.

By day two, it was evident that I hadn't let go enough, and I had brought the build-up of energy from the month into my moontime. I wanted to go to the forest with some sisters, paint our bodies with sweetly rich, earthy mud, roar, scream, or weep at the moon and dance to the beat of a drum. I took some moments to do that in my mind's eye alone in the shower. It helped, but I am struggling with this whole motherhood thing and finding time and space for myself.
I have been acutely aware of how much I push my body to keep going. I was able to stop at least 1% of the time and rest when my womb was calling out.

I'm feeling unsettled at the thought of my period finishing. I haven't had time to give myself to the quiet, soulful connection in my moontime. I'm seeking to regain my balance, rediscover my core and step into my wild power here. I'm sensing that if I can show up in this work, my life will be orchestrated beautifully. I'm feeling shaken but hopeful.

September 2017,
Moontime Day 28. I was lying in bed for a few moments of quiet this morning. I feel slightly foolish, hungover, and still giddy from far too many efforts and projects this summer. But I'd do it all over again! I caught myself in the throws of an external summer season gone wildly off track with cycle awareness and carried away in the splashes of vivid colors and summer's bountiful seductions. What a beautiful garden I had! And how I fought its ending!

A pot of coffee brewing drowned out the fresh scent of a late summer rain. I was finally bringing in the harvest, preparing, turning inward to meet the sweet nectar of Self as one with Source. I am humbled. I surrender. Autumn is carving out the gold. Inner winter, menstruation, here I come.

*March 14, 2018,*
Last night, I had a very healing dream; I was in a retreat led by a shaman. She held my feet, and all of this pain began to exit my body through my feet. She helped me to recognize that my sexual energy is also my power and honored it. It sounds simple, but it was profoundly beautiful, and I feel somehow better this morning, despite my raging cough and getting woken every hour through the night by my teething toddler. And so my day 17 begins.

June 2018,
Remembering me.

The total sum of moments of love in all my life.
Pause. Don't rush this. Taste, feel, touch, connect.
The Eternal.

November 2018,
Moontime, Menstruation Day 1. Sliding through altered states, wrapped in a warm velvet between driving, stoplights, and the fussiness of my teething toddler. I wish to be held in the darkness, embraced by the fire, gliding closer and closer into Spirit and my deepest self. I drive through the sunlight, movement, action, and productivity. Behind my eyes, a veil of dark and vast oceans is calling me. Fuck the patriarchy! I AM WOMAN. I will rise above this, live a life of my feminine purpose, and allow my soul the depths it is capable of diving into and rising above.

Day 2. The inner tides are moving, and my blood washes upon the shores. My blood. My life. My essence. My sacred gift, raw and exposed. I was paraded through the streets, naked. How dare they call it dirty. How dare they look upon it with disgust and shame. My red river runs, streaks of life and mystery marked upon my body. Today, I wear her with dignity, strength, and pride.

# Where was my Tribe of Women

Where was my tribe of women
when I broke through the veil of childhood
and reached my first bleed,
to celebrate with joy
and teach me the ways of nature
inhaling and exhaling, flowing
in the core of my body.

Where was my tribe of women
to hold my tiny, feverish, aching body
after I had been left alone with him
and his pressing, smothering body,
the stench of sickness.

Where was my tribe of women
when the light inside me died
the warmth gone
leaving an empty, lost hollowness that may never be filled.

Where was my tribe of women
when the rage first rose up
wild, fierce, and terrifying
to look me in the eye and say,
"Yes, you are safe. Face into Her, let her voice be known
instead turning her inwards into the crushing silence.

Where was my tribe of women
when my body, who knew,
who could not lie
screamed out to me, for me
in complete and perfect agony
demanding to be seen or die.

*Where was my tribe of women*
*when I witnessed the horrors of this world*
*ravaged by a sickness that was not to be named*
*as I saw the Mother bleeding*
*Her flesh torn open, her forests shaven*
*Her body; breathless and dying.*

*Where was my tribe of women*
*when I lay alone at night as a young girl*
*a single candle lit, crying*
*feeling the crushing weight of a suffering world*
*in my open, loving heart.*

*Where was my tribe of women*
*when I was told that my body was not good enough,*
*is wrong and only here for the pleasure of man.*

*Where was my tribe of women*
*when religion taught me*
*that women are evil*
*and God is male.*

*Where was my tribe of women*
*who would embrace and adorn my fluid spring body*
*and look him in the eyes and say yes, he has a good heart*
*you have chosen well.*

*Where was my tribe of women*
*who could hold together my open, gaping body*
*after giving birth*
*and bring everything back to the center in sacred ceremony.*

*Where was my tribe of women*
*when my fresh, newborn son was taken from me*
*to lay alone in an empty, sterile place*

*as I heard his cries and screams from being pierced with needles*
*for tests and tests and more tests*
*too exhausted to stand again*
*and walk the length of the hall to his room,*
*but doing it one hundred times more.*

*Where was my tribe of women*
*when I cried alone in the dark*
*terrified that my son would never be loved and accepted*
*by a culture that fears something different*
*because he has one extra, perfect, little chromosome.*

*WHERE WAS MY TRIBE OF WOMEN?*
*(Sobbing)*

*I called to them again and again.*
*And their love came rushing in.*

*They answered in the echoes of my ancestors*
*from days long before the disease of Patriarchy set in.They*
*answered from deep down in my roots*
*rising up in the cells of my body,*
*a hidden network of mothers, daughters, and grandmothers*
*facing their own demons.*

*Where is my tribe of women?*
*They are here in this sacred circle*
*like a grove of budding trees*
*awakening from a long, dark winter*
*as we stretch and move, shudder and dance*
*weep and laugh, embraced in one another*
*held by Mother Gaia.*

# The Death of a Master

"**M**aybe Sara knows why I get dizzy when I stand up." I could hear Leonard's weak voice in the background.

He had already been through a liver infection, which had cleared with the help of a little-known Ayurvedic herbal juice that I had mailed to him called Bhringraj. I did not yet know that he had already had symptoms of a heart attack.

Heike had called a few of us close to him to come together for online meetings to discuss her concerns. It was then that I learned he had been hospitalized while in California not only with the liver infection but also for a stroke, which he described as a kundalini crisis. More reports came out about repeated symptoms of heart attack. Leonard had refused hospitalization or surgical interventions.

This was in addition to the melanoma cancer he had been living with off and on for forty years, which he had been successfully treating with Hoxsey herbs. Over the years, he would proudly display the scars where a recent tumor had been and receded. It continued appearing in other areas of his body, but he had faith that it was a healing in progress. Given that the tumors were disappearing, I couldn't argue that healing was happening.

However, Leonard had also stopped bathing or sleeping

by the fire, which was unheard of, as this had been his daily practice since the early 1980's.

At home in Oregon, I was going stir-crazy. I was unable to leave my son who was still quite young with any other caretaker for several days, let alone several weeks. He also had a stubborn ear infection that was not clearing up, so I could not travel with him. To take him on an airplane would have caused horrific pain. Even if I could remedy this, I was still far too sleep-deprived myself. In my current state, I would very likely have been an added burden to his caretakers while also caring for a young child.

It was an agonizing realization. I could not go to help with Leonard's care, nor could I go to see him. I could not be in his presence and gaze into his eyes just one more precious time. I prayed and helped from afar as much as I could. The weeks rolled by.

## *Journal*

August 2019,
Right now, I want, no, I need to be in my community of Rebirthers who love and serve Leonard! My heart is in Virginia and North Carolina.

Thanks to Leonard, I have met Babaji, Mother Mary, Yogananda, and who we believed to be Mary Magdalene. I don't even know how to be vocal about these experiences publicly yet. *Leonard, there is so much more fun and healing to be enjoyed, please, please stay.*

∞∞∞

"Leonard passed this morning at 9:35." I read the text from my friend and one of Leonard's closest supporters, Virginia Peace Arnold. She kept several of us informed throughout the night of Leonard's status. It was the morning of September 5, 2019.

*Leonard passed.* The words seared into my mind. Given the circumstances surrounding him, I knew this moment was coming, but I had prayed and hoped for some miracle as they all so often happened around Leonard. It had been a week of flurries of texts, emails, calls, and group check-ins with those close to Leonard. He had been taken to a hospice facility, laughing when his caretakers said where they were going and that he was dying. It seemed clear to me that not once did he believe or feel that he would die. He never stopped trusting life, Babaji, or existence.

I squinted through tears as they came falling, gasping for air and filled with a deep, heart-stabbing pain. Leonard, my teacher, my immortal friend, had died. I would never look into his eyes again. Never feel the dynamic energy of his Presence in a physical body. Never walk with him, listen to his voice, or go on life-altering adventures with him.

Where was he? I tried to connect with his essence, but the pain was overwhelming. I found my way to the shower, where the sobs started cascading through me.

"No! NO!" I shouted in my mind but kept myself quiet to not disturb my son, who was already stirring awake. The shower was spinning as I held my head, attempting to ease the dizziness I felt. I struggled to breathe through the tight muscles of my throat, my heart constricting. The breaths became more profound and faster, and the next layer of emotional pain hit me harder than the first. I felt I would die from my grief.

And then it happened, within moments; A brilliant flash of light beamed in my mind's eye as I saw Leonard laughing.

"I died. I can't believe I died," he laughed with disbelief.

It was so shocking, so all-encompassing, that my pain left immediately, and I burst into laughter. Leonard was laughing, even at his own death!

How many times had I sat with him, bursting into joy at the hilarity of my case or his, laughing at our dramas? Life was a game for him, a fun, joyful, entertaining game that could never end.

*Our energy body is so strong, it can even survive death,* he had written in a recent article.

The flash of light had gone, and now my agonizing grief returned. I continued to breathe through it, and each time I did, Leonard's image returned with roaring laughter at the hilarity of his predicament.

Here I was, experiencing Leonard in total joy, and I could not help but laugh with him. How could I possibly be sad? What was I grieving for? It dawned on me I was mourning my loss, not his. He was happy and still alive in consciousness and energy.

My grieving process was very different from there on. Yes, I would cry, and yes, I would miss Leonard incessantly. Yes, I felt angry, like I had failed him in some way or others had failed him. But nothing could change the fact that he had passed, and I was feeling him in his Presence, ever so much the same as when he was alive and telepathically checking in on me, perhaps even stronger now. Leonard, in my experience, was the most alive dead person I had ever known.

The days passed by in a slurry of surreal, fog-like activity. I managed Leonard's newsletter, and it was up to me to inform thousands of his closest supporters and students of his passing. I struggled to bring myself to the computer and compile the announcement. I did not want this. I never imagined this day would come. Staring at the computer screen, everything felt empty and void.

Sitting in the silence, I thought of all the years I had coordinated with Leonard; discussing and going over different layers of his life with him, sharing his deepest thoughts as he penned new emerging ideas and articles, and sending out his latest newsletters was an intimate process.

At that moment, I felt very alone. I was still doing the work for him, but he was gone. I drew closer to my colleagues and Leonard's closest supporters for love and support. Eventually, Heike, Peace and I came together to create RIBA, Rebirth International Breathwork Association. Given that the three of us had supported him continuously for decades, it was natural for us to join together.

Each day, I breathed into the grief. And each day, I felt Leonard with me, smiling, loving, lifting, encouraging, still befriending, and mentoring me, even beyond death. This steady experience of a telepathic connection with Leonard and the weekly meetings with RIBA proved invaluable to me.

# Yasoda Ma

Two months after Leonard's passing, my beloved friend, teacher, and spiritual Rebirthing 'mama' Yasoda Deschenes died. It was more than my heart could take. Both of my spiritual parents were gone.

Upon hearing of her passing, I slumped to the floor at the foot of my bed where my son was sleeping. Not wanting to wake him, I stayed on the floor, trying to quiet my sobs as tears streamed down my face. I gasped for breath as I felt myself slipping into a dark inner retreat of depression.

Suddenly, I felt Yasoda standing in my room.

"Sara! What on Earth are you doing? Get up off that floor! This party isn't over yet!" I heard her voice almost audibly in the room.

In shock, I sat up. Yasoda was energetically smiling at me and, of course, dancing. A bit bewildered, I took stock of myself lying on the floor and laughed.

No, this is not what Yasoda would have me doing right now, and she was right. The dance carried on! I breathed in her words and her love. The pangs of loss still visited me over the years, but I knew it was for my selfish longing. Both Leonard and Yasoda seemed to me to be very alive and well in consciousness. This was a very new experience for me, as I had never felt this connection with anyone I knew who had died before.

# Blood and Stone

T wo years after Leonard's passing, I entered the house from my childhood, the home I grew up in, in a lucid dream. We had burgundy red carpets throughout, and while that remained the same in my dream, the house was much bigger now in this dreamscape. There was a jubilant party celebrating Leonard. I scanned the crowd of his family and friends in awe. At last, I spotted him smiling and laughing, as real and full of life as anyone could be.

He stood tall and straight, wearing a white button-up tunic and pants embroidered with delicate gold thread. He was massively alive and exuberant. His life was a total victory, and he was pleased, as were all present at the party. Leonard looked me in the eyes and took my hand as a stream of energy filled me with aliveness and joy. Appearing to me like this, he was giving me darshan, an infusion of energy; a transfer of kundalini life force to me. Tears filled my eyes as I overflowed with vibrancy and joy.

"Do you like my ring?" he asked. I looked down at his hand in mine and noticed a ring on one of his fingers. It was a silver band with a white, inlaid stone with drips of red streaking sparsely within it.

"Blood and bone," I immediately thought. This stone symbolizes his incarnation. Perhaps his next incarnation? Did he know where he was going already? The dream faded as I awoke abruptly.

I felt exuberantly alive and happy. I contemplated deeply the gemstone ring he showed me on his hand. Like drops of blood cradled in bone, it reminded me that we all came here through menstruation: blood embodied and blood created, cradled in the bones of our mother. It reminded me that we are here to love our incarnation.

A quick search online revealed the gemstone I had seen him wearing was Cinnabar Quartz, also known as Cinnabrite. I looked it up in Robert Simmons and Naisha Ahsian's *The Book of Stones, Who They Are & What They Teach*, and it said, *"Cinnabar quartz stones are talismans of the alchemical transformation from self to Self, the full manifestation of one's spiritual blueprint, the fulfillment of the Divine pattern we carry within."* It discussed wealth, prosperity, and manifesting invincibility and described it as the Magician archetype, a conduit between the spiritual and material worlds. That certainly seemed fitting for Leonard.

Several months passed by, and I had found a Cinnabrite amulet to wear. I loved connecting dreams to real life and real life to dreams again. It's all consciousness, and both are equally as rich as the other.

A few nights after my Cinnabrite necklace arrived in the mail, I was going to bed early with joyful anticipation and mild butterflies in my stomach. I had a breathwork session scheduled the following day with Heike. She had served as Leonard's apprentice and Breathwork Master of twenty eight years and carried on with his mission as it had also been her own. I waited two decades to get a session with her. Such is the life of busy

Breathworkers! What I had not anticipated was what was to come in my sleep the night before.

In my final dream sequence before waking, I entered a room with white pillars and a group of friends. I wasn't sure who they were, but they all felt familiar. Babaji was there also, but this time, He appeared like I had never seen Him before. He was like a massive action hero with larger-than-life muscles and strength, the epitome of masculine energy. His skin glowed a bluish-black hue and emanated light.

"We need a volunteer," I heard someone say. Everyone turned and looked at me.

"You," Babaji said, and before I knew it, I was lying on a treatment table where He towered over me in his great height and massive, masculine form.

He lifted his hands over my lower belly, and a radiant bluish-white light blasted out of his hands and filled my entire pelvic bowl. Within a split second the energy was flowing up through my torso and shooting out my crown. It was an energy of such intensity that it was both paralyzing and overpoweringly pleasurable. I awoke in a shock. I had received another Shaktipat, a transmission of spiritual energy from Babaji.

Rushing through my morning routine, I enjoyed singing and dancing with Ademar as we prepared for our day. I dropped him off at school and returned home just in time to set up my camping mat, some blankets on my living room floor, and my computer and headphones for the distance session with Heike. She was in Germany, and I was in Oregon. She laughed when

I told her my dream and Shaktipat. Apparently many people have experiences with Babaji and Leonard in her sessions.

It had been years since I'd had a breathwork session with another Rebirther. When you know how to breathe through a completed energy cycle on your own, it becomes part of a daily lifestyle. I had sadly neglected to get any sessions with a Rebirther for a long time, since before my pregnancy. I began to breathe, and to my surprise, tingles began flowing through my arms and torso. Tingles! I had not felt those in years! Something really must be up. I breathed on.

I became a little drifty and had moments of seeing through Ademar's eyes on the playground at school. He was having a good time but seemed attached to me now. I asked him to let me go to work and told him I would see him after school. We shared an inner smile, and off we went our own ways.

The tingles increased and continued to build and buzz in my abdomen. A massive rush of energy swirled in my pelvic bowl. I could have never imagined such energy there in any of my sessions prior. It became clear to me that it was a build-up of power that had not been released during Ademar's birth. It was life energy that had been created for both of us through pregnancy and birth, to benefit both he and I. However, when I had to stop the birthing process and stand up in the tub of water to get out and lay on the bed, it had become lodged in my pelvis. I relived this moment now in my breathing session.

A few more moments of breathing and WHOOSH.... It

flowed out of my body with an orgasmic surge and into my aura. A swirl of pleasurable, sexual energy mingled in my entire torso. The energy rose into my crown again, and I became aware of a white mist surrounding me. Soft pink, blue, and violet light permeated the atmosphere, and I saw Leonard standing with Babaji, smiling at me as I soaked in the Divine energy and light.

"I am always here for you, in the Silence with Babaji. You can find me here anytime you wish."
Leonard smiled gently.

Basking in their presence, I breathed in the love until at last, I was returned to my living room floor, spilling over with pleasurable tingles of light. I could not stand up; it was already time to leave to pick up Ademar from school. I had breathed for over three hours. Fortunately, Jesus could pick him up from school as I lay on the floor, integrating.

Slowly, I was able to move. Slowly, I found my way to get a glass of water. I was in total physical and emotional bliss. The joy silently singing in my body was profound.

Soon, Ademar came bounding in the front door, exuberantly happy from his day at school. I hugged him, and together, we took some deep breaths. I felt a new, wonderful sense of completion and victory around his birth. I sensed that he felt this shift in energy, too.

∞∞∞

The following week, I relaxed on the acupuncture table

at Peter's new office. It was a cloudy, rainy, Oregon winter's day, but streams of sunlight were now parting the clouds and bathing me in gold. I had been thinking of Leonard and Yasoda. I missed them and felt their presence in the room, loving me for much of the session. I was now aware that both he and Yasoda were standing over me, blessing me with their hands raised towards my body. It felt like a light bath. I had been struggling with migraines that no amount of breathwork could stop.

"You have a fantastic capacity to heal; you just don't know it. You can't use something you don't know is there." Leonard said. Yasoda stood by him with tears in her eyes, oozing adoration and love as she and I had so often mutually shared. I was floating lighter than air.

Peter opened the door to the treatment room and paused immediately. I felt his response to the energy. He gently walked to me quietly and reverently.

"Thank you for the light bath," I managed to say, halfway to him and halfway to Leonard and Yasoda.

"Yes, I feel it," Peter replied softly.

There were no more words needed. He knew the tremendous depths a journey of acupuncture could bring and had indeed brought me that day. It was Divine Grace.

Just five days later, another migraine came on. I woke up feeling terrible, and my face was all puffy. I felt slightly hungover from my road trip to the beach with Ademar the day before. We had been picking huckleberries and got caught in a rainstorm later on, while playing on the beach.

By the afternoon, I felt I would pass out. I slept intermittently and heard Leonard repeating, "You have so much spiritual power, but you don't know how to use it, and so it's creating challenges in your body."

I felt it was the endometriosis he was talking about. No matter how much I tried over the entire span of my adult life, my symptoms kept coming back and persisted. I entertained the idea that I could have so much spiritual power yet not know how to use it and that this could create physical problems. Maybe this is true for everyone. Maybe we have a tremendous life force that can heal and do many things, but we don't know how to use it. Therefore, it creates havoc in our suppressed energy bodies. I relaxed into this idea and pondered how I might discover a platform to express this spiritual power and potential to heal. Realizing I could not think my way through it, I let it go and trusted the process to unfold.

Two days later, my period started, and although I was tired and needed to rest, I was once again symptom-free.

Aum Namaha Shivaiya!

## *Journal*

October 26, 2020,
How I miss strolling the streets of Staunton. Oh, and to visit the house, Leonard's home that he opened up to so many people wanting to learn from him, the home that I lived in with the trees, stars, moon, freshwater spring,

and the old bathtubs caked in mineral water from the land.

How I would love see the patio tub and drain ditch that I dug, that he and I cemented in tenderly with soft hands, as I was processing the deepest layers of low self-worth I had ever touched on in my life, that I have never had to revisit since then because Rebirthing and physical immortality erased those painful lies and healed those seemingly bottomless wounds. I am healed in so many ways. I am whole. And Leonard is an integral part of that.

My ability to even consider being self-employed or to imagine I could be financially solvent and independent all started with Leonard and has been supported and nurtured by Leonard for seventeen years! Every victory and major struggle along the way: my money, my spiritual wholeness, my inner confidence and trust in life, my health and physical healing, my greatest friends and community, meeting my husband, and even the liberation of fears that have enabled me to become a mother, all came to be through my time with Leonard. He has touched and greatly impacted every aspect of my life.

How can I ever be thankful enough for that? How can I even dream of repaying that? How can I tell him enough that I love him, that I now love who I am, and I love who I have become in his presence?

January 29, 2020,
In loving memory of Leonard D. Orr and Susan Yasoda Deschenes

Yours was a friendship of simple, pure, total grace. Your Presence transformed every aspect of my life for the better, and you showered me with an abundance of blessings that will perpetuate beyond just 'me' and expand with each breath I take.

There is nothing left but to ride through the waves of grief, and with each liberation, I surrender more deeply to the immense love and unspeakable gratitude you have written upon my being.

You are gone, but I feel your presence. The play has ended, but I hear your whispers of encouragement. The dance is over, but I can still hear your music. I know I shall see you again, and so in those moments, I am enlivened. The page turns, and a new chapter is to be written. Breathing in, I am standing on the shoulders of giants. Exhaling, the dance eternal once again rebirths and begins.

Om Namaha Shivaiya

September 28, 2020,
Last week, I dreamt of Len. He was attending another life celebration dedicated to him. This one was in a large room with chairs. He was serious and intent on studying the cause of his death.

Today, I heard his voice in my mind, laughing and saying, "I was blinded by love, and the need for my mother. The bond we seek in relationships is, in truth, the love we need in infancy from our mothers. The love we did not get from our mothers. It is a crucial relationship for the individual's health, preservation and cultivation of their natural divinity and overall well-being."

Entertaining the thoughts in my mind, I responded with, "How am I doing as Ademar's mother?"

"Well, you are doing ok, but you could do better," I heard him laughing in my mind again. Leonard was always so perfectly light and playful about my seriousness in a profoundly healing way.

December 15, 2021
I just woke up from the most beautiful dream! I was in a temple meditating with Babaji and Leonard. Afterward, I approached Leonard, so happy to see him. I was holding a clear crystal, an apophyllite, and sharing how much I loved seeing him again and how much he meant to me. I gave him the crystal, and he said, "meet me in twenty minutes," then left.

Knowing how easily and quickly Leonard could slip away and disappear from people, I hurried after him. He had put the crystal in a pot with a spider plant and a smaller, vining plant. He had placed a string around it in the infinity shape. I don't know if the string was real or energetic, but it looked like a Brahmin's string.

"The answer is always so simple. Now we're always connected here," Leonard said.

# Conversations with Leonard

With tears welling up in my eyes, I lay in bed watching a video of Leonard playing on screen. Heike had sent it, and it was both magical and painful to listen to Leonard's stream of consciousness again. It was September 2021, two years since his passing.

Aside from my usual evening-lit candles, all the lights in my room were off. I put the phone down, feeling fatigued.

*Leonard, I miss you,* I whispered in my thoughts.

What occurred next was both a delight and a surprise. I felt Leonard's presence very strongly in my room. I could feel his loving energy and flow of consciousness, and in my mind, I audibly heard a response from him.

*"I should have devoted myself to my healing full time; I would have made it. But with it this way, overworking, I didn't stand a chance. Our working relationship can continue, I just don't have a body."*

"Leonard, this wasn't in my job description," I laughed.

*"Well, we have to make do with what we have,"* I felt him respond in a teasing way.

"Hahaha!" I nearly laughed out loud at the imagined conversation unfolding in my head.

*"You'd better light a candle."*

I opened my eyes just as the last of my candles were burning out. I lit my temple lamp from India, happy for this new line of consciousness I was in and wondering if I was half crazy.

"Is sleep deprivation finally getting to me? Am I going crazy?"

*"You're more sane than many people I know."*

Was it my mind? Was it actually him? Did that even matter? This play of thought, whether it was his or just mine, felt deeply healing for me and insightful. I decided to flow with it, and it turned into an ongoing play and exploration.

August 5, 2021

Today, out of nowhere, I just felt Leonard's presence come into the room. I contemplated the changes facing the Breathwork community now that Leonard had passed.

*"We are all going through a big process."* I felt him say.

That is true; perhaps Leonard was going through the biggest process of all of us!

September 10, 2021

I was having a 'conversation' with Leonard while in my bath. Jesús arrived home with Indian food, and I was so hungry! Salivating, I began to get out of my bath, and Leonard laughed incredulously, *"You're going now? I ate myself to death, and you are going to end your bath now to go eat?"*

Leonard, it is Indian food. And it is vegan! I can't pass this up!

*"You are very spiritually advanced and need to give yourself time to be with it, in long baths, fasting, etc. DEPENDENCY CONSCIOUSNESS IS INFANCY CONSCIOUSNESS."*

September 26, 2023,

Tonight, I am eating an apple in the bath. I'm sure Leonard is laughing at me.

October 28, 2021,

*"Death is an illusion like you are looking through a prism, and it distorts what you are viewing."*

Leonard, you used to say channeled content came from frustrated teachers without a body.

*"Well, that's very true and humbling. But teachers who have crossed over into the illusion of death can teach us a lot about how death works and what death actually is.*

*"So, it is an illusion that distorts not only what you see but also what you think. And the quality of your thoughts just goes downhill. It's a slippery slope when someone you love dies.*

*"So you have to watch your thoughts and watch your feelings, and arrest all the bad ones and praise and keep all the good ones. To arrest a thought means to put it to rest. To let it go and forget it. And remember only the good thoughts. You have a question?"*

Yes. So what is death?

*"It's a change in consciousness. It's a total shift in what you are thinking and believing. It's very challenging to describe because humanity is locked into this 3-dimensional space and can't see outside of the confines of this thought system."*

What do you mean by three-dimensional?

*"Well, you have height, depth, and width. And spiritual space knows none of them and all of them. (Laughing). So that's good for today. Let's keep the conversation going, and I'll check back in with you soon."*

Ok, Len. I love you.

*"I love you too; now get some rest, fire, bathing, and breathing. Another session with Heike would do you some good."*

November 4, 2021,

*"I healed my death urge and reconnected with my natural divinity so much that it stirred up a lot of emotional material in men when they came into my presence. Women retain their natural divinity and have to work to keep it. But Men have to work to find and restore it within themselves."*

Leonard, how can you say you healed your death urge when you are now dead?

*"Well, I healed my death urge in 1967 and became very successful in the world as a result of that. But I relearned the death urge from my students, and it was ten times worse than mine. So, I had to keep healing it in myself and others until I was no longer successful at healing it on my own. I*

*needed the support of an ongoing spiritual community that was deep into the practices of spiritual purification.*

*"But it's alright; I am healing it again now, and I have an unlimited supply of lifetimes to master bringing the physical body into the impermeable world of spirit."*

You say 'impermeable' as a way to describe the world of spirit?

*"Yes, it is unchanging, eternal, unlimited, and totally successful. There is nothing 'wrong' in the world of spirit. It is all beautiful and perfect all of the time. It is perfect consciousness, perfect existence, and perfect bliss.*

*"And so we can live this way in our physical bodies also; it just takes time with enough energy and stamina to overcome the death urge that we are born into from our family traditions and the death urge in others. Good, so that's enough for tonight."*

Ok, thank you, Leonard.

December 21, 2021,

In the bath, I had an intense experience, unable to move, barely breathe, or get out of the tub.

Leonard, what is this intense loneliness, sadness, and pain about? It reminds me of when I did a combination hypnotherapy and Rebirthing session and went into an experience of being utterly alone that there was no one else but me in all of creation and the Universe. It hurts so much I can't sleep or eat. I can barely breathe. I've felt this a few times throughout my life. A lot of the time when I was a teenager.

*"Well, there are states of being that are not human. They exist and are there to experience because creation has unlimited potential. Some people naturally go there. You have an affinity for it. Do you get something from it?"*

Well, wow, yes... I'm in this state now and internally asking what I get from it. The answer is that having this pain is how I know I am alive.

*"Yes, because this was your experience at birth. You were imprinted with the experience of being alone, totally alone, and separated from your mother's voice, touch, presence, breath, and everything. The mother's presence is like the Presence of God when you're in the womb and it just disappeared instantaneously. And so this extreme deprivation and loneliness is the imprint your body received as to what love and life, or living, is. These experiences are very damaging to the tissues of the heart. There are so many traumas to the heart, even at the moment of birth. And as a result, heart disease is the number one killer of humanity.*

*"You experienced this more so in your teenage years because, in your teen years, birth trauma surfaces spontaneously to be healed. But once we are aware of this within ourselves, we can overcome it and heal it. And transcend it. And become the masters of life that we were meant to be. But it is hard work.*

*"And so now you know why I shared all the details of my process and told my struggles repeatedly in all my newsletters. I wanted people to see the depth of what it takes to move through these memories and cleanse them from the body. And also the ease of moving through these*

*memories and purifying the body so that it can heal, using spiritual purification practices, of course.*

*"And so you've had this experience in your bathtub, of this experience or memory that has been with you your whole life. And you've had the experience of getting out of the bathtub when it felt impossible to you, and you had succumbed to it. So, it is a victory. And there will be many more.*

*"And so, there are many ways to avoid feeling these sensations and memories. You use overworking as an escape. And also not sleeping and eating. (Smiling gently).*

*It's good to be aware of our patterns and methods of distraction.*

*"And so you are working as an infant would to get her mother's attention. And you are eating because you crave her and that nourishment. And staying awake so that you don't miss her if she comes. You are waiting for her.*

*"So, intimate relationships with a high level of oxytocin naturally bring up these states of emotional material and body memories.*

*"There has to be a high level of commitment to the purification practices and each other to transcend it. Otherwise, people succumb to it and break the relationship."*

So Leonard, what is procrastination about?

*"Well, procrastination is a form of self-sabotage and not wanting to be here. It comes from being repeatedly forced to do things against one's will in early childhood. These memories can also take a lot to wash away.*

*"It's a form of rebellion and exerting control over a situation in which you feel powerless and out of control. Procrastination feels like the appropriate response, and it is very seductive and challenging to pull away from. But once you start doing it, you build trust within yourself and your capacity and capability to deal with any task that life sends your way. I loved overcoming my procrastination and spending time with people who overcame it. They became very successful people in life."*

December 31, 2021,

Sitting in prayer, I asked for liberation from this pain during another migraine and endometriosis symptoms.

Divine mother's sweet, soft voice came in, saying, "My dear child. You manifested this to understand the suffering of others. If you are done with it, let it go."

January 21, 2022,

*"All of time exists in the present moment. You can look back through memories, using your personal connection to infinite intelligence. With your personal connection to infinite intelligence, you have access to everything, the entire storehouse and wealth of information, throughout all time and all of space because it all exists simultaneously in this present moment of now, this eternal moment of now. Going into the silence is how you can access this. Being in the space between your thoughts, not necessarily stopping the thoughts, is very difficult to do (laughing), but being and residing in the space between your thoughts is more accessible to most people."*

Is that connected to being in our heart space?

*"Yes, very much so."*

January 26, 2022,

*"I am very happy with the life I had. I am so grateful."*

February 27, 2022

Leonard, what do you think about the idea that to live in bliss we need to welcome what's uncomfortable?

*"Well, that depends on the context. In a Rebirthing session, welcoming each sensation, whether it's pleasurable or painful, can bring you into a full state of ecstasy. Resisting the sensations, thoughts, and feelings can become quite painful and more dramatic. But in a Rebirthing session, you only need to continue breathing to get through it. It's the simplest thing in the world."*

March 11, 2022,

Leonard, I feel so wide open energetically when I go out. I can feel everyone's energy, and it's overwhelming today. What can I do about this?

*"Well, you can focus on your solar plexus and repeat the mantra Om Namaha Shivaiya. As we clear our mental clutter, excess energy pollution, and painful memories, we become more sensitive to the energy, excessive thinking, and memories that others contain in their body and their energy field. It's only a problem if you let it be a problem.*

*"Don't feed your energy and upset into this. Just relax into the sensations and energetic information and let it*

*pass through you effortlessly. Don't become attached to the experiences and sensations everyone carries around you. Focusing on the solar plexus and repeating the mantra (Aum Namaha Shivaiya) helps to spin off the energy from your aura faster and prevents it from becoming lodged into the body."*

Leonard, why do you say 'the body' instead of 'your body'?

*"Well, we are all one body in many forms. We are all the eternal spiritual substance that permeates time, space, and consciousness. There is no separation except within the boundaries of your conscious creation. You can dissolve yourself back into the oneness, or you can maintain your identity, borrowing from the eternal substance of one body.*

*"It takes a lot of conscious effort to dissolve and annihilate the individual self into the oneness completely, but it can be accomplished. There is no right or wrong. We are all here manifesting as the eternal spirit."*

"Leonard, on a more physical, body-centered level, I'm losing weight, but I can't seem to lose my belly fat. Why is this?

*"Well, you are carrying the energy pollution of others in your solar plexus. And as you know, spending time with the fire can help with this."*

April 9, 2022,

*"I could never be 'gone'. I am more available to you now than before. I am with Babaji and the Eternal Spirit."*

Leonard, who is Babaji?

*"He is the space between your thoughts and all the thoughts that spring from it. He is Divine love in human form and the formless. He is closer than your breath. He is everyone's closest friend. He can be found in the space between your thoughts and all the infinite possibilities that lie there."*

What kind of possibilities?

*"Anything you can imagine and dream. Anything your heart desires. It is your desires that lead you to Him. Suffering is useless and pointless. He is love. And you are love."*

May 10, 2022,

*"It's not enough to just know about a past life; you have to heal it."*

How do I heal it?

*"By releasing it from the cells of your body and your memory through the purification practices. You have to become new and fresh like a child again."*

July 6, 2022,

Me, entering the space between thoughts. I eventually felt Leonard's presence. It is very soft now. I sensed him giving me a blessing. I'm thinking of Sierraville, California, and the many times we shared there.

*"It's a beautiful place."*

I don't think I could go there again. I felt a tremendous heart ache welling up.

*"Don't let the grief stop you from doing what you want in life."*

August 17, 2022,

*"Emotional energy pollution is the biggest biggie of human trauma. It's the source of almost all miseries: negative habitual thinking, suicidal tendencies, and compulsive behaviors like overeating, drinking, smoking, etc."*

And so how does one participate in the world but not eat of the world and succumb to it?

*"Purification with the practices is not enough. We have to have a spiritually enlightened community doing the practices with us and supporting each other. Otherwise, there is no way. We would have to be isolated. But there are ways to isolate and still have a direct, positive impact on the world. Bhartriji influenced his local government to give him his forest reserve, where he lives freely. Other immortals have influenced politics and human behaviors for thousands of years. Their impact seems limited, but it's still something to consider."*

August 31, 2022,

Thank you, Leonard. I feel I am learning more deeply, perhaps truly, for the first time, or the first time of many times, about spiritual cause and effect. I can feel the path I was going on was going into destruction. Now, these core beliefs and identities have surfaced and revealed what needs to be healed to receive the results I want. I know you are guiding me on this path.

*"Yes, every step of the way."*

Gentleness. Thank you.

September 29, 2023,

Today, I feel Leonard here, but in a different way. It is as though he is more distant and working with my higher self. He's there with my higher self!

Leonard, I thought there was no separation between me and my higher self.

*"Thought is the separation. In the silence, there is no separation. A thought is just a thought, a vehicle for creation. There is no power in thought. It is lifeless, a thing, a tool.*

*"YOU give the thoughts your life force energy. You are the driver of the vehicle, which is your thoughts. Most people have it the other way around and think that their thoughts are powerful and the guiding principle. People are in the car and have forgotten that they are the driver, and then there are all kinds of bumps, accidents, and crashes. And people wonder, 'Why is this happening to me?'*

*"You have to take control of your consciousness and your thoughts. You have to take the time to go into the silence, the space between the thoughts, and access your higher self and higher powers.*

*"The thoughts themselves are not going to change. They are just things; they have no power. You have to choose the thoughts you want to empower, enliven, bring life to, and neglect the others. It is okay to forget the thoughts that hurt and don't serve us.*

*In the silence, you can access Babaji, the ascended masters, every immortal master, all of the Divine. There are no limits.*

*"But you have to choose it with dedication and commitment. You have to study like you're going for an exam, the ultimate test of your life. The good news is that the elements make this easy. The elements can clean the mind faster than the mind can clean the mind.*

*"People get excited about fasting and the power of long, extended fasts. But that's only one part of the earth element they are utilizing. People get excited about breathwork, but that's only the element air. People get excited about fire ceremonies and fire walks; they find the power there, but they don't combine it with water purification.*

*"Imagine if people combined all of these elements in their healing. Human beings would become the masters of their reality and universe. There is great potential in humanity. But humanity has to choose it. We are waiting patiently."*

*Leonard Orr and Sara Dawn, Sierra Hot Springs, CA, 2007.*

# Jharra

With my compass in hand, I gently repositioned the poster-sized framed image of Babaji on my new altar to face precisely North. It was the poster I purchased almost twenty years ago from Isabelle in Leonard's bookstore. The sweet scent of a burning Nag Champa incense stick swirled through the room in gentle curls and waves of white smoke.

I had just started a four-week *Home Ashram* course with Marge DeVivo, a longtime devotee of Babaji who had built an ashram in Nebraska and spent her life sharing his teachings, in person and online through www.TruthSimplicityLove.com
and www.TeachingsofBabaji.com

She was a fountain of wisdom and insight. Incidentally, she was also a longtime friend of Yasoda's, and after her passing, Marge and I had come together as comrades and cheerleaders on 'team Yasoda.' It was beautiful to share our love for her and for Babaji together. Now, I was learning the fine art of maintaining a home altar to Herakhan Babaji and Divine Mother from her years of experience.

It occurred to me that I had received her eBook on Jharra healing years ago but never followed up on it. Jharra is a beautiful, gentle healing technique of sweeping a person with peacock feathers while repeating specific healing mantras in silence. Babaji explained it was the first form of healing for humanity before there were herbs and medicines. He also said that Jharra works at the level of cause in consciousness and accesses healing in places that medicines cannot.

Marge described Jharra healing as the following;

*"The charged-up healing mantra goes from the energy field of the practitioner, through the instrument (feathers), and into the auric field of the patient, thereby removing dis-harmony and restoring harmony. Those who can perceive auras can tell you where the dis-harmony is in the body by observing the auric field. Sometimes, the "problem" sits in the auric field for weeks, months, or even years before it manifests into a dis-ease in the physical body. The sweeping restores harmony and balance, thereby eliminating dis-ease and dis-comfort."*

Swami Fakiranand, a devotee who lived with Babaji for years, was initiated into Jharra healing by Babaji directly. He was the first Jharra Master. In 1986, he initiated Marge into Jharra. With Marge as my Jharra teacher, I would be third in line from Babaji. That felt exciting to me.

Since childhood, I had always felt an affinity for peacocks. I loved to go to the Saturday markets, where there were bundles of peacock feathers for sale from local farmers. Peacocks naturally molt their tail feathers every year and grow new ones. My mom would buy a few for me, and I would play with them for hours. Peacocks are a magical bird associated with the phoenix, so in retrospect, my affinity for them made sense, knowing that my main animal totem is the phoenix.

After studying some initial materials, Marge and I arranged a time for the initiation to be done over the phone. We spoke for some time about our love for Babaji and shared a few of our experiences with Him. Marge spent time with Him at his ashram in Herakhan in the 1980s, so her understanding, wisdom, and depth of love and devotion were just magical to me.

As she introduced Jharra more deeply, she spoke of the principal Hindu Deity of Jharra, Kalbhairav. Kalbhairav is the black form of Lord Shiva, the protector and healer. She described him as having the appearance of a superhero, with strong, huge muscles and massive masculine energy. He is the ultimate Divine masculine, all of the masculine's healthy and empowered aspects.

Upon hearing her description of Him, I asked to share my last Shaktipat dream with Babaji. She listened to my story and confirmed that yes indeed, that was undoubtedly KalBhairav whom I had met in my dream.

KalBhairav, the protector and overseer of Jharra, had already given me Shaktipat! My mind was reeling in a very good way. This felt like a huge confirmation that I was moving in the right direction to become a Jharra practitioner.

The initiation over the phone was surprisingly energetic. I felt Babaji's presence and a download of information and energy through my crown. My heart filled with a warmth that felt all-encompassing. I was transported into a deep meditative state where the silence was palpable and filled with energy. I felt blissful and filled with light.

As is the process of initiation into Jharra, Marge gave me the assignment to repeat specific mantras a certain number of times per day to charge up the energy and clear my energy field. It was no small task. I did hundreds of repetitions on my malas over the following weeks. I quickly found that one of the mantras was best for me to do in the mornings, as it was very energizing, and the others I could do later in the day to enter a deeply peaceful state.

Once my assignment of mantras was completed, I began offering sessions to complete my initiation and receive certification. I found that I love offering Jharra, as it also heals me in the process. And it is simply delightful to sweep people gently with peacock feathers and perceive them as embodying their highest Divine Self and masterful potential.

I was quickly amazed by what people shared about their experiences of Jharra;

*"Thank You for the Jharra session, Sara. That was nice. I hadn't expected it to be like a meditation because I was consciously feeling my body and trying not to meditate. I don't normally close my eyes in meditation, as that would normally put me to sleep. Nor do I typically focus on body sensations.*

*I concentrated on my body sensations head to toe and connected to the sacred heart in Earth and Soul Star. About mid-way through, it seemed like things got brighter and more colorful as though someone turned on a light, not in my 3rd Eye or Crown but mid-way in front of my head.*

*Afterward, when it was completed, it felt like my Crown was open, I felt a dull sensation there. Now five minutes later, the sensation is in the back of my head on the left." - R.M.*

∞ ∞ ∞

*"That was so sweet! Right away, at the beginning, I felt activation in my crown. It evolved to warmth and activation at the top and back of my head. This was a new sensation for me.*

*Marge DeVivo and Herakhan Babaji, 1982.Throughout the session, I felt tingling energy moving down my legs. At one point, it was particularly noticeable in my left leg running down the outside from the hip.*

*Overall, it was very relaxing, and my mind fell back & forth between sleep and wakefulness. Thank you!" - H.K.*

∞ ∞ ∞

*"I loved it, Sara. I'm so grateful! My experience: the first part had a lot to do with my eyes. I could feel the energy moving behind my eyes and some twitching. My neck was also involved, and some adjustments were made to that part of my body. Subsequently, I could feel a sensation of attention to the ring finger of my left hand.*

*Later, I envisioned being in meditation, possibly in a room of an ashram where the floor and walls were cement. I was alone and in deep meditation there. The 15-minute session seemed like it was only 5 minutes, so there was a distortion of time. After it ended, I was left with a feeling of being peaceful and somewhat tired." - N.W.*

∞ ∞ ∞

*"I felt solid in my spine and then my core, like a central channel that was solid, rooted, and weighted into my body. I then felt very light. I don't know precisely when that happened, but I realized I was feeling light. I felt some tension in the back of my solar plexus, which I've often*

*felt when I meditate. I then felt my heart opening. Afterwards, I felt my third eye opening. That was really nice! Thank you!"* - D.K.

Marge DeVivo and Herakhan Babaji, 1982.

Swami Fakiranand (photo provided by Marge DeVivo.)

# Sexual Alchemy

Exhausted late in the night, I fell fast asleep. Between full-time parenting during the Covid pandemic, managing the house and yard care, working with RIBA, and carrying on late night 'conversations' with Leonard, I wasn't getting enough rest. Despite all that, since my last Shaktipat and the intense energy I experienced in my session with Heike, my sexual energy was over the top. Things were getting interesting.

Somewhere around two am in the morning, I awoke, rolling around on my bed in uncontrollable sexual ecstasy. It was as if an ethereal lover was with me, and we were having a full-on, passionate night. I energetically felt his deep, spiritual love for me, his higher spiritual connection, and his warm hands, lips, and tongue running all over my body. It took all I had not to begin moaning out of fear of waking everyone in the house!

Waves of pleasure rolled through my body endlessly, over and over. An hour went by. Then two. I could not bring myself to orgasm, nor could I go back to sleep. I kept reaching mini peaks, and then it would fade away. I began to worry about how this would stop and how I would get any sleep with my demanding schedule as a mom! What was happening?

To my surprise, the rich, smooth, sweet voice of my imagined spiritual mate illuminated my mind and simply said, "Love, focus on your own pleasure."

After a split second of blissful silence, the energy continued again and I could not stop rolling, now letting out small sighs of ecstasy. I finally let all thoughts fade, focusing only on my body and sensations. I found I could have as many 'mini' vaginal orgasms as I wanted, something I had never experienced before. At last, I had what felt like a deliciously long, intense, freeing orgasm and drifted off to sleep.

Over the following months, my experiences deepened, beginning with a warm pressure in my skull with each orgasm. Soon, it was expanding and swirling behind my eyes, eventually growing into intense tingles in my crown. I recalled Marge's words from one of our previous conversations. She said many people don't understand that sex energy *is* life energy.

One evening, I quietly pondered the act of sex and contemplated this in meditation. I intuited the following:

*"Each spiritually-filled, tantric orgasm is a victory. It transcends the flesh and brings the body further into the light. In logistical terms, sexual energy is like the pump or engine that powers the system. If you are in your heart, the energy goes up into the heart, which then amplifies it. The heart is the amplifier. If your mind is clear and quiet, the energy goes to the brain. It swirls in the entire skull, nourishing the nervous system, awakening expanded states of being and perceiving the whole body-mind-spirit, the entire energetic Being that is you."*

I had lightly studied a little Tantra before, and there were often jokes among Rebirthers about how much sex improved for experienced Breathworkers. Still, in my twenty years of breathwork, I had never experienced anything like this. I was in totally new territory. Now, it seemed to me it was a path of kundalini activation and self-realization.

∞∞∞

Several days later, back at my acupuncturist's office, I was again having a phenomenal experience. This time, feeling so sexually alive and radiant, I was filled with gratitude, love, joy, and vibrancy. As I lay on my stomach, with needles in my back, legs, and feet, I began to feel a swirling sensation in my pelvic bowl. Out of the dark goddess void of my womb, an image of two dragons appeared. They were long and fiery-looking. They grew in energy and intensity until, at last, they broke free and shot up through my spine and out my crown. I saw them in my mind's eye, finally freed from the cage they had been held in at the base of my spine.

Now, they were flying wildly in the sky, snacking on little energetic 'bugs' that represented my life's problems. They swallowed them whole like they were nothing but pesky little mosquitoes. My two dragons, which I hadn't even realized were caged there in my body, were now set free in the world!

# This girl

Who didn't know she mattered
Who didn't think her presence was worth one iota
Who didn't know YES, she could have that too.
Who thought she was not worth the time or the effort
Who didn't know what she wanted to be or who she could become
Who was too shy to speak a word in public, let alone in a small group.
Who feared motherhood.
Who feared life.
This girl, who couldn't find her voice.
Who couldn't find her YES! until it came crashing toward her with all the love and power of heaven.
Who discovered she could laugh, sing, play, and dance in the moonlight.
Who realized she could be and do more.
Who found her value.
Who found her heart and healed the wounds.
Who saw the shining radiance in everyone around her until she was moved to tears.
Who saw the galaxies expanding and unwavering in the eyes of God.
Who found the absolute simultaneous bliss and suffering of motherhood.
Who would climb out of hiding, once again, over and over again to reach for her soul's destiny.
This girl.
I am learning to love her.
To be amazed by her.
To be ever so grateful to her.

*Who are you at this moment?*
*How are you doing with your self-love?*
*What ecstasies are calling to you from the depths of your heart?*
*Who are you really, in your core essence?*
*When will YOU become?*
*Maybe you are already here and want to shine a little brighter.*
*Regardless, we all need your love right now.*
*We all need YOU.*
*Your love, your unique spiritual signature.*
*It starts with daring to love and fully accept that beautiful being called 'Your Self'.*

# Courting the Spiritual Power of Menopause

Not yet in menopause, I sensed it was courting with me. For certain, in my mid-forties, it was approaching. I was in my last decade of menstruation.

With my eyes closed and a candle lit, I listened to a guided meditation. I was shocked at what was unfolding for me as I passed easily through one vivid, energetic image after another.

I gazed down at the rondure of a floating sphere where my bare feet balanced steadily. I drifted in the open sky as if beyond all gravity or density. A deep burgundy-red hue permeated the atmosphere like a soft, ominous cloud. Stars twinkled all around in a magical dance of light that fully enveloped me. Dainty, puffy clouds scattered across the field of my vision as if there were no up or down, no horizon. I could easily step on the clouds and traverse across the ethers at will if I desired.

Still standing on the small globe suspended in the ethers, an intricately ornate golden scale appeared before me. It stood as tall as I, its organic lines flowing and curving as if it were a living and breathing life of its own. A closer study revealed that my current moon time (menstrual period) was resting in the weight pan, which was formed of a pristine, golden crescent moon centered on a shining fulcrum.

Each moon time I had ever embodied appeared to me poised perfectly in each one's turn, glowing with a luminous blood red, polished now like precious gems worth their weight in gold. Warm, welcoming, inviting, safe; all my lunar phases were arranged in a circle, offering me an exquisite horizon. This mandala was my unique menstrual signature, an energetic record of every bleed and all the personal lessons unique to me that each encompassed.

This horizon of my own 'period moons' and the scale before me were my only reference to space and matter, of anything solid in this etheric realm.

The wisdom, the learning, the pain, and grieving, the totality of my menses was now held as a treasure house of stunningly beautiful, rich, deep knowledge, and spread before me like a vast library of wealth. My time of menstruating would soon be drawing to an end. I felt a pang of sadness as I stood in awe of her beauty, my beauty, as a menstruating woman.

The timeless enchantress, a woman's blood, my blood, and my spiritual journeys were held together rhythmically like clockwork. But not the dry, lifeless mechanical workings on the face of a clock. No, no. This was the hand of the Goddess herself, the unseen natural order of all women, of all who have ever cyclically bled, of all who embody the menstruating Goddess Divine, the Mother of us all.

A cool breeze pulled at me from my right, gently calling my gaze away from this stunningly beautiful scene. A corridor of trees in autumn beckoned me, and I walked down the pathway with their golden leaves falling to the ground beneath my bare feet. As the last few leaves dropped from their branches, everything fell under a veil of blackness. I stood in total darkness, facing the gentle, calm wind, still playing softly with the tresses of my hair and kissing my cheek.

Searching, I looked deeper into the darkness. A single white snowflake appeared, lacy and intricate. I stepped toward it only to realize it was a single dandelion seed floating in the breeze. I reached for it, but the wind swept it away from me and into a deep blue night with more stars and the final glow of a setting sun.

Wherever I was, whatever strange land had manifested for me was now in the full warmth of a late summer night. A bit tired, I lay down and was wrapped in the Earth as the wind continued to sweep at my hair and the tall grasses surrounding me. An intoxicating sea of sweetly-smelling pollen and fragrances filled my mind and body. Yet, I felt very alone in this place that was so peaceful and quiet. A realization drew upon me that this really would soon be my last menstruation. A tinge of uncertainty crept in. Am I prepared? Maybe not? Perhaps I need more allies to help me through this night.

I stood up now in flowing robes of white and turned towards the shining moon smiling above me. A symphony of crickets and fireflies caressed me through the warm summer air. I stepped into a white boat, seated on a still, shining lake, dark as night and smooth as glass. The moon above guided the boat's path: a slow, smooth sail through the still water, with gentle ripples disappearing into the now silent stillness.

I traversed the dark, starry sky mirrored in this glossy lake and reached the edge of the other shore, which, to my surprise, was covered in snow. I stepped off the boat, my white robes magically transforming into thick, warm layers and white boots softly pressing into the untouched snow. I began a gradual ascent up the side of a wintery mountain.

Halfway through, I realized this mountain was a great, wise man who awoke as I reached his heart center, and he embraced me. I fell fast asleep and dreamt peacefully in his all-encompassing embrace. I floated into the dark sky, entering another galaxy through my dreams. White light sparked at my fingertips, filled with energy and aliveness. I awoke gently from my dream to find that I had returned to the center of my collective moon time circle and menstrual scale.

The warm embrace of Medicine Mountain Man still held me. I breathed in, empowered, supported, and loved. I exhaled, confident and determined.

∞ ∞ ∞

Several days later, I entered another guided journey that proved to be just as remarkable as the first. I slipped into a deeply relaxed sort of dream state with ease.

Entering a glass room of stars on all sides, above and below, I had a sense of spinning and spiraling, alone. A guardian, *my guardian*, entered the room dressed in all white and handed me a staff. This gift was to see and know that I am not alone and never was alone. The staff represented my spiritual power, and I was ready to wield it in the world.

Leaving the room of stars, I passed through a jungle and then onwards to a warm sunny beach, finally resting in a softly lit forest amidst the gentleness of springtime. I saw a wooden door and opened it, passing through into a space of total whiteness.

There was only light, a heavenly sound, and an inverted v-shaped corridor above me as naked, wintery trees held hands high above my head. A dove landed before me and transformed into a woman wearing a golden crown. No words were exchanged, only peace, love, light, and tonal sounds.

I flew off the planet and into the stars. Soon, they faded behind me as I entered the sun. I embodied the Light that is brighter than the sun. I stepped out of the sun and into a dark Universe. Stars appeared in the distance, along with other galaxies and planets. I was spinning again. I saw a vision of the Earth's silhouette and went there, landing in a forest of dark trees backlit by the night sky. All was rotating, spiraling, in the spinning of the Universe.

*I am with fire. I am pure magic. I can play within the darkness and heal it. I am connected to galaxies rooted in the Earth, which are equally rooted in other galaxies. I am in this world but no longer of it.*

Walking through another door of light, it was as if I was nothing but a golden light. I entered a stage with a screen in the background; first, it showed a cityscape, then snowy skies, the north and south poles, forests, rivers, oceans, and deserts flashed upon the center stage screen before me. The screen disappeared, and I felt the urge to fall off the stage and into the stars and black nothingness surrounding it. I sensed a slight tinge of fear, but I flew.

Phoenix came once again to see me. Remembering her first appearance to me as my animal totem years ago, I reached for her talons and we spun in the darkness and stars, locked together. She was burning with light inside. Her message to me was that I AM eternal. A white pearlescent egg in her claw was given to me.

My body again tingled as I brought my attention back to my physicality. The guided meditation was over. Breathing in softly, I was stunned. I truly had stepped into a new level of spiritual power. Only time could reveal where the masterful Phoenix would guide me next.

∞ ∞ ∞

# Affirmations for Healing

With my thoughts, language, feelings, body, and every reference, I am healthy. The disease does not serve me anymore. I am free from disease.

I love and accept who I AM today.

I AM grateful for all the decisions I have ever made.

My life is a blessing to myself and those around me.

I rejoice in being 100% responsible for my life and my health.

I AM complete, whole, and fully alive right now.

I AM an expression of Eternal Life.

I Trust my abundant, Divine imagination.

I Trust my Higher Self, the very essence of my Being.

I AM at peace within and of myself, regardless of any outer circumstances.

I AM living Forever, Now.

There is no limit to my Reality. It just keeps getting better and better!

Every choice I make contributes to my good health and

aliveness.

I love to nourish and take care of mySelf.

Everything about my body is sacred.

All my bodily functions are normal, and my normal state of being is Bliss.

I AM pleased with my body.

I AM honored and appreciated just for being me. My body is immersed in pleasure and peace.

I love my body!

I love my life!

Others love me and my body.

Others love that I AM alive, and I feel their love deeply.

I claim this body and this planet in the name of LOVE.

I AM here, fully and completely.

The Universe Loves and supports me.

# Affirmations for Healthy Menstruations

I have an Abundance of rich, nourishing, life-giving blood.

My menstrual blood is a sacred gift to the Earth.

My menstruations are healthy, purifying, and bringing me joy.

Menstruation is highly pleasurable.

Life and nourishment are so abundant in me that it is safe for me to allow them to flow forth into my world.

I rejoice in my femininity!

It is my Gift and my joy to be a Woman.

I AM safe to be a Woman in this world.

I AM a Divine Woman.

I AM fully awakened to the Goddess within, and I express myself safely and freely.

I AM innocent and fully empowered with my sexual nature.

I rejoice in my body, and I deserve pleasure!

My female body is my sacred vessel, which I embody wholly and completely.

I Trust the wisdom of my body.

I AM one with nature, and my body is at peace.

I AM one with the Divine flow of nature, and it is good.

It is a blessing to be a woman!

I am connected to the creative power of my ovaries.

My body is a sacred space of life, and life is ecstatic!

There is nothing I and God/dess cannot heal.

# Affirmations for Sexual Healing

I now reclaim my inner child; my innocence, my magic, my joy of being and my safety and belonging in the world.

My sexual energy and life force are sacred and mine to behold.

I am sexually empowered and safe in the world. I claim my physical, bodily space and autonomy.

I am my own sovereign entity, free to choose and express my love with safety and mutual consent.

I deserve love and have always deserved only love. I am love.

I reject the sadistic idea that I needed trauma and pain to learn, grow, evolve, or become enlightened.

The painful events of the past have not created who I am today.

I choose to be free and to heal.

I am whole and complete, and always have been, regardless of any circumstances.

I choose my liberation.

I declare that I am and forever shall be safe, protected, loved, and nourished.

I enjoy loving, kind relationships with people who are authentic, caring, affectionate, and present.

I am filled with the love of Spirit and the healing Light of God/dess.

∞ ∞ ∞

# Resources

## Sara Dawn

SaraDawn.com - offerings of Jharra, Rebirthing Breathwork, and Affirmative Prayer. For a complete list of resources related to this book, please visit SaraDawn.com/resources

## Rebirthing Breathwork

RIBA, Rebirth International Breathwork Association
RebirthingAssociation.com

It is my hope that you will discover, experience, and receive as much joy as I do from Rebirthing Breathwork. Once you do, it will become your life-long friend and trustworthy companion. In learning the Connected Breathing rhythm and completing at least ten individual sessions, it can commonly be practiced safely and securely on your own, enabling you to breathe through emotions, stress, fatigue, and pain anywhere you go.

Rebirthing Breathwork has been, in my experience, the fastest and most pleasing way to undergo a transformational healing process. Unlike other forms of therapy, it does not necessitate and is not limited to the use of your mind. It is a full-blown conversation between your body and God/Spirit/Source (call it what you will) on a cellular level. You don't have to figure anything out. You are not trying to get anywhere or get anything. You just breathe and become purified.

I am eternally grateful that Rebirthing Breathwork became a part of my life path. It has been essential to my healing. It is irreplaceable. Nothing can come close or even compare to the impression it has permanently left on my life. Breath is the vehicle of life. Breath takes care of us!

## Babaji

TruthSimplicityLove.com
TeachingsofBabaji.com

## The Physical Immortality Consciousness Consultation; Part I, Ii And Iii: With Articles From Leonard D. Orr

First published in 2016, this consultation was used by Leonard Orr in his training center in Virginia, USA with great reviews from his personal trainees. Written by Sara Dawn, this consultation is the culmination of her years of study with Leonard and her work leading seminars on physical immortality and healing the death urge. It includes Leonard's articles 'Two Powerful Words; Physical Immortality', and 'The Body Mediation; Victory Affirmations'.

Physical Immortality can be a modern day lifestyle and way of living. These practices come from his learning and observation of yogis who have lived for a very, very long time, more than the Western mind has ever been conditioned to comprehend.

If you are interested in longevity and going for total healing and physical mastery, this consultation is for you! You can use this text not only to practice, learn and contemplate ideas about Physical Immortality, but also to offer as a consultation for your clients, friends, and family. This can be done for free as a gift, a barter, or professionally with a financial exchange. This consultation itself can be a vehicle that supports life and prosperity.

As Leonard Orr said, even if you don't believe in or achieve physical immortality, exploring these ideas can give you a more fulfilling, enjoyable, and rich life.

Welcome to the Physical Immortality Consultation. This is more than an intellectual exercise, it is an experience and purification. It can increase your quality of living and level of happiness, satisfaction, joy, and gratitude to no limits! We are here living Eternal Life. It's here in the eternal moment of Now. It is never too late to begin. The opportunity is present each moment of every day. So let's have some fun!

## Learn To Breathe Energy

A simple guide to Conscious Energy Breathing; easy to use breathing techniques you can begin today to heal your inhibited breathing patterns.
14 pages.

# About The Author

## Sara Dawn

Sara is a Master Breathworker and co-founder of RIBA, Rebirth International Breathwork Association. She spent seventeen years working closely with Leonard D. Orr, founder of the modern day Breathwork movement.

Sara has worked in the field of personal growth and human development for over 20 years , focusing on Breathwork, Jharra healing, feminine wisdom teachings, nature mysticism, and formerly as a licensed Religious Science Practitioner with the United Centers for Spiritual Living (founded by Ernest Holmes).

In her writings, she aims to instill all the beauty, aliveness, and joy she has been blessed with in her personal spiritual awakening into the hearts and minds of her readers.

"The more people who can achieve living in their bliss and divine Union, the more we all will get swept up in that energy and transform life as we know it into heaven on earth." ~Sara Dawn

www.ingramcontent.com/pod-product-compliance
Lightning Source LLC
Chambersburg PA
CBHW030909090426
42737CB00007B/135